Kaskaia   Shienne Chief   Awappaho

ACCOUNT

OF AN

EXPEDITION

FROM PITTSBURGH

TO

THE ROCKY MOUNTAINS,

PERFORMED

IN THE YEARS 1819, 1820.

BY ORDER OF THE
HON. J. C. CALHOUN, SECRETARY OF WAR,

UNDER THE COMMAND OF
MAJ. S. H. LONG, OF THE U. S. TOP. ENGINEERS.

COMPILED
FROM THE NOTES OF MAJOR LONG, MR. T. SAY,
AND OTHER GENTLEMEN OF THE PARTY,

By EDWIN JAMES,
BOTANIST AND GEOLOGIST TO THE EXPEDITION.

IN THREE VOLUMES.
VOL. III.

Rediscovery Books

Reproduced by kind permission of the
Royal Geographical Society

Published by
Rediscovery Books Ltd
Unit 10, Ridgewood Industrial Park,
Uckfield, East Sussex,
TN22 5QE England
Tel: +44 (0) 1825 749494
Fax: +44 (0) 1825 765701

This edition © Rediscovery Books Ltd 2006

To find out more about Rediscovery Books
and its range of titles visit
www.rediscoverybooks.com

Published in association with
Royal Geographical Society
with IBG

Advancing geography and geographical learning

The **Royal Geographical Society with IBG** was founded in 1830 to advance geographical science. Today it supports geographical research, promotes geography in schools and through outdoor learning, in society and to policy makers. Geography connects us to the world's people, places and environments.
The **Rediscovery Books** series allow us to see how previous geographers and travellers understood and recorded the world.

In reprinting in facsimile from the original, any imperfections are inevitably reproduced and the quality may fall short of modern type and cartographic standards.

CONTENTS

OF

THE THIRD VOLUME.

CHAP. I.

Inconveniences resulting from want of Water. — Wood Ticks. — Plants. — Loss of One of the Party. — Honey Bees. — Forests. — Gray Sandstone. — Indications of Coal. — Limestone - - - Page 1

CHAP. II.

Osage Orange. — Birds. — Falls of the Canadian. — Green argillaceous Sandstone. — Northern and Southern Tributaries of the Canadian. — Cottonwood. — Arrival at the Arkansa. — Cane Brakes. — Cherokees. — Belle Point - - - - 22

CHAP. III.

The Party proceed upon their Route. — Thunderstorm. — Some Account of the Kiawa, Kaskaia, Arrapaho, and Shienne Indians. — New Species of Toad - - - - - - 39

CHAP. IV.

Arrapaho War-party. — Tabanus. — Rattlesnakes. — Burrowing Owl. — Departure of Bijeau and Ledoux for the Pawnee Villages. — Scarcity of Timber. — Great Herds of Bisons. — Wolves - - - 56

CHAP. V.

Termination of the Great Bend of the Arkansa. — Ietan War-party. — Little Arkansa. — Red River Fork. — Little Neosho and Little Verdigrise Creeks - - 70

CHAP. VI.

Indian hunting Encampment. — Brackish Water. — The Party pressed by Hunger. — Forked-tailed Flycatcher. — An elevated, almost mountainous, Range of Country. — Desertion of Three Men. — Red Water - - - - - - - 85

CHAP. VII.

The Party meet with Osage Indians. — Some Account of this Nation. — Manner of taking Wild Horses - 101

CHAP. VIII.

Verdigrise River. — Mr. Glenn's Trading-House. — New Species of Lizard. — Neosho or Grand River. Salt Works. — Large Spider. — Illinois Creek. — Ticks. — Arrival at Belle Point - - - 115

CHAP. IX.

Journey from Belle Point to Cape Girardeau. — Cherokee Indians. — Osage War. — Regulator's Settlements of White River - - - - - 124

CHAP. X.

Hot Springs of the Washita. — Granite of the Cove. — Saline River - - - - - - 148

CHAP. XI.

Red River. — Exploring Expedition of 1806. — Return to the Arkansa. — Earthquakes - - - 163

CONTENTS.

	Page
A GENERAL DESCRIPTION of the Country traversed by the exploring Expedition, being the Copy of a Report of Major Long to the Hon. J. C. Calhoun, Secretary of War	189
OBSERVATIONS on the MINERALOGY and GEOLOGY of a Part of the United States West of the Mississippi	271
NOTES	333

EXPEDITION

FROM PITTSBURGH

TO THE ROCKY MOUNTAINS.

CHAPTER I.

INCONVENIENCES RESULTING FROM WANT OF WATER. — WOOD TICKS. — PLANTS. — LOSS OF ONE OF THE PARTY. — HONEY BEES. — FORESTS. — GRAY SANDSTONE. — INDICATIONS OF COAL. — LIMESTONE.

August 22d. So much rain had fallen during the night, that, soon after commencing our morning march, we enjoyed the novel and pleasing sight of a running stream of water. It had been only two weeks since the disappearance of running water in the river above, but during this time we had suffered much from thirst, and had been constantly tantalized with the expectation of arriving at the spot where the river should emerge from the sand. By our computation of distances we had travelled more than one hundred and fifty miles along the bed of this river without having once found it to contain running water. We had passed the mouths of many large tributaries, but they, like the river itself, were beds of naked sand. The narrative of Lewis and Clarke has been thought deserving of ridicule, on account of the frequent mention of " dry rivers;" but if not rivers, what are these extensive drains, carrying off the occasional surplus of water from large districts, to be called ? It is to be remembered also, that all the more considerable of them are constantly conveying away, silent and unseen, in the bottom of their deep beds, streams of water of no trifling magnitude. This is probably the case with all such as have their sources in the primitive country of the Rocky Mountains, likewise with those which traverse any great extent of the floetz trap district, as both of these formations afford a more abundant supply of water than the sandstone tracts.

In the afternoon we saw a dense column of smoke rising suddenly from the summit of a hill at some distance, on the right hand side of the river. As at the moment the air happened to be calm, the smoke rose perpendicularly in a defined mass, and after continuing for a few minutes, ceased suddenly. Having recently observed the signs of Indians, we took this as a confirmation of our suspicions, that an encampment or a village was not far distant. We have observed that parties of Indians, whether stationary or on their marches, are never without *videttes*, kept constantly at a distance from the main body, for the purpose of giving timely notice of the approach of enemies. Several methods of telegraphic communication are in use among them, one of which is this, of raising a sudden smoke; and for this purpose they are said to keep in constant readiness a supply of combustibles. During the remainder of this and the day following we were in constant expectation of falling in with Indians. Towards evening, on the 23d, we saw an unusual number of horses, probably four or five hundred, standing among the scattered trees along the river bottom. We saw them while more than a mile distant; and from the dispersed manner of their feeding, and the great intermixture of colours among them, we concluded they must be the horses belonging to a band of Indians. We accordingly halted, and put our guns in order for immediate use; then, approaching cautiously, arrived within a few rods of the nearest before we discovered them to be wild horses. They took fright, and dispersing in several directions, disappeared almost instantly.

At eleven P. M. the double meridian altitude of the moon's lower limb, observed for latitude, was 72° 18′ 15″, index error 0° 8′ 0″. For the two last days our average course had inclined considerably to the south; the water, visible in the river, had increased rapidly in quantity, and the apparent magnitude of the stream was nearly equal to what it had been four hundred miles above.

August 24. Our supply of parched corn meal was now entirely exhausted. Since separating from our companions on the Arkansa, we had confined ourselves to the fifth part of a pint each per day, and the discontinuance of this small allowance was at first sensibly felt. We however became gradually accustomed to the hunter's life in its utmost simplicity, eating our bison or bear meat without salt or condiments of any kind, and substituting turkey or venison, both of which we had in the greatest plenty, for bread. The few hungry weeks we had spent about the sources of the river had taught us how to dispense with superfluous luxuries, so the demands of nature could be satisfied.

The inconvenience we felt from another source was more serious. All our clothing had become so dirty as to be offensive both to sight and smell. Uniting in our own persons the professions of traveller, hostler, butcher, and cook, sleeping on the ground by night, and being almost incessantly on the march by day; it is not to be supposed we could give as much attention to personal neatness as might be wished. Notwithstanding this, we had kept ourselves in comfortable condition as long as we had met with water in which to wash our clothes. This had not now been the case for some weeks. The sand of the river bed approaches in character so near to a fluid, that it is in vain to search for or to attempt to produce any considerable inequalities on its surface. The utmost we had been able to accomplish, when we had found it necessary to dig for water, was to scoop a wide and shallow excavation, in the bottom of which a few gills would collect, but in so small a quantity, that not more than a pint could be dipped up at a time; and since the water had appeared above the sand, it was rare to find it more than an inch or two in depth, and so turbid as to be unfit for use. The excessive heat of the weather aggravated the inconvenience resulting from the want of clean clothing, and we were not without fears that our health might suffer.

The common post oak, the white oak, and several other species, with gymnocladus or coffee-bean tree, the cercis and the black walnut, indicate here a soil of very considerable fertility; and game is so abundant, that we have it at any time in our power to kill as many bison, bear, deer, and turkies as we may wish, and it is not without some difficulty we can restrain the hunters from destroying more than sufficient to supply our wants. Our game to-day has been two bears, three deers, one turkey, a large white wolf, and a hare. Plums and grapes are very abundant, affording food to innumerable bears and turkies.

August 25. Our eventless journey affords little to record, unless we were to set down the names of the trees we pass, and of the plants and animals which occur to our notice. Our horses have become so exhausted by the great fatigues of the trip, that we find it necessary to content ourselves with a slower progress than formerly. According to our expectations when we first commenced the descent of this river, we should ere this time have arrived near the settlements; these, however, we can plainly perceive, are still far distant. The country we are traversing has a soil of sufficient fertility to support a dense population; but the want of springs and streams of water must long oppose a serious obstacle to its occupation by permanent residents. A little water is to be seen in the river, but that is stagnant, the rise occasioned by the late rains having subsided.

Leaving our camp at an early hour, we moved down the valley towards the south-east, passing some large and beautiful groves of timber. The fox squirrel, which we had not seen since we left the Missouri, the cardinal and summer red bird, the forked-tail tyrant, and the pileated wood-pecker, with other birds and animals belonging to a woody country, now became frequent. The ravens, common in all the open plains, began to give place to crows, now first noticed. Thickets of oak, elm, and nyssa, began to occur on the hills, and the fertile soil of the low plains to be covered with a dense growth of ambrosia, helianthus, and other heavy weeds. As we were riding forward, at a small distance from the river, two noble bucks and a fawn happened to cross our path, a few rods in front of the party. As the wind blew from them to us, they could not take our scent, and turned to gaze at us without the least appearance of alarm. The leader was shot down by one of the party, when his companion and the fawn, instead of taking fright, came nearer to us, and stood within pistol-shot, closely watching our movements, while the hunters were butchering the one we had killed. This unusual degree of tameness we could discover more or less in all the animals of this region; and it seems to indicate that man, the enemy and destroyer of all things, is less known here than in any portions of the country we have passed. In some parts of our route we have seen the antelopes take fright when we were more than a mile to the windward of them, when they could have received no intimation from us only by sight, yet it does not appear that their powers of vision are in any degree superior to those of most other ruminant animals.

Sunday, August 27th. We were able to select for this day's rest a delightful situation at the confluence of a small creek from the south. The wide valley of the river here presented a pleasing alternation of heavy forests, with small but luxuriant meadows, affording a profuse supply of grass for our horses. The broad hills, swelling gently one above another as they recede from the river, are diversified with nearly the same intermixture of field and forest as in the most highly cultivated portions of the eastern states. Herds of bisons, wild horses, elk and deer, are seen quietly grazing in these extensive and fertile pastures; the habitations and the works of man alone seem wanting to complete the picture of rural abundance.

We found, however, the annoyance of innumerable multitudes of minute, almost invisible, wood ticks, a sufficient counterpart to the advantages of our situation. These insects, unlike the mosquitoes, gnats, and sand flies, are not to be turned aside by a gust of wind or an atmosphere surcharged with smoke, nor does the closest dress of leather afford any protection from their persecutions. The traveller no sooner sets foot among them, than they commence in countless thousands their silent and unseen march; ascending along the feet and legs, they insinuate themselves into every article of dress, and fasten, unperceived, their fangs upon every part of the body. The bite is not felt until the insect has had time to bury the whole of his head, and in the case of the most minute and most troublesome species, nearly his whole body, under the skin, where he fastens himself with such tenacity, that he will sooner suffer his head and body to be dragged apart than relinquish his hold. It would perhaps be advisable, when they are once thoroughly planted, to suffer them to remain unmolested, as the head and claws left under the skin produce more irritation than the living animal; but they excite such intolerable itching, that the finger nails are sure very soon to do all finger nails can do for their destruction. The wound, which was at first almost imperceptible, swells and inflames gradually, and being enlarged by rubbing and scratching, at length discharges a serous fluid, and finally suppurates to such an extent as to carry off the offending substance. If the insect is suffered to remain unmolested, he protracts his feast for some weeks, when he is found to have grown of enormous size, and to have assumed nearly the colour of the skin on which he has been feeding; his limbs do not enlarge, but are almost buried in the mass accumulated on his back, which extending forward bears against the skin, and at last pushes the insect from his hold. Nothing is to be hoped from becoming accustomed to the bite of these wood ticks. On the contrary, by long exposure to their venomous influence, the skin acquires a morbid irritability, which increases in proportion to the frequency and continuance of the evil, until at length the bite of a single tick is sufficient to produce a large and painful phlegmon. This may not be the case with every one; it was so with us.

The burning and smarting of the skin prompted us to bathe and wash whenever we met with water; but we had not long continued this practice, when we perceived it only to augment our sufferings by increasing the irritation it was meant to allay. [1]

It is not on men alone that these blood-thirsty insects fasten themselves. Horses, dogs, and many wild animals are subject to their attacks. On the necks of horses they are observed to attain a very large size. It is, nevertheless, sufficiently evident that, like mosquitoes and other blood-sucking insects, by far the greater number of wood ticks must spend their lives without ever establishing themselves as parasites on any animal, and even without a single opportunity of gratifying that thirst for blood which, as they can exist and perform all the common functions of their life without its agency, would seem to have been given them merely for the annoyance of all who may fall in their way.

Among many other plants, common to the low and fertile parts of the United States, we observed the acalypha, and the splendid lobelia cardinalis, also the cardiospermum halicacabum, sometimes cultivated in the gardens, and said to be a native of the East Indies. It is a delicate climbing vine, conspicuous by its large inflated capsules. The acacia (robinia pseudoacacia), the honey locust, and the ohio æsculus are among the forest trees, but are confined to the low grounds. The common black haw (viburnum lentago), the persimmon or date plum, and a vitis unknown to us, occur frequently, and are all loaded with unripe fruit. The mistletoe, whose range of elevation and latitude seems to correspond very nearly with that of the miegia and the cypress, occurs here parasitic on the branches of elms. In the sandy soils of the hills, the formidable satropha stimulosa is sometimes so frequent as to render the walking difficult; it is covered with long and slender prickles, capable of inflicting a painful and lasting wound, which is said to prove ruinous to the feet of the blacks in the West Indies. The cacti and the bartonias had now disappeared, as also the yucca, the argemone, and most of the plants which had been conspicuous in the country about the mountains. The phytolacca decandria, an almost certain indication of a fertile soil, the diodia tetragonia, a monarda, and several new plants, were collected in an excursion from our encampment. The red sandrock is disclosed in the sides of the hills, but appears less frequently and contains less gypsum than above, though it still retains the same peculiar marks, distinguishing it as the depository of fossil salt; extensive beds of red argillaceous soil occur, and are almost invariably accompanied by saline efflorescences or incrustations. We search in vain, both in the rocks and the soils, for the remains of animals; and it is rare in this salt formation to meet with the traces of organic substances of any kind. The rock itself, though fine and compact, disintegrates rapidly, producing a soil which contains so much alumine as to remain long suspended in water, tinging with its peculiar colour all the rivers of this region. It has been remarked, that the southern tributaries of the Arkansa, particularly the Canadian, the Ne-gracka, and the Ne-sew-ke-tonga, discharge red waters at the time of high freshets, in such quantity as to give a colouring to the Arkansa all the way to its confluence with the Mississippi; from this it is inferred that those rivers have their sources in a region of red sandstone, whose north-eastern limit is not very far removed from the bed of the Arkansa. We attempted to take sets of equal altitudes, but failed on account of a trifling inaccuracy in our watch; the variation of the magnetic needle was found to be the same as on the 25th, namely $11° 30'$ east.

Our hunters had been sent out in quest of game, as, notwithstanding the plenty we had enjoyed, and the great number of animals we had killed, we found it impossible, on account of the heat of the weather, and the frequency of the blowing flies, to keep a supply of meat for more than one day. At evening they returned, having killed a large black bear; the animal finding himself wounded, had turned with great fury upon the hunter, who, being alone, was compelled to seek his safety by climbing into a tree. It is well known that the black bear will sometimes turn upon his pursuers, and this it is probable is more frequently the case at this season than at any other, as they are now unincumbered with that profusion of fat, which for a part of the year renders them clumsy and inactive, and the males are moreover excited by that uncommon ferocity which belongs to the season of their loves.

August 28th. The weather during the night had been stormy, a thunder-shower from the north-west on the preceding evening had been succeeded by rain and high winds; the morning was cool, the thermometer at 64°.

We had observed, that the sand-drifts, extending along all that part of the river we had passed in the three last weeks, were piled almost exclusively along the northern bank. The country we were now passing is too fertile, and too closely covered with vegetation, to admit the drifting of the sand, except from the uncovered bed of the river; yet along the northern side of the valley we frequently saw naked piles of sand, which had been wafted to considerable distance by the winds. From the position of these sand-banks, as well as from our experience, we were induced to believe, that the high winds of this region are mostly from the south, at least during the dry season.

We left our encampment at half-past five in the morning, and followed the river; the aggregate of our courses for the day was about east, and the distance twenty-one miles. Our last course led us out of the river valley, and for a few miles lay across the open plain. Here we passed a large and uncommonly beautiful village of the prairie marmots, covering an area of about a mile square, having a smooth surface, and sloping almost imperceptibly towards the east. The grass which covers this plain is fine, thick, and close fed. As we approached the village, it happened to be covered with a herd of some thousands of bisons; on the left were a number of wild horses, and immediately before us twenty or thirty antelopes, and about half as many deer. As it was near sunset the light fell obliquely upon the grass, giving an additional brilliancy to its dark verdure.

The little inhabitants of the village were seen running playfully about in all directions, and as we approached they perched themselves on their burrows, and proclaimed their terror in the customary note of alarm. A scene of this kind comprises most of what is beautiful and interesting to the passing traveller in the wide unvaried plains of the Missouri and Arkansa.

In the course of the day we passed two large creeks, one entering from the south, the other from the north; also several springs on the south side at the base of a rocky hill, rising abruptly from the bed of the river; but notwithstanding all these tributary supplies, no running water appeared above the sands of the river bed.

We passed great numbers of carcasses of bisons recently slaughtered, and the air was darkened by flights of carrion birds, among which we distinguished the obscene vulture aura, and the vulture atrata, the black vulture of the Southern States. From the great number of carcasses and skeletons, we were induced to believe ourselves on the hunting ground of some nation of Indians, and our expectations of seeing the Pawnees of Red river began to revive. Our hunters killed two fine bucks, both in uncommonly good condition for the season. The fat on the ribs of either of them was more than an inch thick. They were both changing their hair to what is called the *blue*, which at this season is a sure indication that the animal is in good condition.

August 29th. Finding the valley of the river somewhat contracted in width and extremely circuitous, we ascended into the open country on the north side, and made our way across the hills, taking a course a little south of east. At the distance of a mile or two from the river we enjoyed a delightful view of the elevated country, beautifully varied with gentle hills, broad vallies, fertile pastures, and extensive woodlands. The soil we found superior, the timber more abundant than that of any region we had passed since we left the Missouri. Extensive forests appeared in the distant horizon, and the prairies in every direction intersected by creeks and ravines, distinguished by lines of trees. The surface of the country is undulating, very similar to that of Grand river and the lower part of the Missouri, but the soil is more fertile. The first elevations rise from forty to fifty feet above the bed of the river, and these are succeeded by others, ascending by an almost imperceptible slope towards the interior. Among the trees on the uplands are the black cherry, the linden, and the honey locust, all affording indications of a fertile soil.

A little before we halted to dine, Adams, our interpreter of Spanish, having dropped some article of baggage, returned on the track for the purpose of recovering it; and as he did not join us again, we concluded he must have missed his way.

At evening we returned to the valley of the river, and placed our camp under a small cotton-wood tree, upon one of whose branches a swarm of bees were hanging. These useful insects reminded us of the comforts and luxuries of a life among men, and at the same time gave us the assurance that we were drawing near the abodes of civilization. Bees, it is said by the hunters and the Indians, are rarely if ever seen more than two hundred and fifty or three hundred miles in advance of the white settlements.

On receiving the first intimation of the absence of Adams, who had been following in the rear of the party, a man was sent back to search for and bring him to our encampment; but as he could not be found, we concluded he had missed our trail, and probably gone forward. We were confirmed in this belief when, on the following morning, we discovered the track of a solitary mule which had passed down along the bed of the river. This we accordingly followed, not doubting but Adams must soon perceive he had passed us, and would wait until we should overtake him.

The loose soft sands of the river-bed yielding to our horses feet, made the travelling extremely laborious; and the intense reflection of the rays of the sun almost deprived us of the use of our eyes. Mr. Peale's horse soon became unable to proceed at an equal pace with the remainder of the party; but as no suitable place for encampment appeared, he dismounted, and by great exertions was able to urge his animal along in the rear. The travelling in the bed of the river became so extremely inconvenient, that we resolved upon attempting to penetrate the thick woods of the bottom, and ascend to the open plains. We found, however, the woods so thick, and so interlined with scandent species of smilax cissus, and other climbing vines, as greatly to retard our progress, and we were soon induced to wish ourselves again upon the naked sands. Notwithstanding the annoyance they gave us, we took a pleasure in observing the three American species of cissus growing almost side by side. The cissus quinquefolia *, the common woodbine, cultivated as an ornament about yards and summer-houses, grows here to an enormous size, and, as well as the cissus hederacea, seems to prefer climbing on elms. The remaining species, the cissus bipinnata, is a smaller plant, and, though much branched, is rarely scandent. All of them abound in ripe fruit, which, notwithstanding its external resemblance and its close affinity to the grape, is nauseous to the taste, and does not appear to be sought with avidity even by the bears. In ascending the hills, we found them based upon a variety of sandstone, unlike the red rock of the salt formation, to which we had been so long accustomed. With this change a corresponding change takes place in the conformation of the surface and the general aspect of the country. The hills are higher and more abrupt, the forests more extensive, the streams of water more copious

* Ampelopsis quinquefolia of Michaux.

and more serpentine in their direction; in other words, we here begin to recognize the features of a mountainous region. The sandstone which appears in the beds of the streams, and the sides of the hills, is coarse and hard, of a dark gray colour, and a horizontally laminated structure. It is deeply covered with a soil of considerable fertility, sustaining heavy forests of oak. Among these trees the upland white oak is common, but is of rather diminutive size, and often hollow. In a tree of this description we observed, as we passed, the habitation of a swarm of bees, and as it was not convenient at that time to stop, we fixed a mark upon it, and proceeded to make the best of our way towards the river. On descending the hills, we found the valley of the river much contracted in width, and the bed itself occupying less space by half than where we had left it above.

On the following day the party remained encamped to take observations, and afford an opportunity for rest to the horses. Some of the men went back about six miles to the bee-tree we had passed on the preceding day, and brought in a small quantity of honey enclosed in the skin of a deer recently killed. About our camp we examined several lodges of sandstone, of the coarse dark grey variety above mentioned; in some instances we found it nearly approaching in character the glittering crystalline variety of the lead mines, but we sought in vain for an opportunity to observe the manner of its connexion with red sandstone.

As we were now at the western base of that interesting group of hills, to which we have attempted to give the name of the almost extinct tribe of the Osarks, and as we believed ourselves near the extreme southern bend of the river we were descending, we thought it important to ascertain our latitude and longitude by as complete sets of observations as was in our power to make; and this the favourable position of the moon enabled us to do in the most satisfactory manner. The results will be seen on the map.

During the extreme heat of the day the mercury stood at 99° in a fair exposure. This extraordinary degree of heat may have been in some degree connected with the stagnation of the air between the hills, and possibly with the reverberation of the sun's rays from the naked sands; but the instrument was one of an approved character, and was exposed in the deep shade of an extensive grove of trees.

As yet no running water appeared in the river; but as the pools were large, and some of them little frequented by the bisons, we were no longer under the necessity of digging.

September 1st. The sycamore, the æsculus, the mistletoe, and the paroquet, are conspicuous objects in the deep and heavy forests of the Ohio and Mississippi; with these we now found ourselves surrounded. Bisons were comparatively scarce along this part of the river, but whether this was owing to the near approach of inhabited countries, or to the great extent and almost impenetrable density of the forests on each side of the river, we were unable to determine; at night we still heard the growling of the herds in the distant prairies, and occasionally saw bisons in small bodies crossing the river.

The Kaskaia Indians had told us, that before we arrived at the village of the Pawnee Piquas, we should pass a range of blue hills. These we concluded could be no other than hills whose sides were covered with forests, like those we were now passing, and accordingly we watched with some anxiety for the appearance of something which should indicate the vicinity of an Indian village. As we pursued our way along the serpentine bed of the river, the valley became narrower, the hills more elevated, and as we crossed the rocky points of their bases, we could not but observe that the sandstone was of a different character from any we had before seen. It contains more mica than that of the Alleghanies, or that of the secondary hills along the base of the Rocky Mountains; it glitters conspicuously, like mica-slate when seen in the sunshine; and this, as we found by examination, does not depend entirely on the great proportion of mica it contains, but also in some degree upon the crystalline surfaces of the minute particles. Its cement is often argillaceous, and this, as well as the impressions of some organic relics * we observed in it, induced us to expect the occurrence of coal-beds.

On ascending the hills from the place of our midday encampment, we found this sandstone at an elevation of about two hundred feet (according to our estimate) from the bed of the river, succeeded by a stratum of limestone of the common compact blue variety, abounding in casts of anomias, entrochi, &c. This rests horizontally upon the summits of the hills, and disintegrating less rapidly than the sandstone which forms their bases, it is sometimes left projecting in such a manner as to render access impossible. Climbing to the summit of some of the hills near the river, we had the view towards the south and east of a wild and mountainous region, covered with forests, where, among the brighter verdure of the oak, the nyssa, and the castanea pumila, we distinguished the darker shade of the juniper, and others of the coniferæ.

A little before arriving at the place of our evening encampment, we observed the track of a man who had passed on foot, and with bare feet, down the river. This we were confident could be no other than the track of our lost interpreter Adams. What accident could have deprived him of his mule we

* Strobilaria of Nuttall, belonging to the heteromorphous genus phytolithus of Martin.

were at a loss to conjecture. We found it equally difficult to account for his pushing forward with such perseverance, when he must have had every reason to believe we were behind him.

September 2d. The morning was fair, and we had commenced our journey by sunrise. At a little distance below our encampment, we passed the mouth of a large tributary from the south. It was about sixty yards wide, and appeared to contain a considerable quantity of water, which was absorbed in the sands immediately at its junction with the larger stream. About the mouth of this creek we saw the remains of several gar-fish (esox osseus); this fish is protected by a skin so flinty and incorruptible, as to be invulnerable to the attacks of birds and beasts of prey; and even when the internal soft parts have been dissolved and removed by the progress of putrefaction, the bony cuticle retains its original shape, like that of the trunk and limbs of the canoe birch, after the wood has rotted away. The gar is usually found in deep water, lying concealed in the places where small fish resort, and seizing them between his elongated jaws, which are armed with numerous small and sharp teeth. This fish, though not held in high estimation as an article of food, is little inferior, as we have often found by experiment, to the boasted sturgeon of the Hudson. Its unsightly aspect produces a prejudice against it; and in countries of such abundance as those watered by the Mississippi and its tributaries, a creature so disgusting in appearance and of so unpromising a name is rarely eaten. We had passed the creek above mentioned about a mile, when we discovered a little column of smoke ascending among some scattered oaks on the right hand bank of the river; approaching the spot, we perceived our lost interpreter, who had parted from us five days previous, sitting a few feet in advance of his fire. When we discovered him, his appearance was peculiarly striking, and indicative of the deepest despondency.

He had kindled a fire upon a little rocky eminence projecting to the verge of the river, and seated himself near it on the ground, with his face turned up the river, as if in expectation of relief from that quarter. His elbows rested upon his knees, and his hands supported his head. Having sat in long expectation of seeing us, he had fallen asleep; and on being waked, it was some minutes before he recovered entire self-possession and consciousness. His long sun-burnt hair hung loosely about a face it could scarcely be said to shade, and on which famine and terror had imprinted a frightful expression of ghastliness. Perhaps some consciousness of having acted an imprudent and reprehensible part, prevented any demonstrations of joy he might otherwise have shown at sight of us. Under the apprehension that accidents of this kind might occur, it had repeatedly been enjoined upon all of the party, never to lose sight of the main body when on the march. But on this occasion no regard was paid to this necessary regulation.

From his statement we learned, that after separating from us, on the morning of the 29th August, he had returned a mile or two to search for his canteen; but not finding it, in his hurry to rejoin the party, he had missed the trail, and presently found himself bewildered. Taking the bed of the river as his guide, he urged on his mule, without allowing it time to rest or to feed, till, on the third day, it refused to proceed, and was left. He then took his baggage, musket, &c. and pushed forward on foot, evidently with the hope of arriving at the Pawnee village, but by the end of the day found his strength so exhausted that he could go no farther, and was compelled to encamp. Having expended his ammunition in unsuccessful attempts to shoot turkies, he had been trying to make a substitute for fish-hooks by bending up some needles; but this project he had not brought to perfection, and assured us he had not tasted food since the breakfast of the 29th, a period of more than five days.

The small-leaved and the white elm*, the nettle-tree or hackberry, the cotton-wood, mulberry, black walnut, pecan, ash, sycamore, and indeed most of the trees common to the low grounds of the Mississippi, are intermixed here to form the dense forests of the river valley, while, in the more scattered woods of the highlands, the prevailing growth is oak, with some species of nyssa, the dyospiros, and a few other small trees. At evening a large flock of white pelicans passed us on their way up the river.

On the morning of the 3d, not having been able to select a suitable place for a Sunday encampment, we moved on, searching for a supply of grass, that we might halt for the day. The hunters preceded the party, and meeting with a herd of bisons and good pasturage in the same place, they killed a bull of a most gigantic stature, and waited until the remainder of the party came up, and encamped near the carcass. We have often regretted that we had not taken the dimensions of this animal, as it appeared to surpass in size any we had before killed, and greatly to exceed the ordinary stature of the bison.

Having arranged our camp, and done in the way of washing, dressing, &c. the little in our power to do, we made an excursion into the adjoining forest to collect plants, and to search for honey, which, from the great number of bees we had seen, we were conscious must be abundant. Since leaving the open country, we had remarked a very great change in the vegetation. The dense shade, and perhaps the somewhat confined air of the forest, are unfavourable to the growth of many of those grasses, and those robust perennials, which seem to delight in the arid soils and the scorching winds of the sandy deserts. The sensitive (cassia nictitans), the favourite food of the bees, some species of hedysarum, and a few

---

* Ulmus americana and ulmus alata.

other legumina, are, however, common to both regions.

Our search for bee-trees was unsuccessful; but in our way we saw great numbers of gray squirrels, and killed a fat buck, one of whose quarters we found a heavy load to carry a mile or two to our camp.

A considerable part of the day we spent in unavailing contest with the ticks. The torment of their stings increased upon us if we were a moment idle, or attempted to rest ourselves under the shadow of a tree. We considered ourselves peculiarly fortunate when we could find the shade of a tree extending some distance on to the naked sands of the river-bed, for then the ticks were less numerous. In the middle of the day the mercury again rose to $97°$, and the blowing flies swarmed in such numbers about our blankets and clothing as to allow us no rest.

About the pools near our camp we saw the little white egret; the snowy heron had been common for some days. Great numbers of cranes, ducks, pelicans, and other aquatic birds, induced us to believe that larger bodies of water than we had recently seen must be near.

Bears and wolves were still frequent; among the latter we observed a black one of a small size, which we believed to be specifically different from any one of those we had seen above. All our attempts to capture this watchful animal were without success. Since entering the region of forests, we had found the number of small animals, birds, and insects considerably increased. An enormous black hairy spider, resembling the mygale avicularia of South America, was often seen; and it was not without shuddering that we sometimes perceived this formidable insect looking out from his hole within a few feet of the spot on which we had thrown ourselves down to rest.

On the 4th we met with nothing interesting except the appearance of running water in the bed of the river. Since the 13th of the preceding month, we had travelled constantly along the river, and in all the distance passed in that time, which could not have been less than five hundred miles, we had seen running water in the river in one or two instances only, and in those it had evidently been occasioned by recent rains, and had extended but a mile or two, when it disappeared.

CHAPTER II.

OSAGE ORANGE. — BIRDS. — FALLS OF THE CANADIAN. — GREEN ARGILLACEOUS SANDSTONE. — NORTHERN AND SOUTHERN TRIBUTARIES OF THE CANADIAN. — COTTON-WOOD. — ARRIVAL AT THE ARKANSA. — CANE BRAKES. — CHEROKEES. — BELLE POINT.

September 5th. The region we were now traversing is one of great fertility, and we had daily occasion to regret that our visit to it had not been made earlier in the season. Many unknown plants were observed, but their flowering season having passed, the fruit of many of them have ripened and fallen, we were deprived of the means of ascertaining the name and place of such as had been heretofore described, and of describing such as were new. We had, however, the satisfaction to recognize some interesting productions, among which we may enumerate a very beautiful species of bignonia, and the bow-wood or osage orange. [2] The rocky hills abound in trees of a small size, and the cedars are sometimes so numerous, as to give their peculiar and gloomy colouring to the landscape. We listened as we rode forward to the note of a bird, new to some of us, and bearing a singular resemblance to the noise of a child's toy trumpet; this we soon found to be the cry of the great ivory-billed wood-pecker (picus principalis), the largest of the North American species, and confined to the warmer parts. The picus pileatus we had seen on the 25th of August, more than one hundred miles above, and this with the picus erythrocephalus were now common. Turkies were very numerous. The paroquet, chuck-wills-widow, wood-robin, mocking bird, and many other small birds, filled the woods with life and music.

The bald eagle, the turkey buzzard, and black vulture, raven and crow, were seen swarming like the blowing flies about any spot where a bison, an elk, or a deer had fallen a prey to the hunter. About the river were large flocks of pelicans, with numbers of snowy herons, and the beautiful ardea egretta.

Soon after we had commenced our morning ride, we heard the report of a gun at the distance of a mile, as we thought, on our left; this was distinctly heard by several of the party, and induced us to believe that white hunters were in the neighbourhood. We had recently seen great numbers of elk, and killed one or two, which we had found in bad condition.

September 6th. Numerous ridges of rocky hills traverse the country from north-east to south-west, crossing the direction of the river obliquely. They are of a sandstone, which bears sufficient evidence of belonging to a coal formation. At the spot where we halted to dine, one of these ranges, crossing the river, produces an inconsiderable fall. As the whole width of the channel is paved with a compact horizontal sandstone, we believed all the water of the river must be forced into view, and were a little surprised to find the quantity something less than it had been almost six hundred miles above in the same stream. It would appear, that all the water which falls in rains or flows from springs in an extent of country larger than Pennsylvania, is not sufficient to supply the evaporation of so extensive a surface of naked and heated sands.

If the river of which we speak should at any season of the year contain water enough for the purposes of navigation, it is probable the fall occasioned by the rocky traverse above mentioned will be sufficient to prevent the passage upwards. The point is a remarkable one, as being the locality of a rare and beautiful variety of sandstone. The rock which appears in the bed of the river is a compact slaty sandstone, of a deep green colour, resembling some varieties of chloritic slate.

Whether the colour depends upon epidote chlorite, or some other substance, we were not able to determine. The sandstone is micaceous, but the particles of mica, as well as those of the other integrant minerals, are very minutely divided. The same rock, as we found by tracing it to some distance, becomes of a light grey colour, and contains extensive beds of bituminous clay-slate. Its stratifications are so little inclined, that their dip cannot be estimated by the eye.

This point, though scarce deserving the name of a cataract, is so marked by the occurrence of a peculiar bed, or rocks crossing the river, and by the rapid descent of the current, that it may be readily recognized by any who shall pass that way hereafter. In this view we attach some importance to it, as the only spot in a distance of six hundred miles we can hope to identify by description. In ascending, when the traveller arrives at this point, he has little to expect beyond, but sandy wastes and thirsty inhospitable steppes. The skirts of the hilly and wooded region extend to a distance of fifty or sixty miles above, but even this district is indifferently supplied with water. Beyond commences the wide sandy desert, stretching westward to the base of the Rocky Mountains. We have little apprehension of giving too unfavourable an account of this portion of the country. Though the soil is in some places fertile, the want of timber, of navigable streams, and of water for the necessities of life, render it an unfit residence for any but a nomade population. The traveller who shall at any time have traversed its desolate sands, will, we think, join us in the wish that this region may for ever remain the unmolested haunt of the native hunter, the bison, and the jackall.

One mile below this point (which we call the Falls or the Canadian, rather for the sake of a name than as considering it worthy to be thus designated), is the entrance, from the south, of a river fifty yards wide. Its banks are lined with tall forests of cotton-wood and sycamore, and its bottoms are wide and fertile. Its bed is less choked with sand than that of the river to which it is tributary. Six or eight miles farther down, and on the other side, is the confluence of the Great North Fork, discharging at least three times as much water as we found at the falls above mentioned. It is about eighty yards wide. The beds of both these tributaries are covered with water from shore to shore, but they have gentle currents, and are not deep, and neither of them have in any considerable degree that red tinge which characterizes the Canadian. We have already mentioned, that what we consider the sources of the North Fork are situated in the floetz trap country, nearly opposite those of the Purgatory Creek of the Arkansa. Of one of its northern tributaries we have received some information from the recent work of Mr. Nuttall, who crossed it in his journey to the Great Salt river of Arkansa in 1819.* " Still proceeding," says he, a little to the north of west, about ten miles further, we came to a considerable rivulet of clear and still water, deep enough to swim our horses. This stream was called the Little North Fork (or Branch) of the Canadian, and emptied into the main North Fork of the same river, nearly 200 miles distant, including its meanders, which had been ascended by the trappers of beaver." From his account it appears that the banks of this stream are wooded, and that the " superincumbent rock" is a sandstone, not of the red formation, but probably belonging to a coal district.

Its water, like that of the Arkansa, and its northern tributaries, when not swelled by rains, is of a greenish

* Journal of Travels into the Arkansa Territory, by Thomas Nuttall, &c. page 200.

colour. This colouring is sometimes so intense in the rivers of this region as to suggest the idea that the water is filled with minute confervas or other floating plants, but when we see it by transmitted light, as when a portion of it is held in a glass vessel, the colour disappears.

Three and a half miles below the confluence of the North Fork is a remarkable rock, standing isolated in the middle of the river, like the Grand Tower in the Mississippi. It is about twenty-five feet high, and fifty or sixty in diameter, and its sides so perpendicular as to render the summit inaccessible. It appears to have been broken from a high promontory of gray sandstone overhanging the river on the north side.

Not being able to find grass for pasture, we rode later than usual, and were finally compelled to encamp on a sandy beach, which afforded nothing but rushes for our horses.

September 8th. The quantity of water in the river had now become so considerable as to impede our descent along the bed; but the valley was narrow, and so filled with close and entangled forests, and the uplands so broken and rugged, that no other path appeared to remain for us. We therefore continued to make our way, though with great difficulty, and found our horses much incommoded by being kept almost constantly in the water, as we were compelled to do to cross from the point of a sand-bar on one side the river, to the next on the other. Quicksands also occurred, and in places where we least expected it, our horses and ourselves were thrown to the earth without a moment's notice. These sudden falls, occasioned by sinking in the sand, and the subsequent exertion necessary to extricate themselves, proved extremely harassing to our jaded horses, and we had reason to fear that these faithful servants would fail us almost at the end of our journey.

Above the falls, the width of the river, that is of the space included between its two banks, varies from three hundred yards to two miles; below it is uniformly narrower, scarce exceeding four hundred yards. The beaches are sloping, and often covered with young cotton-wood or willow trees. In the Missouri, Mississippi, and to some extent in the Arkansa and its tributaries, the islands, sand-bars, and even the banks, are constantly shifting place. In the progress of these changes, the young willows and cotton-wood trees which spring up wherever a naked beach is exposed, may be supposed to have some agency, by confining the soil with their roots, and arresting the dirt and rubbish in times of high water. On the Missouri, the first growth which springs up in these places, is so commonly the willow, that the expressions "willow-bar" and "willow-island" have passed into the language of the boatmen, and communicate the definite idea of a bar, or an island recently risen from the water. These willows become intermixed with the cotton-wood, and these trees are often almost the exclusive occupants of extensive portions of the low grounds. The foliage of the most common species of willow (S. angustata) is of a light green colour, and, when seen under certain angles, of a silvery gray, contrasting beautifully with the intense and vivid green of cotton-wood. [3] Within a few yards of the spot where we halted to dine, we were so fortunate as to find a small log canoe made fast on shore. From its appearance we were assured it had been some months deserted by its rightful owner; and from the necessity of our situation, thought ourselves justified in seizing and converting it to our use. Our pack-horses had become much weakened, and reduced by long fatigue; and in crossing the river, as we had often to do, we felt that our collections, the only valuable part of our baggage, were constantly exposed to the risk of being wetted. We accordingly made prize of the canoe, and putting on board our packs and heavy baggage, manned it with two men, designing that they should navigate it down to the settlements. Aside from this canoe, we discovered in the adjoining woods the remains of an old camp, which we perceived had been occupied by white men, and saw other convincing proofs that we were coming near some inhabited country.

We halted at evening in a small prairie on the north side of the river, the first we had seen for some time. The difficulties of navigation, arising from the shallowness of the water, prevented the arrival of the canoe and baggage until a late hour. The men had been compelled to wade a great part of the way, and drag the canoe over the sand.

September 9th. We had proceeded a mile or two from our encampment, when we discovered a herd of twenty or thirty elk, some standing in the water, and some lying upon the sand-beach, at no great distance before us. The hunters went forward, and singling out one of the finest bucks, fired upon him, at which the whole herd plunged into the thicket, and disappeared instantly. We had, however, too much confidence in the skill of the hunter to doubt but his shot had been fatal, and several of the party dismounting, pursued the herd into the woods, where they soon overtook the wounded buck. The noble animal, finding his pursuers at his heels, turned upon the foremost, who saved himself by springing into a thicket which the elk could not penetrate, but in which he soon became entangled by his enormous antlers, and fell an easy victim. His head was enveloped in such a quantity of cissus smilax and other twining vines, that scarce the tips of his horns could be seen; thus blind-folded, he stood until most of those who had followed into the woods had discharged their pieces, and did not finally yield up his life until he was stabbed to the heart with a knife. He was found in excellent condition, having more than two inches of fat on the brisket. The meat was carried to the river, and deposited on a projecting point of rocks, with a note addressed to the men who were behind with the canoe, directing them to add this supply of provisions to their cargo.

At this point, and again at an inconsiderable distance below, a soft green slaty sandstone forms the bed of the river, and occasions a succession of rapids. At noon an observation by the meridian altitude of the sun's lower limb gave us $35°\ 30'$, as an approximation to our latitude. This was much greater than we had anticipated from the position assigned to Red river on the maps, and tending to confirm the unpleasant fears we had entertained of having mistaken some tributary of the Arkansa for the Red river.

Thick and extensive cane brakes occurred on both sides of the river, and though the bottoms were wide and covered with heavy forests, we could see at intervals the distant sandstone hills, with their scattered forests of cedar and oak.

September 10th. We left our camp at the usual hour, and after riding eight or ten miles, arrived at the confluence of our supposed Red river with another of a much greater size, which we at once perceived to be the Arkansa. Our disappointment and chagrin at discovering the mistake we had so long laboured under, was little alleviated by the consciousness that the season was so far advanced, our horses and our means so far exhausted, as to place it beyond our power to return and attempt the discovery of the sources of Red river. We had been misled by some little reliance on the maps, and the current statements concerning the position of the upper branches of Red river, and more particularly by the confident assurance we had received from the Kaskaia Indians, whom we did not suspect of a wish to deceive us in an affair of such indifference to them. Knowing there was a degree of ambiguity and confusion in the nomenclature of the rivers, we had insisted particularly on being informed, whether the river we were descending was the one on which the Pawnee Piquas had their permanent residence, and this we were repeatedly assured was the case. Several other circumstances, which have been already mentioned, led us to the commission of this unfortunate mistake.

According to our estimate of distances on our courses, it is seven hundred and ninety-six and a half miles from the point where we first struck the Canadian to its confluence with the Arkansa. If we make a reasonable allowance for the meanders of the river, and for the extension of its upper branches some distance to the west of the place where we commenced our descent, the entire length of the Canadian will appear to be about one thousand miles. Our journey upon it had occupied a space of seven weeks, travelling with the utmost diligence the strength of our horses would permit.

On arriving at the Arkansa, we waited a short time for our canoe, in which we crossed our heavy baggage, and then swimming our horses, we ascended the bank in search of a place to encamp, but soon found ourselves surrounded by a dense almost impenetrable cane brake, where no vestige of a path could be found. In this dilemma, no alternative remained, but to force our way forward by the most laborious exertions. The canes were of large size, and stood so close together that a horse could not move forward the length of his body without breaking by main force a great number of them. Making our way with excessive toil among these gigantic gramina, our party might be said to resemble a company of rats traversing a sturdy field of grass. The cane stalks, after being trod to the earth, often inflicted, in virtue of their elasticity, blows as severe as they were unexpected. It is not to be supposed our horses alone felt the inconvenience of this sort of travelling. We received frequent blows and bruises on all parts of our bodies, had our sweaty faces and hands scratched by the rough leaves of the cane, and oftentimes, as our attention was otherwise directed, we caught with our feet and dragged across our shins the flexible and spiny stalks of the green briar.

This most harassing ride we commenced at eleven in the morning, and continued without a moment's intermission till sunset, when finding we were not about to extricate ourselves, we returned near a mile and a half on our track, to a spot where we had passed a piece of open woods large enough to spread our blankets on. Here we laid ourselves down at dark, much exhausted by our day's journey.

Our fatigue was sufficient to overcome the irritation of the ticks, and we slept soundly until about midnight, when we were awakened by the commencement of a heavy fall of rain, from which, as we had not been able to set up our tent, we had no shelter.

On the following morning, after several hours spent in most laborious travelling, like that of the preceding day, we found ourselves emerging from the river bottom, and, to our great satisfaction, exchanging the cane brakes for open woods. At the foot of the hill lay a deep morass, covered with the nelumbo and other aquatic plants. It had probably been the former bed of the Arkansa. Observing water in some part of it, several of the party attempted to penetrate to it to drink, but the quaking bog was found so deep and soft as to be wholly impassable.

After ascending the hills we pursued our course nearly due north, through open woods of oak and nyssa, until we reached the prairie, and soon after discovered a large and frequented path, which we knew could be no other than that leading to Fort Smith. On emerging from the low grounds we had no longer the prospect of boundless and monotonous plains. We were in a region of mountains and forests, interspersed with open plains, but these were of limited extent.

September 12th. We resumed our journey at sunrise. The weather was cool, and the morning fair. The wide and densely-wooded valley of the Arkansa lay on our route. The course of the river was marked by a long and undulating line of mist, brightening in the beams of the rising sun; beyond rose the blue summits of the Point Lucre and Cavaniol mountains, "in the clear light above the dews of morn." Though the region about us had all the characters of a mountain district, we could discover little uniformity in the direction of the ranges. The Cavaniol and Point Lucre mountains are situated on opposite sides of the Poteau, above the confluence of James's Fork, and are part of low ridges running from S.W. to N.E. On the north side of the Arkansa is a ridge of considerable elevation, nearly parallel in direction to the aggregate course of the river.

In the path we were travelling we observed tracks indicating that men on horseback had recently passed, and in the course of the morning we met a party of six or eight Indians, who informed us they were of the Cherokee nation; that we should be able to arrive at the military post at Belle Point on the following morning. They were on horseback, carrying guns, kettles, and other articles suited to a hunting excursion, which it was their purpose to make in the territory of the Osages; one or two of them had on round hats; all had calico shirts, or some other article of foreign fabric, as part of their dress; and all had a mean and squalid appearance, indicating that they had been in habits of frequent intercourse with the whites. They were unable to speak or understand our language, but communicated with considerable ease by means of signs.

At eleven o'clock we halted, and as our provisions were nearly exhausted, most of the party went out to hunt, but were not fortunate in meeting game. We found, however, some papaw trees with ripe fruit of an uncommon size and delicious flavor, with which we were able to allay our hunger. The papaw tree attains a much larger size, and the fruit arrives at greater perfection, in the low grounds of the Arkansa, than on the Missouri, Ohio, and Upper Mississippi, where it is also common. The papaws fall to the ground as soon as fully ripe, and are eagerly sought after by the bears, raccoons, oppossum, &c.

In the afternoon one of our mules failed so far that the undivided attention and the most active exertions of two men were required to keep him moving at the rate of a slow walk. This made it necessary we should encamp, and we accordingly selected a spot in a fine open grove of oaks, where we pitched our tent. Among other interesting plants we collected here the beautiful vexillaria * virginica of Eaton, which has the largest flower of any of the legumina of the United States, as is remarked by Mr. Nuttall. We saw also the menispermum lyoni, hieracium marianum, rhexia virginica. As we encamped at an early hour, the party dispersed in several directions in search of game. Nothing was found except a swarm of bees, affording as much honey as we chose to eat for supper. While engaged in felling the tree we heard guns discharged at a distance, and by sending persons to examine, learned they were those of a party of men accompanying Mr. Robert Glen on his way from Fort Smith to the trading-house at the mouth of the Verdigrise. In the evening we received a visit from Mr. G., whose camp was distant only about a mile from ours. He was the first white man not of our own party whom we had seen since the 6th of

* We have adopted this name from the author of the " Manual of Botany," as a substitute for that of the 1712 genera of Persoon, which has been so severely censured by President Smith in Rees's Cyclopedia. It is equally appropriate with the old name, and contains no offensive allusion.

the preceding June. From him we received a highly acceptable present of coffee, biscuits, a bottle of spirits, &c.; also the welcome intelligence that Captain Bell, with his division of the exploring party, had arrived at Fort Smith some days previous.

Early on the 13th we took up our march in a heavy fall of rain, which continued until we arrived at the little plantation opposite Belle Point. Here we emerged from the deep silence and twilight gloom of the forest, and found ourselves once more surrounded by the works of men. The plantation consisted of a single enclosure, covered with a thick crop of maize, intermixed with gigantic stalks of the phytolacca decandria and ricinus palma christi; forming a forest of annual plants, which seemed almost to vie with miegias and annonas occupying the adjacent portions of the river bottoms. As we followed the winding pathway past the little cottage, at the corner of the field we were saluted by several large dogs, who sprang up from the surrounding weeds. Urged by our impatience to see human faces, we called out to the people in the cottage to direct us to Belle Point, although we knew the path could not be mistaken, and that we were not ten rods from the ferry. Notwithstanding our inquiries might have been thought impertinent, we were very civilly answered by a young woman, who came to the door, and attempted to silence the clamours of the dogs. We were not surprised to find our uncouth appearance a matter of astonishment both to dogs and men.

On arriving at the beach opposite Fort Smith, and making known our arrival by the discharge of a pistol, we perceived the inhabitants of the garrison and our former companions coming down to the ferry to give us welcome; and being soon carried over, we met from Major Bradford and Captain Ballard a most cordial and flattering reception. Captain Bell, with Mr. Say, Mr. Seymour, and Lieutenant Swift, having experienced numerous casualties, and achieved various adventures, having suffered much from hunger, and more from the perfidy of some of their soldiers, had arrived on the 9th, and were all in good health. The loss most severely felt was that of the manuscript notes of Mr. Say and Lieutenant Swift. Measures for the apprehension of the deserters and the recovery of these important papers were taken immediately, and a reward of two hundred dollars offered. Mr. Glen had kindly volunteered his assistance and his influence to engage the Osages in the pursuit. But these efforts were unavailing.

We arrived at Fort Smith at about nine o'clock, and were soon afterwards invited to a bountifully furnished breakfast-table at Major Bradford's. Our attentive host knowing the caution necessary to be used by men in our situation, restrained us from a too unbounded indulgence in the use of bread, sweet potatoes, and other articles of diet to which we had been long unaccustomed. The experience of a few days taught us that it would have been fortunate for us if we had given more implicit heed to his caution.

The site of Fort Smith was selected by Major Long in the fall of 1817, and called Belle Point, in allusion to its peculiar beauty. It occupies a point of elevated land immediately below the junction of the Arkansa and the Poteau, a small tributary from the south-west. Agreeably to the orders of General Smith, then commanding the ninth military department, a plan of the proposed work was submitted to Major Bradford, at that time and since commandant at the post, under whose superintendance the works have been in part completed, not without some deviation from the original plan. The buildings now form two sides of a hollow square, terminated by strong block-houses at the opposite angles, and fronting towards the river.

The hill which forms the basis of the fort is a dark gray micaceous sandstone in horizontal laminæ, and is elevated about thirty feet above the water. The country back of the fort has an undulating surface, and rises gradually as it recedes, being covered with heavy forests of oak, tulip tree, sassafras, &c. Towards the south and south-east, at no great distance, rise the summits of the mountainous range already mentioned. The Sugar-loaf and Cavaniol mountains (the former being one of a group of these similar conic summits), are visible from some points near Fort Smith. The Poteau, so called by the French from the word signifying a post or station, rises sixty or seventy miles south of Belle Point, opposite to the sources of the Kiamesha, a branch of Red river. Nearly the whole of its course is through a hilly or mountainous region, but it is one so sparingly supplied with water, that the Poteau, within two miles of its confluence with the Arkansa, is in the dry season no more than a trifling brook. In an excursion which we made from Fort Smith, we ascended the Poteau about a mile and a half, where we observed an extensive bed of bituminous clay-slate, indicating the neighbourhood of coal. Tracing this slate to the south and east, we found it to pass under a very considerable sandstone hill. Several circumstances induce us to believe that it is also underlayed by a sandstone similar to that at the fort. Attentive examination will show that these rocks have a slight inclination towards the east; and if the bituminous slate in question had been underlayed by compact limestone, as has been conjectured *, it is highly probable this rock would have emerged near where the sandstone appears at Belle Point. We make this remark because, although we have often seen both limestone and bituminous clay-slate in various parts of the Arkansa territory, it has never been our fortune to meet with them in connexion. A few rods above this bed of bituminous slate we crossed the Poteau almost at a single step, and without wetting the soles

* Nuttall's Travels into the Arkansa Territory, p. 144.

of our mockasins, so inconsiderable was the quantity of water it contained. The point between the confluence of the Poteau and the Arkansa is low and fertile bottom land, and, like that on the opposite side of the river, covered with dense and heavy forests of cottonwood, sycamore, and ash, intermixed with extensive and impenetrable cane brakes. In these low grounds the beautiful papaw tree, whose luscious fruit was now ripe, occurs in great abundance. It rises to the height of thirty or forty feet, and its trunk is sometimes not less than a foot in diameter.

Grape vines, several scandent species of smilax and cissus, and a most singular vine allied to menispermum, are so intermixed with the sturdy under growth as to render the woods almost impassable. Paths have been opened by the people of the garrison where they have been found necessary by cutting away the canes and small trees; but they may be said to resemble subterranean passages, to which the rays of the sun never penetrate. We found the air in these, and indeed in every part of heavy forests, stagnant, and so loaded with the effluvia of decaying vegetable substances as to be immediately oppressive to the lungs. After spending an hour or two in an atmosphere of this kind, we found ourselves perceptibly affected with languor and dizziness.

The gardens at Fort Smith afforded green corn, melons, sweet potatoes, and other esculent vegetables, which to us had for a long time been untasted luxuries. It is probable we did not exercise sufficient caution in recommencing the use of these articles, as we soon found our health beginning to become impaired. We had been a long time confined to a meat diet, without bread or condiments of any kind, and were not surprised to find ourselves affected by so great and so sudden a change. It may be worth while to remark, that we had been so long unaccustomed to the use of salt, that the sweat of our faces had lost all perceptible saltness, and that the ordinary dishes which were brought to our mess-table at the Fort appeared unpalatable, on account of being too highly seasoned.

In a region of extensive river alluvion, supporting, like that of the Arkansa, boundless forests, impervious to the winds, and the rays of the sun, it is not surprising that a state of the atmosphere should exist unfavourable to health; intermitting, remitting, and continued bilious fevers prevail during the summer and autumn, and in many instances terminate fatally. Among recent settlers, the want of the most common comforts, of the advice and attendance of skilful physicians, and, above all, the want of cleanliness, and the destructive habits of intemperance, are causes operating powerfully to produce and aggravate these diseases. The settlements about Fort Smith were sickly, and we saw numbers with that peculiar sallowness of complexion which accompanies those chronic derangements of the functions of the liver, so often the consequence of bilious fevers. It is obvious, that the causes of the acknowledged sickliness of the recent settlements in the south and west, are in a great measure local and unconnected with the climate; by the increase of settlements, and the progress of cultivation, they will be in part removed.

Fort Smith is garrisoned by one company of riflemen, under the command of Major Bradford. Among other important designs contemplated in the establishment of this post, one was to prevent the encroachments of the white settlers upon the lands still held by the Indians. Some of the most fertile portions of the Arkansa territory are those about the Verdigrise, Skin Bayon, Illinois, Six Bulls, &c.; in which some unauthorised settlements were heretofore made, but have recently been abandoned, in compliance with the requirements of the commandant at Fort Smith.

AN ACCOUNT

OF

THE EXPEDITION OF THE DETACHED PARTY

ON THE ARKANSA RIVER.*

CHAPTER III.

THE PARTY PROCEED UPON THEIR ROUTE. — THUNDERSTORM. — SOME ACCOUNT OF THE KIAWA, KASKAIA, ARRAPAHO, AND SHIENNE INDIANS. — NEW SPECIES OF TOAD.

Monday, 24th. After the departure of so great a portion of our numbers, combined with whom we could hardly be regarded as sufficiently powerful to contend successfully with a force which we were daily liable to encounter, we were well aware of the necessity of exerting an increased vigilance, and of relying still more implicitly upon our individual means of defence, than we had hitherto done. Our small band now consisted of Captain Bell, Lieut. Swift, Mr. Seymour, Mr. Say, and the interpreters Bijeaux, Ledoux, and Julien, with five soldiers.

We were cheered by the reflection, that we had successfully performed a very considerable and most important part of our expedition, harmonizing well

* The following six chapters are from the pen of Mr. Say.

with each other, and unassailed by any urgent visible dangers, such as had been anticipated by ourselves, and predicted by others. We could not however look forward to the trackless desert which still separated us from the utmost boundary of civilisation, and which we had no reason to believe was less than a thousand miles in breadth, traversed in many portions of its extent by lawless war-parties of various nations of Indians, without an emotion of anxiety and of doubt as to the successful termination of our enterprize.

We were this afternoon assailed by a very severe thunder-storm, and Julien, who had skirted the timber for the purpose of hunting, was electrified by a flash of lightning, which entered the earth within a few yards of him. The wind was violent, and blew the drops of rain with so much force into our faces, that our horses refused to proceed, constantly endeavouring to turn themselves about from the storm; we at length yielded to their obstinacy, and halted upon the plain. The storm did not abate until we were thoroughly drenched to the skin, when, after being delayed some additional space of time, until a straggler had joined us, we continued our journey.

Wednesday, 26th. Late in the afternoon we saw, at a great distance before us, evident indications of the proximity of Indians, consisting of conic elevations, or skin lodges, on the edge of the skirting timber, partially concealed by the foliage of the trees. On our nearer approach we observed their horses grazing peacefully, but becoming suddenly frightened, probably by our scent, they all bounded off towards the camp, which was now full in view. Our attention was called off from the horses by the appearance of their masters, who were now seen running towards us with all their swiftness. A minute afterwards we were surrounded by them, and were happy to observe in their features and gestures a manifestation of the most pacific disposition; they shook us by the hand, assured us by signs that they rejoiced to see us, and invited us to partake of their hospitality. We however replied, that we had brought our own lodges with us, and would encamp near them. We selected for this purpose a clear spot of ground on the bank of the river, intending to remain a day or two with this little known people, to observe their manners and way of life. We had scarcely pitched our tents, watered and staked our horses, before presents of jerked bison meat were brought to us by the squaws, consisting of selected pieces, the fattest and the best, in sufficient quantity for the consumption of two or three days. After the usual ceremony of smoking, they were informed to what nation we belonged, and that further communication would be made to their principal men to-morrow, whom we wished summoned for that purpose. About sundown they all retired, and left us to our repose. The Indians were encamped on both sides of the river, but the great body of them was on the opposite bank, their skin lodges extending in a long single line; the extremities of which were concealed from our view by the timber of the islands in the river, whilst about ten lodges only were erected on the side we occupied, and within a quarter of a mile of our camp.

Soon after our arrival, an Indian well stricken in years inquired if we had seen a man and squaw within a day or two on our route: we described to him the appearance of the calf and his squaw. "That is my wife," said he, "who has eloped from me, and I will instantly go in pursuit of them." He accordingly procured a companion, and both were soon on their way, well armed and mounted.

Thursday, 27th. Notice having been sent to the opposite party of our arrival, and of our wish to see the principal men, four chiefs presented themselves at our camp this morning at an early hour, as representatives of the several bands, of the same number of different nations, here associated together, and consisting of Kiawas, Kaskaias or Bad-hearts, Shiennes (sometimes written Chayenne), and Arrapahoes. Several distinguished men accompanied them. We had made some little preparation for their reception, by spreading skins for them to sit on, hoisting our flag, and selecting a few presents from our scanty stores. They arranged themselves with due solemnity, and the pipe being passed around, many of them seemed to enjoy it as the greatest rarity, eyeing it as it passed from mouth to mouth, and inhaling its fragrant smoke into their lungs with a pleasure which they could not conceal. One individual of a tall emaciated frame, whose visage was furrowed with deep wrinkles, evidently rather the effect of disease than of age, after filling his lungs and mouth topfull of smoke, placed his hands firmly upon his face and inflated cheeks as in an ecstacy, and unwilling to part with what yielded the utmost pleasure, he retained his breath until suffocation compelled him to drive out the smoke and inhale fresh air, which he effected so suddenly and with so much earnestness, and singular contortion of countenance, that we restrained ourselves with some effort from committing the indecorum of a broad laugh. We had the good fortune to find one of them who could speak the Pawnee language tolerably well; he had acquired it in his early youth, whilst residing in a state of captivity in that nation; so that, by means of our interpreters, we experienced no difficulty in acquainting them, that we belonged to the numerous and powerful nation of Americans *, that we had been sent by our great chief, who presides over all the country, to

* In contradistinction from Spaniards, near whose frontier these Indians rove.

examine that part of his territories, that he might become acquainted with its features, its produce and population; that we had been many moons on our journey, and had passed through many red nations, of whose hospitality we largely partook, &c. This was translated into French, then into Pawnee, and afterwards into Kiawa, and the other languages, by their respective interpreters. In reply, a chief expressed his surprise that we had travelled so far, and assured us that they were happy to see us, and hoped that as a road was now open to our nation, traders would be sent amongst them.

We assured them, that traders would be soon amongst them, provided we could report on our return that we had been hospitably treated while travelling through their country.

A few presents, such as knives, combs, vermilion, &c., were then laid before the chiefs, who, in return, presented us with three or four horses, which terminated the proceedings of the council. We afterwards understood that our guests thought we gave but little; and it is perhaps true, that the value of their presents was far greater than ours, yet our liberality was fully equal to our means.

The whole population had now deserted their edifices and crowded about us, and, agreeably to our wishes, which were announced in the council, the women brought jerked meat, and the men skin and hair ropes for halters, to trade with us for trinkets; and we were enabled to obtain a sufficient quantity of each, at a very moderate price. The trading being completed, we expected the crowd to diminish, but it seemed rather to augment in magnitude and density, until, becoming a very serious inconvenience, we requested the chiefs to direct their people to retire, which they immediately complied with, but, with the exception of the Shienne chief, were not obeyed. All the Shiennes forthwith left us, in compliance with the peremptory orders of their chief, who seemed to be a man born to command, and to be endowed with a spirit of unconquerable ferocity, and capable of inflicting exemplary punishment upon any one who should dare to disobey his orders. He was tall and graceful, with a highly-ridged aquiline nose, corrugated forehead, mouth with the corners drawn downward, and rather small, but remarkably piercing eye, which, when fixed upon your countenance, appeared strained in the intenseness of its gaze, and to seek rather for the movements of the soul within, than to ascertain the mere lineaments it contemplated. The other chiefs seemed to possess only the dignity of office, without the power of command; the result, probably, of a deficiency of that native energy with which their companion was so pre-eminently endowed. They scarcely dared to reiterate their admonitions to their followers, not to press so closely upon the white people, but to limit their approaches to the line of our baggage. Still our tents were filled, and our persons hemmed in by the ardent and insatiable curiosity of the multitude, of both sexes and of all ages, mounted and on foot. To an observer of mankind, the present scene was abundantly fruitful and interesting. We could not but remark the ease and air of security with which their equestrians preserved their equipoise on the naked backs of their horses, in their evolutions beyond the crowd; nor could we restrain a smile, in the midst of vexatious circumstances, at the appearance of the naked children, mounted on horses, sometimes to the number of three or four on each, carelessly standing erect, or kneeling upon their backs, to catch a glance, over the heads of the intervening multitude, at the singular deportment, costume, and appearance of the white strangers.

In the rear of our tent, a squaw, who had become possessed of a wooden small-toothed comb, was occupied in removing from her head a population as numerous, as the individuals composing it were robust and well fed. She had placed a skin upon her lap to receive the victims as they fell; and a female companion who sat at her feet alternately craunched the oily vermin between her teeth, and conversed with the most rapid and pleasant loquacity, as she picked them up from the skin before her.

Our attention was now arrested by a phenomenon which soon relieved us from the crowd that pressed upon us. A heavy and extensive cloud of dust was observed in the north, obscuring the horizon, and bounding the range of vision in that direction. It moved rapidly towards us. An animated scene ensued; the Indians fording the river with as much rapidity of movement as they could exert, towards their encampment, horse and foot, the water foaming before them. It soon became obvious that the dust ascended into the atmosphere under the influence of a violent current of air; we therefore employed a few moments of interval in strengthening our feeble tenements to resist the influence of the approaching tempest. Within, they were now so nearly filled with our red brethren, that we wedged ourselves in with some difficulty amongst them. It soon became necessary to exert our strength in holding down our tents and supporting the poles, which bowed and shook violently under the pressure of the blast. Thunder, lightning, rain, and hail succeeded. During this play of the elements, our guests sat in stillness, scarcely articulating a word during the prevalence of the electrical explosions.

Our tents were much admired, and previously to the fall of rain (which exposed their imperfection, in admitting the water, modified into the form of a mist) one of the natives offered to exchange an excellent mule for that in which he was sitting; and as the commonalty could not distinguish us in their minds from traders, another offered two mules (valued equal to four horses) for a double-barrelled gun; and a third would willingly have bartered a very good horse for an old and almost worn-out camp-kettle, which we could by no means part with, though much in want of horses.

These Indians differ, in many particulars, from those of the Missouri, with whose appearance we had been for some time familiar. Their average stature appeared to us less considerable; and although the general appearance of the countenance was such as we had been accustomed to see, yet their faces have, perhaps, somewhat more latitude, and the Roman nose is obviously less predominant; but still the direction of the eye, the prominence of the cheek bones, the form of the lips, teeth, chin, and retreating forehead, are precisely similar. They have also the same habit of plucking the hair from various parts of the body; but that of the head, in the females, is only suffered to attain to the shoulders, whilst the men permit theirs to grow to its full extent. They even regard long hair as an ornament, and many wear false hair fastened to their own by means of an earthy matter, resembling red clay, and depending in many instances (particularly the young beau) to their knees, in the form of queues, one on each side of the head, variously decorated with ribbon, like slips of red and blue cloth, or coloured skin. Others, and by no means an inconsiderable few, had collected their long hair into several flat masses, of the breadth of two or three fingers, and less than the fifth of an inch in thickness, each one separately annulated with red clay at regular intervals. The elders wore their hair without decoration, flowing loosely about their shoulders, or simply intermixed with slender plaited queues. In structure and colour it is not distinguished from that of the Missouri Indians, though, in early youth, it is often of a much lighter colour; and a young man, of perhaps fifteen years of age, who visited us to-day, had hair decidedly of a flaxen hue, with a tint of dusky yellow.

Their costume is very simple, that of the female consisting of a leathern petticoat, reaching the calf of the leg, destitute of a seam, and often exposing a well-formed thigh, as the casualties of wind or position influence the artless foldings of the skirt. The leg and foot are often naked, but usually invested by gaiters and mockasins. A kind of sleeveless short gown, composed of a single piece of the same material, loosely clothes the body, hanging upon the shoulders, readily thrown off, without any sense of indelicacy, when suckling their children, or under the influence of a heated atmosphere, displaying loose and pendant mammæ. A few are covered by the more costly attire of coarse red or blue cloth, ornamented with a profusion of blue and white beads: the short gown of this dress has the addition of wide sleeves descending below the elbow; its body is of a square form, with a transverse slit in the upper edge for the head to pass through; around this aperture, and on the upper side of the sleeves, is a continuous stripe, the breadth of the hand, of blue and white beads, tastefully arranged in contrast with each other, and adding considerable weight as well as ornament to this part of the dress. Around the petticoat, and in a line with the knees, is an even row of oblong conic bells, made of sheet copper, each about an inch and a half in length, suspended vertically by short leathern thongs as near to each other as possible, so that when the person is in motion, they strike upon each other, and produce a tinkling sound. The young unmarried females are more neatly dressed, and seem to participate but little in the laborious occupations, which fall chiefly to the lot of their wedded companions.

The dress of the men is composed of a breech cloth, skin leggings, mockasins, and a bison robe. In warm weather the three latter articles of dress are sometimes thrown aside as superfluous, exposing all the limbs and body to view, and to the direct influence of the most ardent rays of the sun. Such are the habiliments that necessity compels the multitude to adopt; but the opulence of a few has gained for themselves the comfortable as well as ornamental and highly esteemed Spanish blanket from the Mexican traders, and of which we had previously seen two or three in the possession of Pawnee warriors worn as trophies. Another species of garment, in their estimation equally sumptuous with the blanket, is the cloth robe, which is of ample dimensions, simple in form, one half red and the other blue, thrown loosely about the person, and at a little distance, excepting the singular arrangement of colours, resembling a Spanish cloak.

Some have, suspended from the slits of their ears, the highly prized nacre, or pearlaceous fragments of a marine shell, brought probably from the N.W. coast.

The Shienne chief revisited us in the afternoon. He informed us, that one of his young men, who had been sent to ascertain the route which the bison herds had taken, and their present locality, had observed the trail of a large party of men, whom, by pursuing the direction, he had discovered to be Spaniards on their way towards the position we then occupied, where they must very soon arrive. As we were now in a region claimed by the Mexican Spaniards as exclusively their own, and as we had for some days anticipated such an event as highly probable, we involuntarily reposed implicit confidence in the truth of the intelligence communicated by the chief, who regarded that people as our natural enemies. Nevertheless his story was heard by our little band, as it was proper that it should have been in our situation and in the presence of Indians, with the appearance of absolute apathy. The chief seemed not to have accomplished some object he had in view, and departed evidently displeased. When he was out of hearing, the Indian interpreter, who had become our friend, told us, that the story was entirely false, and was without a doubt the invention of the chief, and designed to expedite the trade for a few additional horses that we were then negociating.

Mr. Say (accompanied by an interpreter), who made a short visit to the small group of lodges near us, was kindly received, though hooted by the children, and of course snarled and snapped at by the dogs. The skin lodges of these wandering people are very similar to those of the Missouri tribes, but in those to which he was introduced, he experienced the oppression of an almost suffocating heat, certainly many degrees above the temperature of the very sultry exterior atmosphere. A very portly old man, whose features were distinguished by a remarkably wide mouth and lengthened chin, invited him to a small ragged lodge, to see the riches it contained. These consisted of habiliments of red and blue cloth, profusely garnished with blue and white beads, the product of the industry and ingenuity of his squaw, from materials obtained last winter from some white traders, who made their appearance on Red river. The present members of this family were the old man, one wife, and four children, the latter as usual in a state of nudity. The baggage was piled around the lodge, serving for seats and beds; and a pile of jerked meat near the door served also for a seat, and was occasionally visited by the dirty feet of the children. A boy was amusing himself with that primitive weapon, the sling, of an ordinary form, which he used with considerable dexterity; the effect of which he appeared disposed to try upon the stranger, and was not readily turned from his purpose by a harsh rebuke and menacing gesture.

He was informed, that the party of traders who had last winter ascended Red river to their country, were

Tabbyboos (a name which they also applied to us, and which appears to be the same word which, according to Lewis and Clarke, in the language of the Snake Indians, means white men; but it was here applied particularly to the Americans). These traders offered various articles, such as coarse cloths, beads, vermillion, kettles, knives, guns, powder, lead, &c. in exchange for horses and mules, bison-robes, and parchment or parfleche. Such was the anxiety to obtain the merchandize thus displayed before them, that those enterprising warriors, whose stock of horses was but small, crossed the mountains into Mexico, and returned with a plentiful supply of those animals for exchange, captured from the Spanish inhabitants of that country. This illicit trade in horses was conducted so extensively by that party of traders, that he was told of a single Indian who sold them fifty mules, besides a considerable number of horses from his own stock.

At his return to camp he was informed, that an old Indian had been there, who asserted that he never before had seen a white man; and on being permitted to view a part of the body usually covered by the dress, he seemed much surprised at its whiteness.

These Indians seem to hold in exalted estimation the martial prowess of the Americans. They said that a battle had lately been fought in the country which lay very far down Red river, between a handful of Americans and a great war-party of Spaniards, that the latter were soon routed, retreating in a dastardly manner, like partridges running through the grass. They were at present at war with the Spaniards themselves, and had lately killed many individuals of a party of that nation near the mountains.

In the evening, squaws were brought to our camp; and after we had retired to our tent at night, a brother of the grand chief, Bear Tooth, continued to interrupt our repose with solicitations in favour of a squaw he had brought with him, until he was peremptorily directed to be gone, and the sentinel was ordered to prevent his future intrusion.

The Bear Tooth is the grand chief of the Arrapahoes, and his influence extends over all the tribes of the country in which he roves; he was said to be encamped at no great distance, with the principal body of these nations. He is said to be very favourably disposed towards the white people, and to have afforded protection and a home in his own lodge to a poor and miserable American who had the good fortune to escape from the barbarity and mistaken policy of the Mexican Spaniards, and from the horrors of a Spanish prison, to find an asylum amongst those whom they regard as barbarians, but to whose commiseration his wretchedness seemed to have been a passport.

Friday, 28th. This morning at sunrise we were called from our tents by the cry of Tabbyboo, proceeding from two handsome mounted Arrapahoes, who appeared delighted to see us; they had passed our camp in the night, on their way from the camp of the Bear Tooth, with a message from that chief to our neighbours. In consequence of this information or order, the lodges on both sides of the river were struck at six o'clock, and the whole body of Indians commenced their march up the river, notwithstanding the threatening aspect of the heavens, which portended a storm. We could not but admire the regularity with which the preparations for their journey seemed to be conducted, and the remarkable facility with which the lodges disappeared, and with all their cumbrous and various contents were secured to the backs of the numerous horses and mules. As the long-drawn cavalcade proceeded onwards, a military air was imparted to the whole, at the distance at which we contemplated it, by the activity of the young warriors, with their lances and shields, galloping or racing along the line for caprice or amusement.

The Kiawa chief, and a few attendants, called to make his parting visit; an old man, rather short, inelegantly formed, destitute of any remarkable physiognomical peculiarity, and like other chiefs without any distinction of personal ornament. In common with many of his tribe, his system was subject to cutaneous eruptions, of which several indications, besides a large ulcer near the angle of the mouth, exhibited the proof. We were soon all driven into our flimsy and almost worn-out tents, which afforded us but a very partial shelter from the fall of a heavy shower of rain from the N. W. Here we obtained some additional information from the chief, who was disposed to be communicative, to augment the considerable mass which we had already collected from other Indians, and particularly from Bijeau, respecting these wandering herds. The chief seemed to take a pleasure in pronouncing to us words of the Kiawa language, and smiled at our awkward attempts to imitate them, whilst we were engaged in committing them to paper. This vocabulary, as well as that of the Kaskaia language, which we had previously obtained from the Calf, had been for some time the objects of our wishes; as Bijeau persuaded us that they were more difficult to acquire than any other language, and that although formerly he resided three years with those nations, he never could understand the meaning of a single word, not even their expression for Frenchman, or tobacco. Nor does this observation, though perhaps unintentionally exaggerating the idea of the abstruse nature of the language, appear absolutely destitute of foundation, since these nations, although constantly associating together, and united under the influence of the Bear Tooth, are yet totally ignorant of each other's language; insomuch that it was no uncommon occurrence to see two individuals of different nations sitting upon the ground, and conversing freely with each other by means of the language of signs. In the art of thus conveying their ideas they were thorough adepts; and their manual display was only interrupted at remote intervals by a smile, or by the auxiliary of an articulated word of the language of the Crow Indians, which to a very limited extent passes current among them.

These languages abound with sounds strange to our ears, and in the noisy loquacity of some squaws, who held an animated debate near our tents yesterday, we distinguished pre-eminently a sound which may be expressed by the letters koo, koo, koo.

The Shiennes, or Shawhays, who have united their destiny with these wanderers, are a band of seceders from their own nation; and some time since, on the occurrence of a serious dispute with their kindred on Shienne river of the Missouri, flew their country, and placed themselves under the protection of the Bear Tooth.

These nations have been for the three past years wandering on the head waters and tributaries of Red river, having returned to the Arkansa only the day which preceded our first interview with them, on their way to the mountains at the sources of the Platte river. They have no permanent town, but constantly rove, as necessity urges them, in pursuit of the herds of bisons in the vicinity of the sources of the Platte, Arkansa, and Red rivers.

They are habitually at war with all the nations of the Missouri; indeed, martial occurrences in which they were interested with those enemies formed the chief topic of their conversation with our interpreters. They were desirous to know of them the names of particular individuals whom they had met in battle, and whom they described; how many had been present at a particular engagement, and who were killed or wounded. The late battle, which we have before spoken of, with the Loup Pawnees, also occupied their inquiries; they denied that they were on that occasion aided by the Spaniards, as we understood they had been, but admitted their great numerical superiority, and the loss of many in killed and wounded. Their martial weapons are bows and arrows, lances, war-clubs, tomahawks, scalping-knives, and shields. [4]

Tobacco being very scarce, they do not carry with them a pouch for the convenience of having it always at hand, an article of dress invariably attendant on the Missouri Indian. Bijeau informed us, that the smoking of tobacco was regarded as a pleasure so sacred and important, that the females were accustomed to depart from the interior of a lodge when the men indulged themselves with the pipe. The Shienne chief, in consequence of a vow he had made against using the pipe, abstained from smoking whilst at our council, until he had the good fortune to find a small piece of paper which some one of our party had rejected; with this he rolled up a small quantity of tobacco fragments into the form of a segar, after the manner of the Spaniards, and thus contented himself with infringing the spirit of his vow, whilst he obeyed it to the letter.

The rain having ceased, our guest and his attendants took their leave.

These Indians might readily be induced to hunt the beaver, which are so extremely abundant in their country; but as yet, these peltries seem not to have entered amongst the items of their trade.

In the afternoon we struck our tents and continued our journey; we were soon overtaken by a thunder-storm, which poured down upon us a deluge of rain, which continued with partial intermissions during the night.

Saturday, 29th. The sun arose with renewed splendour, and ushered in another sultry day. Two of the horses which had been presented by the chiefs ran off, and were soon observed to rise the bluffs, and disappear; men were despatched in pursuit of them, who, after a long and fatiguing chase, returned about noon unsuccessful. We reconciled ourselves as we might to this privation, and after dining proceeded onward. The alluvial margins of the river are gradually dilating as we descend, and the mosquitoes, which have of late visited our camp but sparingly, are now increasing in number. A fine species of toad (bufo) [5] inhabits this region. It resembles the common toad (B. musicus daud.), but differs in the arrangement of the colours, and in the proportional length of the groove of the head, which in that species extends to the nose; it is destitute of large verrucose prominences intervening between the verrucæ behind the eyes, and of the large irregular black dorsal spots edged with white, observable upon the musicus. In the arrangement of the cinerous lines, it presents a general resemblance to *B. fuscus* saur. as represented on pl. 96. of the *Encycl. Method.* It thus resides in a country almost destitute of timber, where, as well as a variety of the musicus, it is very much exposed to the direct rays of the sun.

CHAPTER IV.

ARRAPAHO WAR-PARTY. — TABANUS. — RATTLESNAKES. — BURROWING OWL. — DEPARTURE OF BIJEAU AND LEDOUX FOR THE PAWNEE VILLAGES. — SCARCITY OF TIMBER. — GREAT HERDS OF BISONS. — WOLVES.

SUNDAY, 30th. About sunrise a dense fog intercepted the view of surrounding scenery, which was soon dissipated as we moved on, exhibiting all the variety of partially revealed and unnaturally enlarged objects, so familiar to observers of rural sights. At noon, a beautiful natural grove of cotton-wood, lining a ravine in which was some cool but stagnant water near the bank of the river, invited us to repose during the oppressive mid-day heat. We had hardly stripped our horses of their baggage, and betaken ourselves to our respective occupations, when a voice from the opposite bank of the river warned us of the proximity of Indians, who had been until now unseen. Nine Indians soon appeared, and crossed the river to our camp. They proved to be an Arrapaho war-party of eight men and a squaw, of whom one was a Kiawa.* This party informed us, that they had left the Bear Tooth's party on a tributary of this river, at the distance of about half a day's journey from us, moving upwards. As no apprehension of mischief was entertained from so small a party, they were invited to encamp near us for the remainder of the day; to which, urged by curiosity, and perhaps by the hope of receiving some presents, they readily assented. The squaw busied herself in erecting a little bowery, of a sufficient size to contain herself and her

---

* The Arrapaho, or Rappaho nation, is known to the Minnetarees of the Missouri, by the name of E-tâ-léh, or Bison-path Indians.

husband, who we afterwards discovered to be a personage of some eminence in their mystic arts. Having supplied our guests with a pipe of some tobacco, we resumed our occupations. Our attention was, however, diverted to the young Kiawa warrior, who had the presumption to seize the Kaskaia horse which was purchased of the Calf Indian, loose him from the stake around which he was grazing, and having the further audacity to lead him near to our tents, proceeded to make a noose in the halter, which he placed over the mouth of the animal, that patiently submitted to his operations. This sudden subjugation of the horse was a subject of more surprise to us than the outrageous attempt of the Indian, as he had hitherto resisted all our endeavours to accomplish the same object, whether conciliatory or forcible. It seemed to corroborate the truth of the observation, that the horse readily distinguishes the native from the white man by his acute sense of smelling. The intention of the Indian to take possession of the horse was now manifest, and one of our party stepped forward and seized the halter near the head of the animal; but the Indian, who held the other extremity of the halter, betrayed no symptoms of fear, or of an intention to relinquish a possession which he had thus partially obtained: he looked sternly at his antagonist, and asserted his right to the horse, inasmuch as he had, he said, formerly owned him, and meant now to repossess him. Supposing that this altercation might eventuate unpleasantly, the remainder of our party stood prepared to repulse any attempt which the other Indians might make to support the claim of their companion, whilst Bijeau, with a manly decision, advanced and forcibly jerked the halter out of the hands of the Indian. His companions sat enjoying themselves with their pipe, and did not appear disposed to take any part in the transaction. He fortunately made no further exertions to obtain possession of the horse, but immediately mounted his own horse, and rode off in high dudgeon, saying he would remain no longer with us for fear we would kill him. Contrary to our expectations, the other Indians loudly condemned his conduct; they said that the horse had never been his property, though they all knew the animal well; that the Kiawa was a very bad Indian, and would either assemble a party to return against us, or he would return himself that night to accomplish his purpose. "If he does come," said they, "you need not give yourselves any trouble; for we will watch for him, and kill him ourselves."

When the excitement of this incident had subsided, we felt desirous to examine the contents of the medicine bag of the man of mysteries, who was at once a magician and the leader of the party. At our solicitation he readily opened his sacred depository, and displayed its contents on a skin before us, whilst he politely proceeded to expatiate on their powers and virtues in the occult art, as well as their physical efficacy. They consisted of various roots, seeds, pappus, and powders, both active and inert, as respects their action on the human system, carefully enveloped in skins, leaves, &c., some of which, to his credulous faith, were invested with supernatural powers. Similar qualities were also attributed to some animal products with which these were accompanied, such as claws of birds, beaks, feathers, and hair. But the object that more particularly attracted our attention was the intoxicating bean, as it has been called, of which he possessed upwards of a pint. Julien recognized it immediately. He informed us, that it is in such high request amongst the Oto Indians, that a horse has been exchanged for eight or ten of them. In that nation the intoxicating bean is only used by a particular society, who at their nocturnal orgies make a decoction of the bean, and with much pomp and ceremony administer the delightful beverage to each member. The initiation fees of this society are rather extravagant, and the proceeds are devoted principally to the purchase of the bean. That old sensualist, Shongotonga (big horse), is the principal or presiding member of the society, and the bean is obtained in some circuitous manner from the Pawnee Piquas of Red river, who probably receive it from the Mexican Indians. With some few trinkets of little value, we purchased the principal portion of our medicine man's store of beans; they are of an ovate form, and of a light red, sometimes yellowish colour, with a rather deeply impressed oval cicatrix, and larger than a common bean, A small number of a differently coloured and rather larger bean was intermixed with them.

The squaw had in her possession a quantity of small flat blackish cakes, which on tasting we found very palatable. Having purchased some of them, we ascertained that they were composed of the wild cherry, of which both pulp and stone were pounded together, until the latter is broken into fragments, then mixed with grease, and dried in the sun.

Not choosing to rely implicitly on the good faith of the strangers, however emphatically expressed, the sentinel was directed to look well to them, and also to keep the horse in question constantly in view during the night, and to alarm us upon the occurrence of any suspicious movements.

All, however, remained quiet during the night, and in the morning, Monday 31st, we resumed our journey. The river now considerably dilates, and is studded with a number of small islands, but the timber that skirts its stream is still less abundant, and more scattered. The alluvial formation affords a moderate growth of grass, but the general surface of the country is flat, sterile, and uninteresting. The day was cloudy with an E. S. E. wind, which at night brought some rain.

Tuesday, August 1st. Set out late; and after having travelled about two miles, a horseman armed with a spear was seen on the bluffs, at the distance of about a quarter of a mile, who, after gazing at our line for a short time, disappeared. Our Pawnee interpreters being at a considerable distance in the rear, Julien was sent forward to reconnoitre. He mounted the bluff to the general level of the country, and abruptly halted his horse within our view, as if appearances before him rendered precaution necessary. The Indian again came in sight, and in full career rushed towards him, passed him, and wheeling, halted his horse. Many other Indians then appeared, who surrounded Julien, and after a short and hurried conference, they dashed at full speed down the steep bank of the bluff to meet us, the whole in concert singing the scalp song. So adventurous and heedless was this movement, that one of the horses stumbled and fell with great violence, and rolled to the bottom. His rider, no doubt prepared for such an accident, threw himself in the instant from his seat, so as to fall in the most favourable manner, and avoid the danger of being crushed by the horse; not the slightest attention was bestowed upon him by his companions, and indeed the disaster, however serious it first appeared, hardly interrupted his song. His horse being but little injured, he almost immediately regained his saddle, and came on but little in the rear of the others, who now had mingled with our party, shaking us by the hand with a kind of earnest familiarity not the most agreeable. We needed no additional information to convince us that this was a war-party; their appearance was a sufficient evidence of the nature of their occupation. One of us asked an individual if they were Kiawas, and was answered in the affirmative; he asked a second, if they were Kaskaias, and a third, if they were Arrapahoes, who both also answered affirmatively. This conduct, added to their general deportment, served to excite our suspicions and redouble our vigilance. Two or three other little detached squads were now seen to approach, also singing the scalp song. Our interpreters having joined us, it was proposed that we should avail ourselves of the shade of a large tree which stood near the river, to sit down and smoke with them. They reared their spears against the tree with apparent carelessness and indifference, and took their seats in the form of a semicircle on the ground. Having staked our horses in the rear, and stationed the men to protect them and the baggage, we seated ourselves, and circulated the pipe as usual. But as the party opposed to us was nearly quadruple our number, we did not choose to follow their example in relinquishing our arms, but grasped them securely in our hands, and retained a cautious attitude.

Bijeau ascertained that they were a Shienne war-party, on their return from an expedition against the Pawnee Loups. They had killed one squaw, whose scalp was suspended to the spear of the partizan or leader of the party, the handle of which was decorated with strips of red and white cloth, beads, and tail plumes of the war-eagle. He also informed us, that he recognized several of them, particularly a chief who sat next to him, whose person himself and party had formerly seized upon, and detained as a hostage for the recovery of some horses that had been stolen. The chief, however, did not now betray any symptoms of a disposition to retaliate for that act, though, without doubt, he regarded us as in his power. Our interpreter readily conversed with them through the medium of a Crow prisoner, whose language he partially understood.

The partizan who killed the victim of this excursion, and two others, one of whom first struck the dead body, and the other who took off the scalp, were painted deep black with charcoal, and almost the entire body being exposed, rendered the effect more impressive. One of the latter, a tall athletic figure, remained standing behind us, and refused to smoke when the pipe was offered to him, alleging as an excuse, the obligation of a vow he had made against the use of tobacco, on the demise of his late father.

We now drew upon our little store of merchandize, for two or three twists of tobacco and a few knives, which, being laid before the partizan, excited from his politeness the return of thanks. He was of an ordinary stature, and had exceeded the middle age; his face much pitted with the small pox, his nostrils distended by a habitual muscular action, which at the same time elevated the skin of the forehead, and forcibly drew downward that part which corresponds with the inner extremity of the eye-brows, into a kind of gloomy frown. This singular expression of countenance, added to the contrast of the whites of his large eyes, with the black colour with which his features and body were overspread, seemed to indicate the operations of a mind hardened to the commission of the most outrageous actions. He however behaved with much propriety. During these scenes Mr. Say succeeded in ascertaining and recording many of the words of the language, from an Indian who had seated himself behind him.

The party was armed with spears, bows, and arrows, war-clubs, tomahawks, scalping knives, &c.

As many of them now began to ask for tobacco and for paper, to include fragments of it in the form of segars for smoking, and not finding it convenient to gratify them in this respect, we thought it prudent to withdraw, lest a quarrel might ensue. We therefore mounted our horses without molestation, having been detained an hour and a half, and proceeded on our journey, with the agreeable reflection that our deportment had not warranted a supposition that we were conscious of any inferiority in force, but rather that it was dictated by a high courtesy.

A few bisons varied the landscape, which is fatiguing to the eye by its sameness; and after travelling twenty-three miles, we encamped for the night. A large green-headed fly (tabanus) has made its appearance in great numbers, which exceedingly worries our already sufficiently miserable horses. Their range seems to be in a great measure restricted to the luxuriant bottoms, and, like the zimb of Egypt, they appear to roam but little beyond their proper boundaries. If we traversed these fertile portions of the low grounds, which yield a profuse growth of grasses, we were sure of being attacked by them, seizing upon the necks of the horses, and dying them with blood; but the refuge of the more elevated surface, and arid barren soil, afforded speedy relief, by banishing our assailants.

Scarcely were our tents pitched, when a thunderstorm, which had been approaching with a strong west wind, burst over us, but was of short continuance.

Wednesday, 2d. After moving a few miles, we halted, and sent out hunters to kill a bison. [6] The confluent rattlesnakes are very abundant, particularly in and about the prairie dog villages; but neither their appearance nor the sound of their rattle excites the attention of our horses; the sagacity of Mr. Seymour's mule, however, seems superior to that of his quadruped companions. He appears to be perfectly aware of the dangerous qualities of these reptiles, and when he perceives one of them near him, he springs so abruptly to one side, as to endanger his rider. Fortunately none of us have been bitten by them during our pedestrian rambles.

A recent trail of some war-party was this morning observed, leading across the river. The hunters returned unsuccessful, and we proceeded on until sunset to a distance of twenty miles. Great numbers of bisons were seen this afternoon, and some antelopes.

Thursday, 3d. The morning was clear and fine, with a temperature of 57 degrees. The antelopes become more numerous as we proceed; one of them trotted up so near to our line as to fall a victim to his curiosity. A considerable number of the coquimbo, or burrowing owl, occurred in a prairie dog village of limited extent. They readily permitted the hunter to approach within gunshot, and we were successful in obtaining a specimen of the bird in good order. Upon examining the several burrows upon which the owls had been observed to be perched, we remarked in them a different aspect from those on which the prairie dog had appeared; they were often in a ruined condition, the sides in some instances fallen in, sometimes seamed and grooved by the action of the water in its course from the surface to the interior, and in other respects presenting a deserted aspect, and, like dilapidated monuments of human art, were the fit abode of serpents, lizards, and owls. The burrows on which we saw the prairie dog were, on the contrary, neat, always in repair, and evinced the operations of industrious tenants. This contrast, added to the form and magnitude of the dwelling, leads us to the belief that the coquimbo owl does not, in this region, excavate its own burrow, as it is said to do in South America and in the West India islands; but rather that it avails itself of the abandoned burrows of this species of marmot, for the purposes of nidification and shelter.

On our arrival at our mid-day resting-place, on the bank of the Arkansa, the water of the river was potable, but in a few minutes it became surcharged with earthy and stercoraceous matters, from the sweepings of the prairie by the late rain, to such a degree that our horses would hardly drink it. There remained however, a short distance below, a small stream of beautifully pellucid water, which rapidly filtrated through a fortuitous embankment of sand and pebbles, and strongly contrasted with the flood with which it was soon again to intermingle. Our travelled distance to-day was twenty-three miles.

Friday, 4th. Proceeded on about six miles, when we forded a small portion of the river to an island which supported a growth of low and distant trees.

Here the tents were pitched, with the intention of halting a day or two, to recruit our miserable horses, and to supply ourselves with a store of jerked meat. The hunters were accordingly sent to the opposite side of the river, and in a short time they succeeded in killing four fat cows, which gave employment to all the men in preparing the meat for transportation.

A brisk southerly wind prevailed, that rendered the atmosphere less oppressive than usual.

Saturday, 5th. The wind ceased during the night, and the lowing of the thousands of bisons that surrounded us in every direction, reached us in one continual roar. This harsh and guttural noise, intermediate between the bellowing of the domestic bull and the grunting of the hog, was varied by the shrill bark and scream of the jackals, and the howling of the white wolves (canis mexicanus var.), which were also abundant. These wild and dissonant sounds were associated with the idea of the barren and inhospitable wastes, in the midst of which we were then reposing, and vividly reminded us of our remoteness from the comforts of civilised society. Completed the operation of jerking the meat, of which we had prepared two packs sufficient in weight to constitute a load for one of our horses, and disposed every thing for an early departure to-morrow.

Sunday, 6th. An unusual number of wolves and jackals hovered around our encampment of last night, attracted probably by the smell of the meat. Resumed our journey on a fine cloudless morning, with a strong and highly agreeable breeze from the south. We were now traversing the great bend of the river. Travelled twenty-three miles to-day, and shot two bulls, which were now poor, and their flesh of a disagreeable rank taste and scarcely eatable; we therefore contented ourselves with the tongues and marrow-bones.

Monday, 7th. The mercurial column of the thermometer at sunrise, for a few days past, has ranged between 42 and 67 degrees, and the atmosphere is serene and dry. The services of the two French Pawnee interpreters, Bijeau and Ledoux, had terminated, agreeably to their contract, at Purgatory Creek; but having been highly serviceable to us on our route, it became desirable, particularly on the departure of our companions for Red river, that they should accompany us still farther, until we should have passed beyond the great Indian war-path, here so widely outspread. This they readily consented to, as they regarded a journey from that point to their home, at the Pawnee villages, as somewhat too hazardous to be prudently attempted by only two individuals, however considerable their qualifications, and intimate their familiarity with the manners of those whom they would probably meet.

But as we now supposed ourselves to have almost reached the boundary of this region, and they again expressed their anxiety to return to their village, in order to prepare for their autumnal hunt, we no longer attempted to induce their further delay. They departed after breakfast, on a pathless journey of about three hundred miles, the supposed distance from this point to the Pawnee villages of the Platte, apparently well pleased with the treatment they had received, and expressing a desire again to accompany us, should we again ascend the Missouri. We cannot take leave of them, without expressing our entire approbation of their conduct and deportment, during our arduous journey; Bijeau, particularly, was faithful, active, industrious, and communicative. Besides the duties of guide and interpreter, he occasionally and frequently volunteered his services as hunter, butcher, cook, veterinarian, &c., and pointed out various little services, tending to our comfort and security, which he performed with pleasure and alacrity, and which no other than one long habituated to this mode of life would have devised. During leisure intervals, he had communicated an historical narrative of his life and adventures, more particularly in as far as they were relative to the country which we have been exploring. He particularized the adventures of Choteau and Demun's hunting and trading party; their success in beaver hunting, the considerable quantity of merchandize they took with them, their adventures with the natives, and the singular circumstances attendant on their capture by the Mexican Spaniards, and the transfer of the merchandize to Santa Fé, without however venturing to express any conjectures relative to the latter transaction. Much still more important information was derived from him concerning the manners and habits of these mountain Indians, their history, affinities, and migrations.

A copious vocabulary of words of the Pawnee language was obtained from Ledoux, together with an account of the manners and habits of that nation. All these, however, composed a part of the manuscripts of Mr. Say, that were subsequently carried off by deserters from our camp.

Travelled this day twenty-seven miles. The soil is becoming in many districts more exclusively sandy; the finer particles of which, driven by the wind, have formed numerous large hillocks on the opposite side of the river, precisely resembling those which are accumulated on our sea-coast. On the northern side, or that which we are traversing, the prairie still offers its unvaried flatness and cheerless barrenness, so that during a portion of the day's journey not a solitary bush, even on the river bank, relieved the monotonous scene before us.

Tuesday, 8th. Proceeded early, and at the distance of twelve miles, crossed a creek of clear running water, called by Bijeau *Demun's Creek*, from the circumstance of that hunter losing there a fine horse. At a considerable distance above, its stream was slightly fringed with timber, but at our crossing place, it was like the neighbouring part of the river to which it contributed, entirely destitute of trees. Our journey this day was a distance of 24½ miles; towards evening we crossed another creek, over which, being much backed up by the river, we experienced some difficulty in effecting a passage, and were obliged, with this view, to ascend its stream some distance. It was moderately timbered, and amongst other trees we observed the elm and some plum trees, bearing fruit nearly ripe.

Wednesday, 9th. During these few days past, the bisons have occurred in vast and almost continuous herds, and in such infinite numbers as seemed to indicate the great bend of the Arkansa as their chief and general rendezvous. As we pass along, they run in an almost uninterrupted line before us. The course of our line being parallel to that of the Arkansa, when we are travelling at the distance of a mile or two from the river, great herds of these animals were included between us and it; as the prevailing wind blew very obliquely from our left towards the river, it informed them of our presence by the scent which it conveyed. As soon as the odour reached even the farthest animal, though at the distance of two miles on our right, and perhaps half a mile in our rear, he betrayed the utmost alarm, would start into a full bounding run to pass before us to the bluffs, and as he turned round the head of our line, he would strain every muscle to accelerate his motion. This constant procession of bulls, cows, and calves of various sizes, grew so familiar to us at length, as no longer to divert our view from the contemplation of other objects, and from the examination of the comparatively more minute, but certainly not less wonderful works of nature. The white wolves and jackals, more intelligent than their associates, judging by the eye of the proximity of danger, as well as by their exquisite sense of smelling, either dashed over the river, or unhesitatingly crossed our scent in the rear, and at an easy pace, or dog-trot, chose the shortest route to the bluffs.

The soil of the afternoon journey was a deep fine white sand, which rendered the travelling very laborious, under the debilitating influence of an extreme temperature of 94 degrees of Fahrenheit's scale, and affected the sight, by the great glare of light which it so freely reflected. The chief produce of these tracts of unmixed sand is the sunflower, often the dense and almost exclusive occupant. The evening encampment was formed at the junction of a small tributary with the river, at a distance of about twenty-four miles from the last-mentioned creek. The very trifling quantity of timber supported by the immediate bank of the river in this region, is almost exclusively the cotton-wood; we are therefore gratified to observe on this creek, besides the elm, the walnut, mulberry, and ash, which we hail with a hearty welcome, as the harbingers of a more productive territory.

CHAPTER V.

TERMINATION OF THE GREAT BEND OF THE ARKANSA. — IETAN WAR-PARTY. — LITTLE ARKANSA. — RED RIVER FORK. — LITTLE NEOSHO AND LITTLE VERDIGRISE CREEKS.

Thursday, 10th. The great bend of the Arkansa terminates here; and as our horses have fed insufficiently for several days past, we lay by for the day to give them an opportunity of recruiting themselves. A S.S.E. wind prevailed, and at noon exerted a considerable force; the extreme degree of heat was 96 degrees. The hunters brought in a deer and bison.

Friday, 11th. Left the encampment at the confluence of the creek and proceeded onwards. The sandy soil and growth of sunflowers still continue on the river bottoms, and the surface of the opposite bank still swells into occasional hillocks of naked sand. The rice bird (emberiza oryzivora, L.) was feeding on the seeds of the sunflower, and the bald eagle was seen sailing high in the air.

We have hitherto generally been able to procure a sufficient supply of small drift-wood for our culinary purposes, but at this noon-day halting-place we were obliged to despatch a man across the river to collect enough to kindle a fire. From our evening encampment not a tree was within the range of sight.

This day was extremely warm, the mercury at three o'clock indicating 96 degrees, a temperature not decreased by a nimbus in the west, pouring rain, with some thunder. In the evening, silent lightning played beautifully amongst the mingled cirrostratus and cumulus clouds with which the heavens became overcast. In the afternoon, we passed the termination of the sand-hills of the opposite shore. A fine male antelope was shot by Lieut. Swift, and a skunk was also the game of the day. Distance, twenty-five miles.

Saturday, 12th. Passed over a very wide bottom, of which the soil, when not too sandy, produces a most luxuriant growth of grasses and other plants; but the river is still in a great measure destitute of trees, of which we passed but three during the morning's ride, and not a bush over the height of about two and a half feet, being a few willows and barren plum bushes. We were again gratified with the appearance of the prairie fowl running nimbly before us through the grass, the first we have seen since leaving the Platte. The bisons have now very much diminished in number; we passed, unheeded, within a few yards of a young bull, whose glazed eye and panting respiration showed the operation of some malady; and it was curious to observe, that though he stood erect and firmly on his legs, the wolves, which fled on our approach, acquainted with his defenceless condition, surrounded him in considerable numbers, awaiting his dissolution, and probably watching their opportunity to accelerate it.

The afternoon was calm, and the mercury, at its greatest elevation, stood at 99 degrees. Soon after our departure from our resting-place of noon, we observed a large herd of bisons on our left, running with their utmost rapidity towards us, from the distant bluffs. This was a sufficient warning to put us on our guard against another unwelcome war-party. Looking attentively over the surface of the country in that direction, a mounted Indian was observed to occupy an elevated swell of the surface, at the distance of a mile from us. Our peace-flag was, as usual, immediately displayed, to let him know that we were white people, and to induce him to come to us, whilst we halted to wait for him. Assured by this pacific display, he approached a short distance, but again halted, as if doubting our intentions. Julien was then sent forward towards him bearing the flag, to assure him of our friendship. The Indian now advanced, but with much caution, and obliquely, from one side to the other, as if beating against the wind. Another Indian was now observed advancing rapidly, who joined his companion. After some communication, by means of signs, with Julien, to ascertain who we were, they approached within gun-shot of us, and halting, desired to shake hands with our chief; after this ceremony they rode to an elevated ground, in order to give information to their party, which, during this short interview, we had discovered at a long distance towards the bluffs, drawn up in line, in a conspicuous situation. One of the horsemen halted whilst his companion rode transversely twice between him and the party. This telegraphic signal was immediately understood by the party, that consequently came on towards us. But their movement was so tardy, that it required the exertion of the greater part of our stock of patience to wait their coming, under the ardour of the heated rays of the sun, to which we were exposed. They seemed peaceably disposed, and desired to accompany us to the river bank, in order to smoke with us; but such was the scarcity of timber, that we were unable to avail ourselves of the shade of a single tree.

We now ascertained that they were an Ietan or Camanch (a band of the Snake Indians) war-party, thirty-five in number, of whom five were squaws. They had marched to attack the Osages, but were surprised in their camp of night before last, by a party of unknown Indians. In the skirmish that ensued, they lost three men, and had six wounded. They however escaped under cover of the darkness, with the further loss of fifty-six horses, and all their clothing, which were captured by the enemy. [7] They were indeed in a naked condition, being destitute of robes, leggings, and mockasins; with nothing to cover their bodies at night, or to protect them from the influence of the sun during the day. The squaws, however, had managed to retain their clothing, and one of the warriors had preserved an article of dress, resembling a coat, half red and half blue, ornamented with beads on the sleeves and shoulders. The usual decoration of beads about the neck and in the hair and ears were preserved, and one warrior only was painted with vermilion. The hair of several was matted into flat braids with red clay, and one individual had seven or eight pieces of the pearl shell suspended from his ears, so highly valued by these Indians. In every particular of form and feature, they were undistinguishable from the Kiawas, Kaskaias, and Arrapahoes. Much attention was devoted to the wounded, who were each accommodated with a horse, of which animals eight had been fortunately retained. These objects of sympathy were assisted in alighting from their horses with great tenderness, particularly one of them, who was shot through the body. Another of them, who was one of the two mounted spies that first approached us, had lost his brother in the late battle; and to prove the sincerity of his grief for his loss, he had cut more than one hundred parallel transverse lines on his arms and thighs, of the length of from three to four inches, deep enough to draw blood, and so close to each other that the width of the finger could not be interposed between any two of them.

They were armed with bows and arrows, lances and shields, and thirteen guns, but by far the greater number carried lances. They begged stoutly for various articles, particularly clothing; and it was found necessary to separate from them a few feet into a distinct body, in order to be prepared to act together in case of necessity. One of us, however, occupied with the appearance of these Indians, still remained amongst them, until one of them attempted to seize his gun, when a slight scuffle ensued, which he terminated by violently wresting the piece from the grasp of the Indian, and warily retreating from the midst of them.

All being seated, the pipe was passed round to a few principal persons who sat directly in front of us. Some presents were likewise laid before the partizan, consisting of a blanket, a skin to make mockasins of, a dozen knives, and five twists of tobacco; and though some of them complained aloud, and with a violent shivering gesticulation, of the cold they suffered during the night, such was the state of our stores, both public and private, that it was not thought prudent further to enlarge our bounty.

One of our number, who was earnestly occupied in endeavouring to obtain a few words of their language, but who succeeded in recording but four, heard one of them, whilst in conversation with the partizan, terminate a remark with a word or phrase so exactly similar in sound to the words *How is it*, that he almost involuntarily repeated them aloud. The speaker seemed pleased with this, and believing, from the exact similarity of the sounds, that he understood the language, immediately directed his discourse to him, but was answered only by signs denoting ignorance of the language. Their words seem less harsh, more harmonious, and easier of acquisition, than those of their neighbours.

Whilst thus occupied, one of the soldiers who were behind us called our attention to an Indian who had the effrontery to seize the Kaskaia horse by the halter, and, as in a former instance, was making a noose to pass over his head; this procedure was pointed out to the partizan, who taking no notice of it, the fellow was ordered, in a peremptory tone of voice and unequivocal manner, to desist, which he reluctantly complied with. Thus this horse is immediately distinguished and recognized by all the parties we have met with since he has been with us.

We had remained about an hour with this party, when, in consequence of this conduct, of their importunateness, and some incipient symptoms of disorder amongst them, we judged it prudent to leave them, in order to avoid a quarrel. We therefore mounted our horses, notwithstanding the earnest solicitations of these Indians that we would pass the night with them, probably anticipating another night attack from some unseen enemy: but hardly had we proceeded an hundred yards, when Julien's voice called our attention to the precarious situation in which he was placed. He had been by an accident detained in the rear, and being separated a short distance from the party, he was now entirely surrounded by the Indians, who appeared determined to strip him of every thing, and by pulling at his blanket, bridle, &c. they had nearly unhorsed him. Several of us, of course, at this critical juncture turned our horses to assist him, and a soldier who was nearest prepared his rifle to begin the onset. Observing our attitude, many of the Indians were in a moment prepared for battle, by placing their arrows across their bows. And a skirmish would no doubt have ensued, had not the partizan, observing our determination, and influenced perhaps by gratitude for the presents he had received, called off his men from Julien, and permitted us, without any further futile molestation, to proceed on our way.

In consequence of the desperate situation of this party, we could not entertain a doubt that they would attempt to capture our horses during the night, and to appropriate to themselves our personal equipments. We therefore continued our movement until a later hour than usual; and after a day's journey of twenty-two miles, during which we saw but three trees, we encamped on a selected position, and made the best arrangements in our power to repulse a night attack. The horses were staked as near to each other and to ourselves as possible; the packs were arranged in a semicircular line of defence, and each man reposed on his private baggage; the guard was doubled, and we remained wakeful during the night. No alarm, however, occurred; and in the morning,

Sunday 13th, set out early. Our way led over a luxuriant bottom of from three to twelve miles in breadth, producing a luxuriant growth of grasses, now glittering with drops of collected dew; crossed a creek which is destitute of timber, as far as the eye can trace its course. The depth of the water being to all appearance considerable, it became necessary to seek a fording-place, which was found about a mile above its confluence. It was here knee-deep, flowing with a moderate current over a bed of sand and gravel, the surface of the water being depressed only about four feet below the general level. About an hundred yards beyond its confluence, we observed a canal of water backed up from the river, which, from a little distance, gave a double appearance to the creek. We remained here until a large elk, which had been shot, was cut up, and the meat packed upon the horses. At our mid-day resting-place were a few trees, and some elevated sand-hills, but as the situation was not an eligible one for the protection of the horses from Indian depredation, we moved a few miles further, and encamped, as usual, on the bank of the river. The day had been very sultry, with an extreme temperature of 95 degrees, and the evening was accompanied by a display of lightning in the north-western horizon.

The bisons are yet numerous, and the white wolves also abundant; packs of the latter are still heard to howl about our camp in the night, thus responding to the harsh bellowing or grunting of the bulls. Our dogs, that formerly took part in this wild and savage concert, by barking fiercely in return, no longer rouse us from our sleep by noticing it.

Monday, 14th. A slight dew had fallen; the wind was S. S. E., nearly calm; and our morning's journey was arduous, in consequence of the great heat of the atmosphere. Our dogs, these two or three days past, had evidently followed us with difficulty. Cæsar, a fine mastiff, and the larger of the two, this morning trotted heavily forwards, and threw himself down directly before the first horse in the line; the rider turned his horse aside, to avoid doing injury to the dog; but had he noticed the urgency of this eloquent appeal of the animal for a halt, it would not have passed unregarded. The dog, finding this attempt to draw attention to his sufferings unavailing, threw himself successively before two or three other horses, but still failed to excite the attention he solicited, until a soldier in the rear observed that his respiration was excessively laborious, and his tongue to a great length depended from his widely extended mouth. He therefore took the dog upon his horse before him, intending to bathe him in the river, which, however, being at the distance of half a mile, the poor exhausted animal expired in his arms before he reached it. To travellers in such a country, any domesticated animal, however abject, becomes an acceptable companion; and our dogs, besides their real usefulness as guards at night, drew our attention in various ways during the day, and became gradually so endeared to us, that the loss of Cæsar was felt as a real evil.

The afternoon continued sultry, the extreme heat being 97 degrees. Towards evening a brisk N. E. wind appeared to proceed from a nimbus which was pouring rain in that direction, and produced so instantaneous and great a change in the atmospheric temperature, that we were obliged to button up to the chin; but it refreshed and revived us all. As we were now approaching a well-wooded creek, we hoped soon to assuage our impatient thirst, but great was the mortification, upon arriving at the naked bank, to see a dry bed of gravel of at least fifty yards in breadth. Crossing this inhospitable tract, which appears to be occasionally deluged with water, with the intention of passing down the opposite bank to the river, we were agreeably surprised to discover a fine limpid stream of cool flowing water, meandering through a dense growth of trees and bushes, which had before concealed it from view. Here we remarked the honey locust and button-wood (platanus occidentalis), though the principal growth was cotton-wood, elm, and ash. This stream of water, we believe, is known to a few hunters, who have had an opportunity to visit it, by the name of *Little Arkansa*.

The distance of the day's journey was twenty-three miles, during which but a single prairie dog village was seen, and proved to be the last one that occurred on the expedition. Partridges and prairie fowls were numerous.

Tuesday, 15th. Much lightning occurred during the night, pervading the eastern heavens nearly from N. to S. At a distance of a mile from encampment, we crossed a timbered ravine, and further on, a small creek; when, upon looking back on our right, we saw the appearance of an Indian village situated near the confluence of the Little Arkansa with the river. Inspired with hope, we turned towards the spot; but on arriving there, it proved to be a large hunting camp, which had probably been occupied during the preceding season. It exhibited a more permanent aspect than three others that occurred on our route of the three past days; much bark covered the boweries; and a few pumpkins, water-melons, and some maize, the seeds of which had fallen from unknown hands, were fortuitously growing as well within as without the rude frail tenements. Of the maize, we collected enough to furnish out a very slight but extremely grateful repast, and the water-melons were eaten in their unripe state.

Resuming our ride, we crossed three branches of a creek, in one of which two of the horses entered in a part not fordable, and as the banks were steep and miry, it was with much exertion and delay that they were recovered. Oak and walnut trees abound upon this creek, besides elm, ash, and locust. A king-fisher (alcedo alcyon) was also seen. The extreme heat was rather more intense than that of the preceding day, the mercurial column standing for a time at $97\frac{1}{2}$ degrees. The bluffs, hitherto more or less remote from the bed of the river, now approach it so closely as to render it necessary to pursue our course over them. On ascending upon the elevated prairie, we observed that it had assumed a different appearance, in point of fertility, from that which we had been familiar with nearer to the mountains; and although the soil is not yet entirely concealed from the view by its produce, yet the grass is from six inches to one foot in height.

But five bisons were seen to-day, a privation which communicates a solitary air to this region, when compared with the teeming plains over which we have passed, and of which these animals formed the chief feature.

Our distance this day on a straight line may be estimated at $14\frac{1}{4}$ miles, though the actual travelled distance was much more considerable.

During the space of one month, our only regular food, besides meat, has been coarsely ground parched maize meal, of which a ration of one gill per day was shared to each individual. This quantity was thrown into common stock, and boiled with the meat, into a kind of soup. This meal is nutritious, portable, not subject to spoil by keeping a reasonable length of time, and is probably to be preferred, as a substitute for bread, to other succedanea, by travellers in an uncivilised country. Our store of meal, however, was now exhausted, and we were obliged to resort to a small quantity of mouldy crumbs of biscuit, which had been treasured up for times of need.

At night almost incessant lightning coruscated in the north-western horizon.

Wednesday, 16th. Several showers of rain, with much thunder and vivid lightning, fell during the night, and the early morning continued showery; but the clouds were evidently undergoing the change from nimbus to cirrostratus, in this instance the harbingers of a fine day. Several ravines occurred on the morning's journey, containing, in the deeper parts of their beds, pools of standing water. The first was of considerable size, with steep banks, and thickly wooded, as far up its course as the vision extended; the trees were principally oak, some walnut, elm, ash, mulberry, button-wood, cotton-wood, and willow.

A horse presented by the Kiawa chief could not be prevailed upon to traverse this occasional watercourse; he evaded the attempts of several men to urge him forward; and after being thus fruitlessly detained a considerable space of time, the animal was shot. If he had been abandoned, he must have perished for want of water, having been accidentally deprived of sight, and more certainly, as that fluid, so indispensable for the support of the animal's life, was here of difficult access.

At the ravine, which served as a halting place during the mid-day heats, we first observed the plant familiarly known in the settlements by the name of *poke* (phytolacca decandria), reclining over the banks with its fecundity, in the midst of a crowded assemblage of bushes, and partially shading a limpid pool that mantled a rocky bed below. A large species of mushroom, of the puff-ball kind, was not uncommon, nearly equal in size to a man's head.

We have now passed the boundary of the summer bison range; and the wolves, those invariable attendants on that animal, are now but rarely seen. The antelopes also have disappeared. The river banks, as well as the creeks and some ravines, from near the Little Arkansa, are pretty well wooded, with but few interruptions, and in many parts sufficiently dense, but always, as yet, strictly limited to skirting those watercourses.

During the afternoon we crossed numerous ravines, some of which, judging by the infallible indications of dried grass and floated wood lodged on high in the croches of the trees, poured down at certain seasons large volumes of water from the prairies into the river.

Near our evening encampment, but on the opposite side of the river, appeared the entrance of a large creek, of the width of 90 or 100 yards, and of considerable depth; it seems to be well wooded, and its course is nearly parallel to the river for a great distance before it discharges into it. This stream is called Red river fork, its waters are turbid, opaque, and red; great numbers of fresh water tortoises, closely allied to the testudo geographica of Le Sueur, inhabit the basin formed by the entrance of this stream immediately below its junction. The bluffs on that side are washed by the stream of the river.

The bottom land, on the left bank, is still confined to a narrow strip. The sun having been, during the chief part of the day, obscured by an interrupted sheet of cirrostratus, and a brisk N. E. wind prevailing, rendered the day temperate and agreeable. Travelled distance miles nineteen and a half.

Thursday, 17th. Having been entirely unsuccessful in hunting since the 13th instant, we remained in our position during the morning, and sent out four hunters to procure fresh meat; but towards noon they all returned with but three turkies, of which two were young; they saw no deer, but much elk sign.

At two o'clock proceeded onward, upon a slightly undulated prairie, over which the eye roves to a great distance without impediment. Indeed the surface of the country, which extends along the upper portions of the Platte and Arkansa rivers, is generally less undulated than that which extends on either side of the Missouri.

VOL. III.   G

The ravines which intersected our path were not so extensive or profound as those of yesterday, and in one of them we observed the common elder (sambucus).

Should military possession ever be taken of this elevated country, eligible positions might readily be selected for military posts, at several different points below the Little Arkansa, where the bluffs almost impend over the river. Such a position was occupied by our evening encampment. This bluff is naked, of a gently rounded surface, presenting a high rugged and inaccessible front upon the river, which it commands to a considerable distance in both directions. An adequate supply of wood, for fuel and architectural purposes, is offered by a ravine, which flanks its lower side, and by other points.

Two fawns were killed during this afternoon's journey of twelve miles, and a black bear was seen. The bitter apple vine occurred now but rarely.

Friday, 18th. The inequality of the surface increases as we proceed, the undulations being now much more abrupt and considerable, belted near their summits with a rocky stratum, and assuming much the same character with those spoken of in the account of our expedition to the Konza village. This stratum, which is of gray and ferruginous sandstone, contains petrifactions of marine shells, so completely assimilated with the matrix in which they repose, and decomposing so entirely simultaneously with it, when exposed to atmospheric action, that even their generic characters cannot be recognised. Amongst other appearances, however, we observed a bivalve, which seemed to differ from terebratula and its congeners.

At the distance of eleven miles we crossed a small river, flowing with a very gentle current over a gravelly bed, with a breadth of fifty or sixty yards, and an extreme depth of three feet; we have named it *Little Neosho*, or *Stinking Fork*. Its western bottom is of very considerable width, well wooded with the before mentioned description of trees, in addition to which the hackberry here first appears, and supporting a crowded undergrowth of pea-vines, nettles, and rank weeds, which obstruct the passage of the traveller. The eastern bank, upon which our noon-day encampment was established, was high rock and precipitous, requiring considerable exertion to surmount it.

Here the organic reliquiæ are somewhat more distinct than those which we examined on the opposite side of this secondary river. They are referable to those generally extinct genera that inhabited the great depths of the primeval ocean. Amongst them we recognized a smooth species of anomia of the length of half an inch, a species of terebratula, an encrinus, and numerous insulated species of a Linnæan echinus.

At two o'clock pursued our journey, under an extreme heat of 92 degrees, which was hardly mitigated by the gentle fanning of a slight S. E. breeze. The appearance of the country here undergoes a somewhat abrupt change. Low scrubby oaks, the prevailing timber, no longer exclusively restricted, as we have hitherto observed it, to a mere margin of a watercourse, now was seen extending in little clusters or oases, in the low grounds. In the ravines, which are numerous, profound, abrupt, and rocky, we observed the hickory (caria of Nuttall), which had not before occurred since our departure from the forest of the Missouri. The bluffs are steep and stony, rendering the journey much more laborious to our horses, that were almost exhausted by traversing a plain country, and their hoofs, already very much worn by constant friction with the grass, will, we fear, be splintered and broken by the numerous loose and angular stones which they cannot avoid. Near the summits of some of these bluffs the stratum of rock assumes an appearance of such extraordinary regularity, as to resemble an artificial wall, constructed for the support of the superincumbent soil.

At the distance of eight miles from the small river before mentioned we encamped for the night, on the east side of a creek which we call *Little Verdigrise*.

It is about forty yards in breadth, and not so deep as the Little Neosho; its bed is gravelly, but the foot of each bank is so miry that we experienced some difficulty in crossing. There is but a slight skirting of forest, which denotes to the distant spectator the locality of this creek.

One of the hunters returned with the information of his having discovered a small field of maize, occupying a fertile spot, at no great distance from the camp; it exhibited proofs of having been lately visited by the cultivators; a circumstance which leads us to believe, that an ascending column of smoke, seen at a distance this afternoon, proceeded from an encampment of Indians, whom, if not a war-party, we should now rejoice to meet. We took the liberty, agreeably to the customs of the Indians, of procuring a mess of the corn, and some small but nearly ripe water-melons, that were also found growing there, intending to recompense the Osages for them, to whom we supposed they belonged. During the night we were visited by a slight shower of rain from the S.W., accompanied by distant thunder.

CHAPTER VI.

INDIAN HUNTING ENCAMPMENT. — BRACKISH WATER. — THE PARTY PRESSED BY HUNGER. — FORKED-TAILED FLYCATCHER. — AN ELEVATED, ALMOST MOUNTAINOUS, RANGE OF COUNTRY. — DESERTION OF THREE MEN. — RED WATER.

SATURDAY, 19th. Several small corn fields were seen this morning along the creek. At a short distance from our place of encampment we passed an Indian camp that had a more permanent aspect than any we had before seen near this river. The boweries were more completely covered, and a greater proportion of bark was used in the construction of them. They are between sixty and seventy in number. Well-worn traces, or paths, lead in various directions from this spot; and the vicinity of the corn fields induces the belief that it is occasionally occupied by a tribe of Indians, for the purposes of cultivation as well as of hunting.

The increasing quantity of forest, partially obscuring the course of the river, renders it now no easy task to trace its inflexions.

After proceeding twelve miles over a rugged country, at present destitute of water, we were rejoiced to find at our dining-place a puddle of stagnant rainwater, which had been protected from the action of the sun by the elevated and almost impending bank of the ravine in which it was situated, and which, though mantled o'er with green, was yet cool and grateful to our pressing thirst.

We left our cool and shady retreat, and again betook ourselves to the prairies, under a temperature of 96 degrees. Our remaining dog, Buck, had been, since the regretted death of his companion, treated with all the kindness and attention due to a humble friend. He was very frequently accommodated with a ride on horseback before one of the men when he betrayed unusual exhaustion. But notwithstanding all such attentions, for which he seemed touched with the feelings of gratitude, he experienced Cæsar's fate, and was necessarily abandoned.

The evening encampment was pitched upon a luxuriant grassy plain on the margin of the river. On tasting the water, it was perceived to be slightly saline, though the proportion of that condiment was not so considerable as to render it unpleasant to the palate. This saline intermixture is, no doubt, due to the Red river fork, inasmuch as the river, above the entrance of that stream, appeared entirely destitute of saline contamination, and no stream enters on this side in which the slightest apparent degree of brackishness is to be detected by the taste.

The cotton tree is less numerous in this vicinity than we have seen it higher up the river, and being intermixed with other trees, forms but an insignificant feature of the forest.

Sunday, 20th. Heavy rain, accompanied with much thunder and lightning, commenced early in the night, and continued until day-light this morning. Hunters who had been sent out detained us until nine o'clock, when they returned unsuccessful; in consequence of which, and of our having made a sparing meal last evening on a turkey that had been shot, we were obliged to depart fasting on our way.

The ravines were muddy and their banks slippery in consequence of the rain; we had, however, the good fortune to fall upon an Indian trace, which complied with our proper direction, and which indicated the best points at which the gullies might be passed. In its course it conducted us to a creek which was pouring down a torrent of water. Here was an encampment that had obviously been occupied within a day or two, there being fresh rinds of water-melons strewed about it.

One of the party, on attempting to cross this creek, was thrown into the water, in consequence of his horse having plunged suddenly beyond his depth; he however avoided being carried down with the rapid current, by seizing the depending bough of a tree; the horse also was fortunately saved; by taking a different direction, we all passed over without further casualty.

But we were unable to trace any farther the party that we thus ascertained to have so recently preceded us, their footsteps being here entirely obliterated by the rain.

At the distance of sixteen miles we encamped at an early hour on the bank of the river, and sent out hunters, who, however, after examining the vicinity, returned unsuccessful. Our three meals were therefore again, by stern necessity, reduced to a single frugal one, and our table, the soil, was set with a few mouldy biscuit crumbs, boiled in a large quantity of water, with the nutritious addition of some grease. Julien, who had been despatched for the peace flag, which was casually left at a ravine, to our great satisfaction returned with a skunk or polecat, that he had fortunately killed. This we determined to preserve for a feast to-morrow.

Monday, 21st. One of our horses strayed away last night, and could not now be found, we therefore set out without him, and as usual without breakfasting. The Indian trace was again discovered, and pursued about nine miles to the dining place at noon. Here we were obliged to have recourse for food to a little treasured store of dried bison meat, which, when all issued, amounted to the pittance of two ounces per man; this, added to the soup maigre of the skunk, and a half pint of the crumbs of bread, afforded a tolerably good though far from abundant meal.

Proceeded on under an extreme atmospheric temperature of 90 degrees; several deer were seen, but they proved to be so shy, that our hunters, perhaps through over-eagerness, did not succeed in approaching them within gun shot. After accomplishing a distance of ten miles, we pitched our camp on the river bank. Here the stream turns rather abruptly to the east, after having preserved a southerly and south of west direction for a considerable distance. A considerable stream of water, called Nesuhetonga, or Grand Saline creek, flows into the river at this point, nearly opposite to our camp.

Supped on a few bread crumbs boiled in water. A black wolf, the first seen since our departure from the Missouri, made his appearance in the distance.

Tuesday, 22d. Three of the horses having strayed detained us until eight o'clock, when a fall of rain commenced, which continued during the morning, and wet us thoroughly to the skin. A few hostile Indians, aware of the state of our fire-arms, might perhaps have disappointed our hopes of a safe return to the settlements, if, in their attack, their bow-strings could have been preserved from the effects of the rain, which tends greatly to relax them.

A note like that of the prairie dog for a moment induced the belief that a village of the marmot was near; but we were soon undeceived by the appearance of the beautiful tyrannus forficatus in full pursuit of a crow. Not at first view recognising the bird, the fine elongated tail plumes, occasionally diverging in a furcate manner, and again closing together, to give direction to the aerial evolutions of the bird, seemed like the extraneous processes of dried grass, or twigs of a tree, adventitiously attached to the tail, and influenced by currents of wind. The feathered warrior flew forward to a tree, from whence, at our too near approach, he descended to the earth at a little distance, continuing at intervals his chirping note. This bird seems to be rather rare in this region, and as the very powder within the barrels of our guns was wet, we were obliged to content ourselves with only a distant view of the bird.

The river margin, on which we now hold our course, is narrow and fertile, supporting a tolerably thick growth of mossy cup oaks, with walnut, cotton-wood, elm, and much underwood, through which it is sometimes rather difficult to force a passage. The river is now more serpentine in its course than it was remarked to be nearer the mountains, but it is here wide and still, thickly studded with sand-bars.

One of the hunters rescued the body of a small fawn from the wolves that had killed and embowelled it. This afforded us all a good dinner, and as we had in the morning drawn upon our almost exhausted store of sweet corn for a gill to each man as a breakfast, we are to-day comparatively well-fed.

Near our evening encampment was a large old Indian hunting camp. Our distance to-day nineteen miles.

Wednesday, 23d. Set out again fasting, and pursued our journey over a beautiful open level bottom. The bluffs on our left, of but moderate height, were partially clothed with oaks, and the river on the right skirted with the cotton tree. But a single ravine crossed our morning route. At eleven o'clock the mercury in the thermometer indicated 93 degrees.

At the distance of about two miles from our resting-place of noon we again halted and pitched the tents, in anticipation of a violent storm, as a nimbus of an unusually menacing aspect was otherwise announced by wind and thunder, and seemed rapidly approaching from the south. In order to avail ourselves of this delay, the hunters were sent out to endeavour to procure some food. But as the storm passed round, they were soon recalled, bringing with them the seasonable supply of four turkies. On the subsequent part of this day we passed over a small stream, which we call Bitter Apple Creek, with but a slow-moving current, of the width of about ten yards, and three feet deep. Its bed was so muddy that two of the pack-horses were mired, but were finally brought out. We then ascended into the prairie, from which, after labouring over an almost continual succession of ravines, we passed down to the river bank, and encamped for the night, having travelled about twenty miles. Numerous deer were seen to-day, but they were very shy.

The last bitter apple vine that occurred on the expedition was seen to-day. We were once again saluted by the note of the blue jay. The pine warbler (sylvia pinus) also occurred.

Thursday, 24th. As the high prairies offered almost continually a succession of steep and rugged ravines, which called for too much exertion for our horses to pass them, it was determined to endeavour to force our way through the underwood of the bottoms. These we found to be now so intricate, that in many places it was really difficult to force a passage through the intertwined briers and climbing plants. Our progress was, however, at length altogether interrupted by a deep and miry sluice of the river over which no ford could be found. Fortunately, however, the sandy bed of the river itself offered a sufficiently firm footing to enable us to pass round the obstacle. Tired of the brambles, we again sought the prairie, and, ascending an elevated hill, enjoyed a fine view of the river in its meanders to a great distance; but the place of destination, Belle Point, which we now all anxiously look out for, was not yet in sight.

A journey of nine miles and three quarters brought us to a large stream of clear water, but hardly perceptible current, passing over a bed of rock and mud; the banks were steep and high, and afforded us a very pleasant resting-place during the presence of the mid-day heats. A flock of paroquets flew over our heads, uttering their loud note, with their usual loquacity. The kingfisher was flying from one withered support to another, over the surface of the creek, and occasionally darting into the water in pursuit of some little scaly victim; and a large white crane (ardea egretta of Wilson) stalked with slow and measured strides in the shallows of the creek. A glass snake (ophisaurus ventralis) approached too near us, and was captured.

In the afternoon small cumulus clouds arose in the horizon, and we again put forward under a temperature of 95 degrees. Three miles farther a large ravine occurred, containing much water in the deeper parts of its bed, but dry at intervals; it is wooded as far as we can trace it with the eye, and in the season of floods must discharge a large volume of water at its confluence, which is distant about five miles from the creek crossed this morning.

We passed by several singular natural elevations, with conical summits, and halted early to hunt, for which purpose four men were sent out, who returned with two turkies, which furnished us with a very light supper.

Friday, 25th. Remained encamped in order to give the hunters an opportunity to procure some game. We had nothing for breakfast or dinner, and as our meals a few days past had been few and slight, we have become impatient under the pressure of hunger; a few fresh-water muscles (unio), two or three small fishes, and a tortoise which had been found in the mud of the ravine, were roasted and eaten, without that essential condiment salt, of which we had been for some time destitute. The hunters so anxiously looked for at length returned, bringing but three ducks (anas sponsa); one of them had shot down three deer, but they all escaped.

As we have no idea of our distance from Belle Point, and know not what extent of country we are doomed to traverse in the state of privation to which we have of late been subjected, we have selected, from our miserable horses, an individual to be slaughtered for food, in case of extremity of abstinence; and upon which, although very lean, we cannot forbear to cast an occasional wishful glance.

Bijeau, before he parted from us, urged by his wishes for our safety, drew for our information a sketch of the country over which we had to pass, as far as he had travelled in that direction on a former occasion, which sketch was terminated by two large streams entering the river near to each other, and diverging in the opposite direction. As the remarkable relative course of these two streams, as represented by Bijeau, corresponded to sufficient exactness with the representation of the Verdigrise and Grand rivers, which terminated a sketch which Major Long drew to depict the country from Belle Point upwards, we believed that by joining the two sketches we had a complete view of the country before us, as far as the settlements. Bijeau's sketch proved to be a pretty faithful transcript of the country, as far as the two watercourses that we passed on the 18th instant; which, as they terminated his map, we then supposed were, of course, the Verdigrise and Grand rivers. But not being able to recognise in Major Long's draft one single feature of the region we have since traversed, we finally concluded, either that we had not yet arrived at the true Verdigrise river, or that we had passed by our place of destination without perceiving it. In this state of uncertainty it was determined to continue our course with as much speed as the exhausted situation of our horses would permit, with the hope of soon arriving at some settlement, where we might obtain the proper direction.

The greatest heat of the day was 97 degrees. Two hunters were this evening sent forwards to encamp, and hunt early in the morning. Another flock of paroquets were seen to day.

Saturday, 26th. Penetrated through an intricate bottom of bushes, interlaced by vines and briers, the timber chiefly oak. The hunters had procured nothing; but Lieut. Swift had the good fortune to kill a fine buck, and one of the hunters afterwards a turkey. These were a happy alleviation to us, and at our noon halting-place we enjoyed the rare luxury of a full meal. At this position was a large ravine, containing much water of the depth of two feet and a half, and width of twenty or twenty-five yards, but without any visible current; its bed was muddy, and in some places rocky.

The journey of the afternoon was equally intricate with that of the morning; our way led along the fertile but narrow eastern margin of the ravine, or as it would be called in the settlements of the Arkansa, *bayou,* and immediately on our left ascended the abrupt and rocky ridge of the bluff.

After a fatiguing journey of 19 miles we encamped on the river bank, in a fine clear bottom, surrounded semicircularly by the forest. The plum-bushes, which abound in the country through which we have for several days been travelling, are generally killed, probably by conflagration, their black and defoliated branches strongly contrasted with the verdure around them; to-day, however, we met with some which had escaped uninjured, and which afforded a few ripe plums.

Sunday, 27th. The river bottom becoming very narrow, obliged us to ascend upon the high grounds, which we found to be little less than mountainous, often rocky and steep, and, as usual, intersected by profound ravines. Mr. Swift having succeeded in killing another deer, we halted, after a journey of twelve miles, in order to jerk the meat which we now possessed, and to rest the horses, whose feet were bruised and broken by the fragments of rock.

The corporal did not join us until evening. The horse which he had rode became so exceedingly feeble as to be no longer able to support the weight of his rider, who therefore dismounted, and attempted to drive him on before him. In spite of his utmost endeavours the horse proceeded so slowly that the corporal was obliged to forsake him, in order to seek our trail, which he had lost on the rocks over which we had passed. Not being able to regain the trail, and supposing we had directed our course towards the river, he wandered along its margin to a considerable distance, until almost exhausted with fatigue and vexation. He at length ascended a considerable hill which commanded a view of the country around, from which he had the satisfaction to see a column of smoke rising above the forest at a distance. This sure indication he had pursued, until approaching with much caution, he was overjoyed to ascertain that his beacon was no other than the smoke from our meat-drying process. Supposing that the horse would be able to travel after having rested during the night, the corporal was directed to accompany Julien to the spot where he had been left, and to bring him on in the morning.

We availed ourselves of this leisure-time to mend our horse-gear, clothes, and mockasins.

In the evening a slight fall of rain took place, accompanied by thunder in the N. E., which at night became heavy and loud.

Monday, 28th. The horse that gave out yesterday was brought in, together with two others that had strayed, and for which we were hunting. We were now traversing a high ridge of country, which, at many points may be safely estimated at five hundred feet above the surface of the river, and wooded to a great distance from that stream.

In the afternoon, having descended to the river, we again laboured through the difficulties of dense underwood, which such productive soils usually present, until towards evening, when we had the happiness to see a well-worn Indian path which had been interrupted by the river, and now took a direction towards our left. Wishing to pursue this route, as well for the facility of travelling as with the hope of soon arriving at some Indian town, we readily persuaded ourselves that it deviated from the course we were pursuing only in compliance with the inequalities of the country. With little hesitation, therefore, we struck into the path, and night gathered around us before we threw ourselves supperless upon the ground to repose, after a fatiguing march of about twenty-one miles, during which the greatest degree of heat was 92.

Several small flocks of the common wild pigeons flew by us, both yesterday and to-day, in a southerly direction.

Tuesday, 29th. After some detention in seeking a troublesome horse that had strayed, we again proceeded forward fasting. This abstinence, to which we have been several times subjected, affects one of our party in a singular and uniform manner; his voice becomes hollow-toned, and his hearing much impaired, a state that is popularly known, as he expresses it, by the phrase of *the almonds of the ears* being *down*.

We pursued the Indian path a considerable distance this morning; but as its course continued its divergence from the river, and we were fearful of deviating too far, we abandoned it, and by an oblique course endeavoured to regain the river. Here, however, the undergrowth being almost impervious, induced our return to the path, which we again attained near an Indian hunting camp of the past season, situated in a beautiful prairie, near a gently swelling hill.

Here finding a little water in a ravine puddle, we halted, and served out a stinted ration of dried meat to each individual instead of dinner, which, so far from gratifying, tended to stimulate our desire of food.

Having been some days entirely destitute of tobacco in any shape, those of the party who are habituated to the use of it experienced an additional formidable privation. One of the men, who was erroneously supposed to have still a remnant of the precious stimulant in his possession, was heard to reply to an earnest and most humble petition for a small taste of it, or to be allowed to apply his tongue to it:—"Every man chaws his own tobacco, and them that hasn't any chaws leaves."

During the prevalence of the greatest heat of the day, which was 94 degrees, we again set forward, and passed over a gently undulated surface, supporting an open forest of young and scrub oak, intermixed with hickory. In the course of a few miles we arrived at the edge of this forest, which here crowned a much elevated region. It was in fact higher in proportion to the surface before us than any other portion of the country we had seen on this side of the mountains. The eye from this height roved over a vast distance of prairie, and comparatively plain country; and it was evident that we had now passed the hilly and even mountainous country, which we have of late been traversing. A few hills still interrupted the continuity of surface below, more particularly on the right of the landscape towards the river. Not a human being was yet to be perceived, nor a single trait indicative of their present existence. It seemed for a moment that our little cavalcade alone was endowed with the vital principle, and that the vegetable world held a silent and solitary dominion. Belle Point still evades our sight; we might have passed it, or it may still be very far before us; yet we can no longer struggle through the tangled underwood that encloses the river, nor pick our passage amongst the loose stones of the bluffs, in order to preserve an uninterrupted view of the bank of the river upon which that post is established. From this position the path winds rather abruptly downward, and, at a little distance on the plain, conducted us through an abandoned Indian hunting camp.

The horse that gave out on Sunday, having been since both packed and rode, this afternoon sunk under his rider to the ground, and resisted our efforts to induce him to rise. As he appeared to be entirely exhausted, we reluctantly abandoned him. He had been a sprightly, handsome, and serviceable animal, and was chosen from a considerable number of horses, and presented to Mr. Say, by Major O'Fallon, when at the Pawnee villages.

After a day's journey of twenty-two miles, a favourable situation for an encampment offering timely at a site which appeared to have been occupied by a tribe of Indians during the late winter, induced us to pitch the tents, and prepare for the night. And Lieutenant Swift, whose dexterity as a marksman had previously relieved us in times of need, now succeeded in killing a turkey for our evening meal.

Wednesday, 30th. We pursued the path about ten miles farther, with the hope of its soon terminating at some Indian village; but as it continued to diverge too widely from our apparent true course, we once again relinquished it, and turned towards the river, which we expected to regain in the course of a few miles, by tracing down the opposite bank of a large ravine, which now presented itself.

At our resting place of noon the banded rattlesnake (C. horridus) occurred, and five young turkies were procured by the hunters.

Resuming our journey, it soon became obvious that the ravine we were tracing did not discharge into the Arkansa, but into some large tributary of that river, and which, from an elevated ground, we could distinctly see meandering to a great distance on the left. Another Indian path was now discovered, which by its direction seemed to comply with our proper course. It led us to recross the ravine,

with its most luxuriant growth of trees, bushes, and
weeds. On emerging from this intricate maze we
observed a large column of smoke arising in the
south-east, as if from the conflagration of some entire
prairie. This occurrence, combined with the effects
of a large *burning* in the vicinity of our evening
encampment, that seemed very recent, and the appearance of the well-worn pathways, inspired us with
a renewed expectation of soon meeting with human
beings, and of arriving at some permanent Indian
village.

The highest temperature of the day was 95 degrees.
Our distance this afternoon was ten miles.

Thursday, 31st. We arose early, and on looking
at the horses that were staked around the camp,
three of the best were missing. Supposing that they
had strayed to a distance, inquiry was made of the
corporal respecting them; who answered that three
of the men were absent, probably in pursuit of them,
and added, that one of those men who chanced to be
last on guard had neglected to awaken him to perform his duty on the morning watch. Forster, a
faithful, industrious soldier, and who, in performing
the culinary services for the party, had not lately
been laboriously occupied, now exclaimed, that his
knapsack had been robbed; and upon examining our
baggage, we were mortified to perceive that it also
had been overhauled and plundered during the night.
But we were utterly astounded to find that our saddle bags, which contained our clothing, Indian presents, and manuscripts, had also been carried off.

This greatest of all privations that could have
occurred within the range of possibility, suspended
for a time every exertion, and seemed to fill the
measure of our trials, difficulties, and dangers.

It was too obvious that the infamous absentees,
Nolan, Myers, and Bernard, had deserted during
the night, robbing us of our best horses, and of our
most important treasures. We endeavoured in vain

to trace them, as a heavy dew had fallen since their departure, and rested upon every spear of grass alike, and we returned from the fruitless search to number over our losses with a feeling of disconsolateness verging on despair.

Our entire wardrobe, with the sole exception of the rude clothing on our persons, and our entire private stock of Indian presents, were included in the saddle bags. But their most important contents were all the manuscripts of Mr. Say and Lieut. Swift, completed during the extensive journey from Engineer Cantonment to this place. Those of the former consisted of five books, viz. one book of observations on the manners and habits of the Mountain Indians, and their history, so far as it could be obtained from the interpreters; one book of notes on the manners and habits of animals, and descriptions of species; one book containing a journal; two books containing vocabularies of the languages of the Mountain Indians; and those of the latter consisted of a topographical journal of the same portion of our expedition. All these, being utterly useless to the wretches who now possessed them, were probably thrown away upon the ocean of prairie, and consequently the labour of months was consigned to oblivion by these uneducated vandals.

Nolan, Myers, and Bernard, though selected by the officers of Camp Missouri, with the best intentions, for the purpose of accompanying our party, proved worthless, indolent, and pusillanimous from the beginning; and Nolan, we ascertained, was a notorious deserter in two former instances.

This desertion and robbery occurred at a most unfortunate period, inasmuch as we were all much debilitated, and their services consequently the less dispensable on that account, in the attentions necessarily due to the pack-horses, in driving these animals, loading and unloading them, &c.

We resumed our journey upon our Indian pathway in silence, and at the distance of sixteen miles we passed through the river forest, here three miles in width, and once again encamped upon the bank which overlooks that stream. No trace of Belle Point, nor any appearances of civilization were yet in view. But we were all immediately struck with the change in the appearance of the water in the river. No longer of that pale clay colour, to which we have been accustomed, it has now assumed a reddish hue, hardly unlike that of the blood of the human arteries, and is still perfectly opaque, from the quantity of an earthy substance of this tint, which it holds in suspension; its banks and bars are, from deposition, of the same colour. This extraneous pigment has been contributed by some large stream flowing in from the opposite side, and which, in consequence of our late aberrance, we had not seen.

The hunters returned without game, but bringing us a few grapes and some unripe persimmons, all of which were eaten.

The extreme heat of the day was 95 degrees, and in the evening thunder and lightning occurred in the western horizon.

CHAPTER VII.

THE PARTY MEET WITH OSAGE INDIANS. — SOME ACCOUNT
OF THIS NATION. — MANNER OF TAKING WILD HORSES.

FRIDAY, September 1st. The hunters, who had been sent out at day-light, returned at eight o'clock again unsuccessful, but after a journey of about three hours we had an opportunity to appease the cravings of hunger, and halted to regale ourselves on a small fawn that was shot. At three o'clock proceeded on under the extreme atmospheric temperature of the day of 96 degrees, and, as the current of air was scarcely perceptible, the day was as usual very sultry. We were at length very agreeably surprised by hearing an Indian whoop in our rear, and on looking back a mounted Indian was observed upon a rising piece of ground, contemplating our movements. The usual ceremony of displaying our flag, and deputing an individual to assure him of the pacific nature of our mission, induced him readily to approach; and after some communication, he consented to encamp with us. He informed us that he was the son of Clermont, principal chief of the Osages of the Oaks, or *Osage des Chênes* of the French traders; in whose territories we then were. Their village was at the distance of about fifteen miles, but by far the greater portion of the inhabitants of it were now on their way to this river for the purpose of hunting. They had heard the report of the guns of our hunters, and, agreeably to their custom, had sent out spies, of whom he was one, to ascertain from whom the firing proceeded; that he had fallen upon our trail, and consequently had no difficulty in finding us, and was moreover glad to see us. Indeed his conduct proved that he entertained towards us the most friendly and generous disposition. He was not tardy in ascertaining our wants, nor parsimonious in his attempts to relieve them. He passed his pipe around, a ceremony which signifies just as much among these people as the drinking to friendship and good fellowship does amongst the lower classes in civilized society; but to us, who had been so long deprived of the use of tobacco, it was an intrinsic gratification. He then laid before us some fine ripe blue plums; and remarking that the small portion of fawn meat, that constituted all our store, was very lean, he said that he would soon bring some more palatable food, and leaving his pipe and tobacco pouch on the ground, with the request that we would partake freely of both, he disappeared in the forest.

It was dusk when he returned with a fat buck hanging in pieces from his saddle; he was accompanied by five or six young warriors. These young men had visited the opposite side of the river, where they had discovered a herd of bisons, and as they were hastening back to Clermont with the intelligence, they observed our trail, which they mistook for that of a Pawnee war-party, and were exerting their utmost speed homeward, when they met with our friendly Indian, who smiled when he informed us of their mistake.

The remnant of our fawn had been cooked, and was partly eaten on their arrival, when they readily accepted our invitation to partake of it. In return for which, when their meat was prepared, the whole was set before us, and they respectfully waited until we were satisfied.

We now ascertained our position with respect to the settlements. We were within about four days march of Belle Point, and the next large stream we would cross was the Verdigrise.

Previous to retiring to rest the Osages performed their vespers by chanting in a wild and melancholy tone a kind of hymn to the Master of life. Very remote lightning in the S.E. horizon.

Saturday, 2d. Our guests awakened early, and one of them, retiring a short distance from his companions, began the well-known ceremony, common to this nation, of crying aloud with a voice of lamentation, intended probably as an invocation of the departed spirit of a relative or friend.

Messengers were despatched before sunrise to Clermont's camp, to inform that chief of the proximity of a party of white men on this side of the river, and of bisons on the other; and soon afterwards the remainder of our guests, with the exception of one that concluded to remain with us, departed to hunt.

Other Indians, attracted by curiosity, visited us in the course of the day, one of whom informed us, that three men, whose appearance corresponded with the description of our deserters, were now at the village; and that the approaching hunting party being already apprised of their character, Clermont, who was himself with the party, had forthwith despatched an order to the village to have them detained there until the decision of our chief respecting them should be known.

This most welcome news induced Lieutenant Smith and Julien, accompanied by Clermont's brother, and two or three of the young warriors who were present, to set out immediately for the village, in order to seize the recreants, and conduct them to camp. Thus we were inspired with the most sanguine expectations, not only of retrieving our losses, but also of subjecting the offenders to that punishment which was their due.

In the afternoon we had the company of numerous Indians from the hunting party; and an individual, that left our camp early in the morning in pursuit of the bisons on the opposite side of the river, brought a horse load of very lean meat. Their demeanour was pacific and kind, and they appeared disposed to serve us. They brought a considerable quantity of plums of a blue colour, and exceedingly agreeable taste, which were collected from trees growing in the adjacent forest. Our cook having intimated to one of them our want of salt, he instantly mounted his horse, and, after a short absence, returned with a supply. One half of the hunting party was soon afterwards observed fording the river in a long line about a mile below our camp; the other portion, we were told, would cross the river at some point above the camp to-morrow morning, and would act in concert with the others, so as to surround the herd of bisons that they were now going in pursuit of.

In the evening Mr. Swift returned unsuccessful; when he left us in the morning he directed his course to Clermont's camp, which he found in the prairie near a little impure puddle of water. He was very cordially and graciously received by the chief, who invited him to partake of some food. He assured Mr. S. of his regret at being unable to induce any of his young men to pursue our fugitives, who, as he had but then been informed, departed from the village early in the morning. This unwillingness on the part of his young men arose from their extreme anxiety to hunt the bisons, that were at this time unusually near; an enjoyment which they would on no account relinquish. He likewise regretted that he was at present so circumstanced as to be unable to comply with his wishes by visiting our camp. "But," said Clermont, "if your chief will visit me at my camp, which will be established near yours in the evening, I will treat him well; I will present him with as much maize and dried meat as he wants. I will, moreover, furnish him with young men to serve as guides, and a horse or two if he wants them, to aid in the transportation of the baggage." Lieutenant Swift assured him that we were much in want of such assistance as he had proffered, and that on our arrival at Belle Point his generosity should be requited; but the chief declared his indifference to any recompence for such services. Mr. Swift further learned that the deserters, during their short stay at the village, had traded freely for provisions with the trinkets they found in our saddle bags; and although dressed in our clothing, they appeared to imagine themselves suspected to be not what they seemed. This idea was in truth well-founded; for the Indians observing that they retained their guns constantly within their grasp, even when partaking of the hospitality of the different lodges, believed them to have committed some crime or outrage, in consequence of which they regarded themselves as unsafe in any asylum.

As the camp was about to move when Mr. Swift arrived there, he now took his leave to return, but inadvertently deviating from the proper course, he struck the river several miles above our camp. Clermont, meeting with his trail, perceived at once that he had gone astray, and immediately deputed one of his sons to pilot him to our camp.

In the acceptation of these Indians white man and trader seemed to be synonymous, and many of those who visited us importuned us much to trade for leather, dried meat, pumpkins both dried and fresh, &c.; in exchange for which they desired our blankets, and even the clothing from our bodies.

The superiority of the hunting qualifications of the Indians over those of our hunters was obvious in an instance which occurred to day. The corporal went to the forest for the purpose of killing a deer, and it was not long before an Indian, who accompanied him, pointed out one of those animals in a favourable situation. The corporal fired, but thought he had missed his object. The Osage, however, insisted that the animal was mortally wounded, and advanced forward a very considerable distance, where our hunter could see nothing of the usual sign of blood, or trodden grass, and found the victim dead upon the ground.

One of the party, on another occasion, saw an Osage shoot at a deer running, and wound him; another Indian, at a short distance further, fired at the same deer and brought him down, both, of course, with single ball.

The extreme heat of the day was 95 degrees.

Sunday, 3d. Our chief, who upon the invitation of Clermont visited the Indian camp accompanied by Julien and Clermont's son, returned this morning with two other sons of that chief, and a handsome young squaw, wife of one of them. His reception was not equal to his anticipations; Clermont, however, and one of his sons, each presented a skin of maize; but that chief could not realize the almost splendid offers he had made of guides and horses.

Word was brought to Clermont that the information received yesterday, of our deserters having departed from the village, was incorrect, and that they still remained there. This induced, at once, the offer of every thing they were in possession of, with the exception of the manuscripts alone, to any persons who should bring them to our camp. With this liberal offer Clermont himself, accompanied by Julien, set out for the village to arrest them, but on their way a messenger, whom they met, assured them that they had actually and finally departed this morning. Thus all our hopes of recovering our lost property vanished.

The stature of the Osages that fell under our observation was by no means superior to that of the Missouri Indians, and in very many instances their form exhibited a beautiful symmetry. They do not seem to differ, in point of features or colour, from the Indians just mentioned. But the custom seems to be still more general in this nation of shaving the head, so as to leave only a scalp on the back part and above, which is, as usual, ornamented with silver plates, brooches and feathers.

Their dresses and decorations are very similar to those of the Omawhaws, Otoes, and Konzas; but, from their proximity to the settlements, they are furnished with a great proportion of manufactured articles from the Whites.

Their government, so far as we could ascertain, was of the same description with that of the other nations; and their manners, though perhaps less fierce and warlike, seem to be, with the exception of their vociferous matins, not very essentially distinct.

They have the usual armature of the bow and arrow, tomahawk, war-club, and scalping-knife; but a large proportion of them have fusees, and we saw but very few who bore the lance and shield. They are freely branded by the Missouri Indians with the epithet of cowards. They are, at present, in amity with the Sauks and Foxes; and their friendship with the Konzas, with whom they freely intermarry, seems to have been uninterrupted since the expedition of Lieutenant Pike.

The horses belonging to the Osages are by much the best we have seen amongst the Indian nations, and they are kept in the best order. The Indians generally of this country appear to be excellent connoisseurs of horses, and to perceive any defects in them with a remarkable readiness. One of Clermont's sons possessed a very fine horse, for which the Kaskaia horse was offered, but the exchange was refused.

Horses are the object of a particular hunt to the Osages. For the purposes of obtaining these animals, which in their wild state preserve all their fleetness, they go in a large party to the country of the Red or Canadian river, where these animals are to be found in considerable numbers. When they discover a gang of the horses, they distribute themselves into three parties, two of which station themselves at different and proper distances on the route, which by previous experience they know the horses will most probably take when endeavouring to escape. This arrangement being completed, the first party commences the pursuit in the direction of their colleagues, at whose position they at length arrive. The second party then continues the chase with fresh horses, and pursues the fugitives to the third party, which generally succeeds in so far running them down as to noose and capture a considerable number of them.

The name of this nation, agreeably to their own pronunciation, is Waw-sash-e; but our border inhabitants speak of them under the names of Huz-zaus, and O-saw-ses. The word Wawsashe, of three syllables, has been corrupted by the French traders into Osage; and though the spelling of the latter has been retained by the Americans, we have still farther swerved from the original, by pronouncing the word agreeably to the genius of our language.

The lodges or huts of their villages are yet covered with the bark of trees, but it is probable that they will adopt the more permanent and preferable architecture of dirt lodges, used by most of the Missouri nations.

As we proceeded to load our horses at ten o'clock, in order to continue our journey, we perceived that several small articles of no great value had been pilfered from us by our visitors. These are the only losses we have sustained from Indian theft during this protracted journey. During the stay of our party at Fort Osage last season, Mr. Sibley, Indian factor at that place, politely furnished us with the following information respecting the Osages; being the copy of a report made by him to government, in the late war with Great Britain. We present it to the reader in Mr. Sibley's own words:

" 1st. The Chancers, or band of the Arkansa, 600 men; town situated near the mouth of the Verdigrise, a branch of the Arkansa; Clermont first chief.

"2d. The Great Osages, or White Hair's band, 400 men; town situated near the head of the Osage river; Che-sho-hun-ga, first chief.

"3d. The Little Osages, 250 men; town situated on the Ne-ozho, a branch of the Arkansa; Ne-zu-mo-nee, first chief.

"These tribes are at war with all their neighbours, except the Konzas, and a part of the Sauks and Foxes; with the Konzas they are and long have been on the most intimate and friendly terms; with the Sauks and Foxes they are at present barely at peace. All their chiefs (except Clermont) are very weak and unpopular. Many of their great war captains are in opposition to their chiefs, and have powerful influence in their respective tribes. Of these are 'The Duck,' 'Big Wolf,' and 'John L. Foe,' of the Great Osage; 'Sansoreille,' 'Big Soldier,' and 'The Soldier of the Oak,' of the Little Osage. Their council are very much distracted by the jealousies and intrigues of the principal warriors, and for want of energy and decision in the chiefs. When I left them last spring, my impressions were, that the Osages were generally disposed to be at peace with us, but they were very much dissatisfied and displeased, and losing their former unbounded confidence in us, in consequence of what they alleged to be a failure on the part of the United States to fulfil the treaty existing between them and the United States. My opportunities for observation and inquiry concerning the temper and disposition of those Indians were very good, and were not neglected. And my acquaintance with the Osages being very general (extending almost to every individual), and of long standing (upwards of eight years), enables me to speak confidently of them.

"In the year 1804 the President of the United States gave his promise to a number of Osage chiefs, then on a visit at Washington, to establish for them a trading-house on the plan authorized by a law of congress. In 1806 the President repeated the same promise to another deputation of Osage chiefs then here. In 1808 the President ordered the establishment to be made, and accordingly in October of that year it was made. So far this was a gratuitous act of the government; but in the following month it assumed a very different character. On the 8th November 1808 Peter Choateau (the U. S. agent for the Osages), arrived at Fort Clark. On the 10th he assembled the chiefs and warriors of the Great and Little Osages in council, and proceeded to state to them the substance of a treaty, which he said Governor Lewis had deputed him to offer the Osages, and to execute with them. Having briefly explained to them the purport of the treaty, he addressed them to this effect (in my hearing) and very nearly in the following words: 'You have heard this treaty explained to you; those who now come forward and sign it shall be considered the friends of the United States, and treated accordingly; those who refuse to come forward and sign it shall be considered enemies of the United States, and treated accordingly.' The Osages replied in substance, 'that if their Great American Father wanted a part of their land, he must have it; that he was strong and powerful, they were poor and pitiful. What could they do? He had demanded their land, and had thought proper to offer them something in return for it. They had no choice; they must either sign the treaty, or be declared the enemies of the United States.'

"The treaty was accordingly signed on the same day; and so much were the Osages awed by the threat of Mr. Choateau, that a very unusual number of them touched the pen; many of whom knew no more the purport of the act than if they had been an hundred miles off; and I here assert it to be a fact, that to this day the treaty is not fairly understood by a single Osage.

"Thus, the trading-house which had been established gratuitously, in conformity with the earnest solicitations of the Osage chief, and repeated promises of the President, was made a part of the price of the lands acquired under that treaty of the United States. In April 1810 this treaty was ratified and confirmed by the Senate, and was duly proclaimed by the President of the United States to be a law of the land. The Osages complained of the delay which took place between its signature (from which time is was binding on them) and the payment of the first and second annuities, which were not made till September 1811. The trading-house was kept up and well supplied until early in June 1813, at which time the establishment was by order broken up, and has been discontinued ever since, contrary to the expectations and entirely against the consent of the Osages, who considered the trading-house as the only benefit they had acquired by the treaty.

"No complaints have been made against the Osages from the signature of the treaty till after the trading-house and garrison were withdrawn from Fort Clark; since that time a party of the Great Osages murdered one of our citizens, and the murderers were promptly demanded (agreeably to the treaty) by Governor Clark, and would have been surrendered, if Mr. Choateau (who was sent after them) had performed his duty. Several other important things are promised the Osages in the treaty. A mill, ploughs, and other implements of husbandry, a blacksmith to mend their guns, ploughs, &c. and block-houses to defend their towns. In short, they were induced to believe, that an establishment was to be perfectly kept up near their towns, which should afford them a ready market at all times for their furs and pelts, encourage and assist them in acquiring habits of civilization, and protect them from their surrounding enemies. A mill and one block-house have been built at an enormous expense, and a blacksmith has been fixed; all at the town of the Great Osages. The mill, I believe, is of some use to those few who are near it. The blacksmith (although expensive to government) is not of the smallest service. The block-house is only useful to the traders who sometimes go to that village.

"All of them would be extremely useful, if properly placed and taken care of; but detached as they are from the agency, and unconnected with an establishment such as was originally contemplated at Fort Clark, they are at present of very little use.

"These facts, concerning the Osage treaty, are stated merely to show that we have not dealt justly with the Osages, and to infer from them, that unless immediate steps are taken to recover that confidence and respect which those Indians once had in the United States, the inevitable consequence will be, their decided and active hostility against the settlements of the Missouri, and those back of the lead mines. British emissaries had repeatedly attempted to engage the Osages in their service previous to the evacuation of Fort Clark, but without effect. The leading men have often declared to me their determination 'never to desert their American Father as long as he was faithful to them.' At a time when we were under serious apprehensions of an attack on Fort Clark, the warriors of the Little Osages offered their services to me to defend the post. In less than two months after those declarations and offers of service Fort Clark was evacuated, and the Osage establishment abandoned, without any notice or apology for so very extraordinary and unnecessary an act. Thus were the Osages left (I may truly say) in the arms of the British agents. How far those agents have succeeded in weaning them from their growing attachment to the United States I am unable to say; they have had full scope for their arts, and it would be idle to suppose they have not made some progress.

"Of all the Missouri Indians, the Osages were the least accessible to British influence, from their strong attachment to the French. They had acquired a *French* prejudice against the English, which, since my acquaintance with them, has rather increased than diminished. Such are the Osages, and such our relations and political standing with them.

" To put an end to the difficulties now existing between the United States and those people, and to relieve our frontier from the additional weight and destructive effects of their hostility, I beg leave to propose the following plan :—

" The Osage treaty should be immediately carried into complete effect, and measures promptly adopted to engage the Osages in the service of the United States: with this view, and to effect the latter important object, it will be necessary to make an establishment near the Osage towns, to consist of a tradinghouse, armourer, or blacksmith, and mill; the tradinghouse to be constantly supplied with a sufficient quantity of suitable Indian goods, to be furnished to the Osages (and such other Indians as the Osages may associate with them in the service of the United States, and request to be furnished,) on liberal terms, either in barter for their furs and pelts, payment of their annuities, payment for their services, and such occasional presents as the safety of Indian affairs may authorize or require. This store should constitute an ample fund always in their country, and always accessible to supply all their wants, and promptly to discharge all their just demands against the United States. During the continuance of the war 40,000 dollars per annum would be requisite. In peace from 10 to 15,000 would be sufficient.

" This establishment should be so regulated in its details as to prevent frauds and abuses, restore confidence among the Osages, and produce the most satisfaction to them, and benefit of the United States. In peace the net profits of the trade will more than defray the whole expense. In war those profits will very much diminish the expense. This establishment should be under the direction of a responsible and confidential agent, who should also be charged with the local superintendance of Indian affairs within the proper sphere of his agency.

"A strong stockade fort and garrison should be fixed in the neighbourhood of the Indian establishment, under such police and regulations as should effectually prevent any clashing between the military and Indian departments, and solely to be confined to military purposes. A system of espionage to be adopted and put into operation at this establishment, and extended as far as possible among the surrounding Indian nations."

The Osages of the Oaks, or Clermont's band, were separated from the other bands, and fixed in their present situation, chiefly, it is said, through the influence of Mr. Choteau, previously to the cession of the territory to the American government. The monopoly of the Missouri trade having been granted to Mr. Manuel Lisa by the Spanish authorities, Mr. Choteau, a rival trader, could no longer traffic with them on the waters, or within a certain distance of the Missouri. He therefore managed to separate a considerable portion of the nation from the interest of his rival, and induced them to establish a town near the Arkansa, of the trade of which river he enjoyed the monopoly.

At a short distance we crossed a small creek which issues from a spring of water. The prairie is now very fertile, interspersed with pleasing groves of oak, and swelling, on either hand, and in the distance, into remarkable pyramidal and conical hills, of which the summits are rocky. The spice-wood (laurus benzoin) and the pecan (carya olivæformis) first occurred to-day. Our distance, twelve miles.

CHAPTER VIII.

VERDIGRISE RIVER. — MR. GLENN'S TRADING-HOUSE. — NEW SPECIES OF LIZARD. — NEOSHO OR GRAND RIVER. — SALT WORKS. — LARGE SPIDER. — ILLINOIS CREEK. — TICKS. — ARRIVAL AT BELLE POINT.

MONDAY, 4th. The face of the country exhibited the same appearance as that of yesterday's journey, until we arrived at a dense forest, which we supposed to margin the Verdigrise river, or Was-su-ja of the Osages. There being no trace to direct us, we were obliged to penetrate the intricate undergrowth as we might, and after a tedious and laborious passage of something more than three miles, we attained, probably by a somewhat circuitous route, the river which we had so long vainly sought. At our crossing-place the stream was probably eighty yards wide, and one foot in depth, running with a brisk stream over a rocky bed, though above and below, as far as we examined, the depth of water is much more considerable. This river is more rapid and pellucid than any tributary we had passed on this side of the mountain streams, and during the season of floods its volume is augmented by the tribute of those ravines over which we passed on the 30th ultimo.

Late in the afternoon, we struck the Osage trace, leading from their village to the trading establishment, at the confluence of the Verdigrise; whither we now direct our course. Our evening encampment was at a small ravine, in which were some plum bushes, bearing fruit, yet unripe, of a fine red colour, and, without the slightest exaggeration, as closely situated on many of the branches as onions when tied on ropes of straw for exportation. Distance, seventeen miles three quarters. Extreme heat, 90 degrees.

Tuesday, 5th. At ten o'clock we arrived at Mr. Glenn's trading-house, near the Verdigrise, about a mile above its confluence with the Arkansa. We were hospitably received by the interpreter, a Frenchman, who informed us that Mr. Glenn was absent on a visit to Belle Point. In reply to our inquiries respecting the best and shortest route to the place of destination, two Americans who were present assured us, that there was a path the whole distance so obvious as not to be mistaken, and that they were so much occupied, as to be unable to spare any one to pilot us. Unfortunately, however, for our informant, a military cap, which was now discovered suspended from a beam, betrayed him to be a soldier, belonging to the garrison of Belle Point, temporarily employed at this place. When asked by what right he entered into any other engagements whilst in the service of the United States, he replied that he had the permission of his officers; but as he could not show a certificate, he was ordered to join our suit forthwith as a guide, and to assist with the pack-horses. The interpreter informed us, that the distance to the town of the Osages of the Oaks is about fifty-five miles; from thence to the village of the second band of Osages, called the Great Osages, situated near the head waters of Osage river, more than fifty miles; thence to the village of the third band, called Little Osages, situated on the Neosho or Grand river, three miles; he assured us, that Clermont had then four wives and thirty-seven children; a number, doubtless, unprecedented amongst the North American Indians, and which may probably be attributed to this chief by mistake. We also learned, that at the distance of twenty-five miles was a copious salt spring, lately worked with the permission of the Indians; but at present it is abandoned, and the apparatus removed. Mr. Nuttall, in his interesting Journal of Travels in the Arkansa territory, has given an excellent account of this saline. It produced, agreeably to his statement, under the management of the company, one bushel of salt from eighty gallons of water, and one hundred and twenty bushels were manufactured in a week.

A beautiful species of lizard [8] (agama), is occasionally met with in this territory. It runs with great swiftness. The form of its scales, their arrangement and proportions, considerably resemble those of polychrus marmorata, with the exception of the caudal ones, the series of which are equal, and the scales near the tip of the tail only are mucronate. A band over the shoulders somewhat resembles that of stellio querto paleo.

In addition to our usual fare, served upon the earth, we here enjoyed the luxury of wild honey and Indian corn, or maize bread, spread upon a table; and felt perhaps a little of that elation which the possession of a new coat communicates to the beau, when we found ourselves mounted on stools and benches around it.

The sassafras (laurus sassafras) occurred this morning; and soon after our departure from the trading-house, we saw the cane (miegia macrosperma), and were soon involved in a dense cane brake. Here we were hardly fanned by a breath of air, and during the prevalence of the extreme heat of the day, which was 96 degrees, the state of the atmosphere was extremely oppressive. A short ride brought us to the Neosho, or Grand river, better known to the hunters by the singular designation of the Six Bulls.

It enters the Arkansa very near to the confluence of the Verdigrise, and at the ripple, which offers us a facility of crossing, is about eighty yards wide, the water clear, above and below moving with a gentle current, and its bed and shores paved with large pebbles. At the entrance of the opposite forest, our guide, to whom the direct and very obvious path was supposed to be so familiar, now became bewildered, and after reconnoitring to his heart's content amongst the entangled briers, vines, and nettles, ushered us into a trace which conducted to an old Indian encampment, and terminated there. Further progress was in a great measure intercepted by the cane brake, which not presenting any path, obliged us to break our passage with much labour. The dusk of the evening found us still pursuing a devious course through a world of vegetation impenetrable to the eye, vainly seeking a spot upon which an encampment could be fixed, when, to our unspeakable joy, and without previous intimation, the prairie of Bayou Menard appeared suddenly before us. The timber of these bottoms is large and various. The extreme heat of the day, 96 degrees. Distance, eighteen miles.

Our pleasure at first seeing civilized white men was of no ordinary kind; it appeared as though we had already arrived at our own homes and families, in anticipation of Belle Point, which had hitherto seemed the utmost boundary and terminus of our pilgrimage.

Wednesday, 6th. A fine morning, and, as on the days of the first instant, and 30th ultimo, no dew had fallen. Crossed the ravine at the head of Bayou Menard, and ascended the elevated hills, clothed with small oaks, and arrived at a branch of Greenleaf Bayou about nine o'clock; a distance of eight miles.

A slight shower of rain fell in the afternoon; and during our ride we first observed the dogwood (cornus florida). In the evening, we arrived at Mr. Bean's salt works. These are situated on a small creek which flows into the Illinois creek about a mile below, and are at the distance of about seven miles from the Arkansa. Mr. Bean commenced his operations in the spring, and has already a neat farm-house on the Illinois, with a considerable stock of cattle, hogs, and poultry, and several acres in Indian corn. Near the springs he has erected a neat log-house, and a shed for the furnace; but his kettles, which were purchased of the proprietors of the Neosho establishment, were not yet fixed. He assured us that the water was so far saturated as not to dissolve any perceptible quantity of a handful of salt that was thrown into it. On the side of a large well, which he had sunk to collect the salt water, and perhaps two feet from the surface of the soil, he pointed out the remains of a stratum of charcoal of inconsiderable extent, through which they had penetrated, and which to a by-stander was a certain proof that these springs had been formerly worked by the Indians. But as no other appearances justified this conclusion, a greater probability seems attached to the idea, that during some former conflagration of the prairies, the charred trunk or branches of a tree was here imbedded. Another agent, however, of sufficient efficacy to operate this carbonization of wood, resides in the sulphuric acid, liberated by the decomposing pyritous rocks, so abundant here.

Whilst waiting with a moderate share of patience for our evening meal of boiled pumpkins, one of the children brought us a huge hairy spider, which he carried upon a twig, that he had induced the animal to grasp with its feet. Its magnitude and formidable appearance surprised us. The boy informed us that he had captured it near the entrance of its burrow, and that the species is by no means rare in this part of the country. Not having any box suitable to contain it, nor any pin sufficiently large to impale it, we substituted a wooden peg, by which it was attached to the inside of a hat. This species so closely resembles, both in form, colour, and magnitude, the gigantic bird-catching spider of South America*, that from a minute survey of this specimen, which is a female, we cannot discover the slightest characteristic distinction. But as an examination of the male,

* Mygale avicularia.

comparatively with that of the avicularia, may exhibit distinctive traits, we refrain from deciding positively upon the species. This animal had been previously mentioned by Mr Nuttall, in his recent and interresting account of his travels in this region. Distance, twenty-four miles.

Thursday, 7th. The Illinois is called by the Osages *Eng-wah-condah*, or *Medicine Stone Creek*. At our fording place near the Saline, it is about sixty yards wide, with clear water and pebbly shores, like those of the Neosho. We proceeded on, through a country wooded with small oaks, and interspersed with occasional small prairies, and crossed a deep ravine called Bayou Viande. The Bayous, as they are named in this country, unlike those of the lower portion of the Mississippi river, are large and often very profound ravines or watercourses, which, during the spring season, or after heavy rains, receive the water from the surface of the prairies, and convey it to the river; but in the summer and early autumn, the sources being exhausted, the water subsides in their channels, occupying only the deeper parts of their bed, in the form of stagnant pools, exhaling miasmata to the atmosphere, and rendering their vicinity prejudicial to health.

The extreme temperature of the day was 93 degrees, but it was rather abruptly reduced by a strong wind from the S. E., which brought up a heavy rain, with much thunder and lightning, and continued to drench us until the evening, when, after a ride of fourteen miles, we encamped at Bayou Salaison or Meat-salting Bayou. At our mid-day refectory, we were much annoyed by great numbers of small ticks, that were excessively abundant amongst the grass, and crawled by dozens up our leggings. Wherever they effected a lodgement upon the skin, their numerous punctures would cause an intolerable itching sensation, that bid defiance to repose. In the evening, in addition to the needful process of drying our clothing and blankets, we had ample employment in scratching and picking the pestiferous arachnides from our bodies. On entering the water, the disagreeable sensation seemed to be mitigated for a time, only to be augmented on our return to the atmosphere. Mosquitoes, which were also abundant, were readily expelled from our tents by the smoke of burning wood; but the ticks, otherwise constituted, frustrated our endeavours to obtain the necessary rest and sleep during the night.

These ticks are of two different species, and, in common with other species inhabiting different parts of the United States, are distinguished by the name of *seed ticks*, probably on account of their small size when compared with others of the same genus.

The larger of the two kinds [9] may be compared, in point of transverse diameter, to the head of a small-sized pin; but the other one is so much smaller, as to elude the sight, except on minute inspection.

The Cherokee Indians frequently visit this vicinity on hunting excursions; and our guide informs us, that a hunting-party of that nation is at present situate at the mouth of this Bayou, at the distance of two miles and a half from our camp.

Friday, 8th. The face of the country presents the same appearance with that we passed over yesterday, offering in the arrangement of forest and fertile prairie, many advantageous scites for plantations, of which one is already established at the confluence of Big Skin Bayou.

During the afternoon's ride, the country was observed to be more hilly. Soon after the occurrence of the greatest heat of the day, which was 91 degrees, several showers of rain fell, accompanied with distant thunder.

On a naked part of the soil, gullied out by the action of torrents of water, we beheld a hymenopterous or wasp-like insect (sphex) triumphantly, but laboriously, dragging the body of the gigantic spider, its prey, to furnish food to its future progeny. We cannot but admire the prowess of this comparatively pigmy victor, and the wonderful influence of a maternal emotion, which thus impels it to a hazardous encounter, for the sake of a posterity which it can never know. Distance, nineteen miles.

Saturday, 9th. Pursued our journey, with every hope of reaching the place of rendezvous appointed by Major Long before noon. Since passing Bayou Viande, we have observed the country on either side of our path to be distinguished by extremely numerous natural elevations of earth, of some considerable degree of regularity. They are of a more or less oval outline, and their general dimensions may be stated at one hundred feet long, by from two to five feet in greatest height. Their existence is doubtless due to the action of water. Should the rivers Platte and Arkansa be deprived of their waters, the sand islands of their beds would probably present a somewhat similar appearance.

An Indian, who observed us passing, hallooed to us from a distance, and expecting some important communication, we waited some time until he came up. He proved to be a Cherokee, dressed much in the manner of the whites, and not a little infected with the spirit of an interrogator, common, no doubt, to those with whom he has been accustomed to associate, and therefore probably regarded by him as a concomitant of civilization. We left him to his own surmises respecting our object and destination, and soon arrived at the path which strikes off for the river. After passing a distance of two miles through a cane brake, we passed a hut and small farm belonging to a soldier of the garrison, and were shortly on the strand of the river, with the long-sought Belle Point before us. We were soon ferried over, and were kindly received on the wharf by Captain Ballard and Mr. Glenn. The former gentleman was at present invested with the command, in consequence of the temporary absence of Major Bradford, on a visit to St. Louis. His politeness and attention soon rendered our situation comfortable, after a houseless exposure in the wilderness of ninety-three days. The greatest heat of the day was 91 degrees, and distance travelled nine miles.

The Arkansa, below the great bend, becomes more serpentine than it is above, and very much obstructed by sand-bars and islands, either naked or clothed with a recent vegetation; they are but little elevated above the water, and are covered to some depth during the prevalence of floods in the river. At Belle Point, and some distance above, these islands almost wholly disappear, but the sandy shores still continue, and are, as above, alternately situated on either side of the river, as the stream approaches or recedes from the opposite river bottoms. The colour of the water was now olive green. All the red colouring matter, with which it is sometimes imbued, is contributed by streams entering on the southern side. The current of the Arkansa is much less rapid than that of the Platte, but the character of these two rivers, in a great degree, corresponds in their widely spreading waters of but little depth, running over a bed of yielding sand. The rise of the waters at Belle Point takes place in the months of March and early in April, with a less considerable freshet in July and August. But to this place navigation is seldom practicable, for keel-boats, from the month of August to February inclusive, though the autumnal freshet of October and November frequently admits their passage.

CHAPTER IX.

JOURNEY FROM BELLE POINT TO CAPE GIRARDEAU. — CHEROKEE INDIANS. — OSAGE WAR. — REGULATOR'S SETTLEMENTS OF WHITE RIVER.

THE opportunity afforded by a few days residence at Fort Smith, was seized for the purpose of ascertaining, by several successive observations, the latitude and longitude of the place. The results of several observations of the sun's meridian altitude, and of lunar distances, had between the 14th and 19th September, give for the latitude of Belle Point, 34° 50′ 54″, and for the longitude 94° 21′ west of Greenwich.

On the 19th, Captain Bell left the fort to proceed on his way to Cape Girardeau, accompanied by Dougherty and Oakly, two of the engagees whose services were no longer required. On the 20th, Doctor James and Lieutenant Swift departed in company with Captain Kearny, who had visited the post in the discharge of his duties as inspector and paymaster. It was the design of this party to descend the Arkansa to the Cherokee agency, and to proceed thence to the hot springs of the Washita.

On the 21st, the party, now consisting of Major Long, Messrs. Say, Seymour and Peale, accompanied by Wilson, Adams, Duncan, and Sweney, the other soldiers being left at the fort, commenced their journey towards Cape Girardeau. We took with us five horses and five mules, two of the latter being loaded with packs. Captain Ballard kindly volunteered his services as guide, and, attended by a servant, accompanied us the first day's journey on our march.

Our route lay on the south side of the Arkansa, at considerable distance from the river, and led us across two small creeks—one called the Mussanne or Massern, and the other the Vache Grasse. [10] The latter stream has a course of several miles, but during the dry season, discharges very little water. The small path we followed lay for the most part through open woods of post oak, black jack, and hickory, occasionally traversing a narrow prairie. In these open plains, now covered with rank grass and weeds, we discovered here and there some traces, such as a skull or a hoof of a bison, indicating that the undisputed possession of man to these regions had been of a very recent date.

It was near five o'clock when we arrived at the solitary cabin of a settler, and though we found no inhabitant about the place, we halted, and encamped near the spring. Our horses were scarce unsaddled, when a man, who seemed to be the occupant of the house, came up, and informed us, that half a mile further on our way, we should find a house and good accommodations. Accordingly, we again mounted our horses, and rode on to "Squire Billingsby's," as our destined host was entitled, where we met a very hospitable reception. As the night approached, we observed that several young women and men, the sons and daughters of the family, disappeared, going to the cottages of the neighbours (the nearest of which seemed to be the one we had passed) to spend the night, that they might leave their beds for our use. Our hospitable landlord had many swarms of bees, some of which had been taken from the neighbouring forests. Wishing to make the addition of some honey to the bountiful table spread for our entertainment, he went with a light, and carefully removing the top of one of the hives, took out as much of the comb as he wished, and then replaced the top without killing or injuring the bees. In this manner, he assured us, honey may at any time be taken without destroying the insects, who will, if the season admits, speedily make up the deficiency thus produced. Some feather beds having been given up by their ordinary occupants expressly for our use, we could not well avoid accepting the accommodation thus offered, but instead of proving an indulgence, we found the use of them partook more of the nature of a punishment. We spent an unquiet and almost sleepless night, and arose on the following morning unrefreshed, and with a painful feeling of soreness in our bones, so great a change had the hunter's life produced upon our habits. Those of the party who spread their blankets, and passed the night on the floor of the cabin, rested much more pleasantly.

On the succeeding morning, Captain Ballard returned to Belle Point, and we resumed our journey, accompanied by one of the sons of our landlord, who undertook to guide us on our way, until we should fall in with a path which we might continue to follow. We passed through a hilly country, crossing two creeks, heretofore called the Middle and Lower Vache Grasse. At the distance of four or five miles from the Arkansa, on each side, the country is broken and mountainous, several of the summits rising to an elevation of near two thousand feet above the surface of the water. Several trees which stood near our path had been in part stripped of their bark, and the naked trunks were marked with rude figures, representing horses, men, deer, dogs, &c. These imperfect paintings, done with charcoal, and sometimes touched with a little vermilion, appeared to be historic records, designed to perpetuate, or at least to communicate the account of some exploit in hunting, a journey, or some similar event. We have already remarked, that this method of communication is sufficiently understood by the Indians, to be made the vehicle of important intelligence.

A little before sunset we arrived at a settlement on the stream, called Short Mountain Bayou. The little cabin we found occupied by two soldiers belonging to the garrison, who were on their return from the settlement at Cadron, whither they had been sent with letters on our arrival at Fort Smith, Cadron being the nearest post-town. We had expected letters from our friends by the return of the express, but were disappointed.

The soldiers informed us, that the house in which they had quartered themselves for the night, had been for a week or two deserted, since its proprietor had died, and his wife, who was sick, had been removed to the nearest settlement. The place is called the Short Mountain Settlement, from a high ridge of sandstone, a little to the north-west, rising in the form of a parallelogram to an elevation of about twelve hundred feet.* Its sides are abrupt, and in many places, particularly towards the summit, perpendicular. The summit is broad and nearly tabular, being covered with small trees, among which the red cedar, or some other ever-green tree, predominates. The plantation is somewhat elevated on a rocky eminence, at a little distance from the creek, but it is surrounded on all sides, save one, by the heavily wooded low grounds, in which we are to look for the causes whose operation have made it so soon desolate. Short Mountain Bayou, if we may judge from the depth and width of its channel, and the extent of its low grounds, is a large stream, or rather one which drains an extensive surface, but at this time it exhibited a succession of green and stagnant pools, connected by a little brook, almost without any perceptible current. On the surface of these pools, we saw the floating leaves of the nymphæa kalmiana, some utricularias, and other aquatic plants.

* It may be proper to remark, that the elevation of none of the Ozark mountains having been ascertained, the estimates which we have made are only to be considered as approximating towards the truth.

September, 23d. After leaving the wide and fertile bottoms of the Short Mountain Bayou, our path lay across high and rocky hills, altogether covered with woods. The upland forests are almost exclusively of oak, with some little intermixture of hickory, dogwood and black gum. They are open, and the ground is in part covered with coarse grasses.

At noon we arrived at the Cherokee settlements on Rocky Bayou, and were received with some hospitality at the house of the Metiff chief, known by the name of Tom Graves. Though entirely an Indian in his character and habits, he has the colour and features of an European, and it was not without some difficulty we could be made to believe that he was in reality allied by birth to the 'people among whom he holds the rank of a chief. His house, as well as many we passed before we arrived at it, is constructed like those of the white settlers, and like them surrounded with enclosed fields of corn, cotton, sweet potatoes, &c., with cribs, sheds, droves of swine, flocks of geese, and all the usual accompaniments of a thriving settlement.

Graves, our landlord, though unable to speak or understand our language, held some communications with us by means of signs, occasionally assisted by a black girl, one of his slaves, who interpreted the Cherokee language. He told us, among other things, that the Osages do not know how to fight; that the Cherokees were now ready to give up the Osage prisoners, if the Osages would deliver into their hands the individuals who had formerly killed some of the Cherokees, &c. He has shown his admiration of military prowess, by calling one of his children Andrew Jackson Graves. He treated us with a good degree of attention, and showed himself well acquainted with the manner of making amends by extravagant charges. Our dinner was brought in by black slaves, and consisted of a large boiled buffaloe, fish, a cup of coffee, corn bread, milk, &c. Our host and his wife, of unmixed aboriginal race, were at table with us, and several slaves of African descent were in waiting. The Cherokees are said to treat their slaves with much lenity. The part of the nation now residing on the Arkansa, have recently removed from a part of the state of Tennessee. They are almost exclusively agriculturalists, raising large crops of corn and cotton, enough for clothing their families, which they manufacture in their own houses.

After dinner we proceeded a few miles, taking with us one of Graves's sons as a guide, who led us to a place affording good pasture for our horses. Here we encamped.

September 24th. From the settlement of the Cherokees, at Rocky Bayou, our route lay towards the south-east, across the succession of rocky hills, sparingly wooded with oak, intermixed with the cornus porida, attaining an unusual magnitude.

As we descended towards the Arkansa, we perceived before us the cabins and plantations of another settlement of Cherokees. Passing near a wretched and neglected tenement, we observed a white man, who appeared to be the occupant, and called upon him to direct us to the place where, as we had been told, the river could be forded. It was not until we had repeated our request several times, that he seemed disposed to give any attention. He then approached at a snail's pace, and setting himself down upon the ground, drawled out his direction, terminating each word with a long and hearty yawn. The depression and misery which seemed written on his features, and the sallowness of his complexion, convinced us that disease, as well as native indolence, had some share in occasioning the apparent insolence he had shewn, and cured us of any wish we might have felt to reproach him.

Following a winding pathway, which led through deep-tangled thickets and heavy cane-brakes, we arrived at the ford, and crossing without difficulty, halted at the settlement of Walter Webber, a young chief of the Cherokees. Here we found the gentlemen of our party who had left the garrison before us.

The chiefs of the Cherokee nation had called a grand council, to meet at Point Pleasant the day after our arrival there, to adopt measures to forward the negociations for peace with the Osages, with whom they had been at variance for many years. The origin of the quarrel, existing between these powerful and warlike nations, is by some referred to the period of the American revolution, when the Osages killed a number of refugees, who had fled to them for protection. Among these were some Cherokees, some Indians of mixed breed, and it is said some Englishmen, to whom the success of the American arms rendered unsafe a longer residence in the country then occupied by the Cherokee nation. Whether the outrage thus alleged against the Osages was in fact committed, it is not at this time easy to determine. It appears, however, agreeably to the information we have been able to collect, that of late years the Cherokees have almost uniformly been the aggressors, while the abuses of the Osages, so loudly complained of, both by the Cherokees and the Whites, have been acts of retaliation. A large number of Cherokees now live on the south side of the Arkansa, upon lands claimed by the Osages; and all the Cherokees of the Arkansa are in the habit of hunting and committing depredations upon the Osage hunting grounds. In 1817, the Cherokees, with a number of Delawares, Shawnees, Quapaws, and eleven American volunteers, the whole amounting to about six hundred men, made an irruption into the territory of the Osages, having previously taken measures to quiet the suspicions of their enemies, by occasional messages, professing a peaceable disposition on their part. When they had arrived near the village, they sent a deputation to the Osages, concealing at the same time their numbers and their hostile intention, and inviting Clermont, the chief, to a council which they proposed to hold at a little distance from the town. Clermont being absent on a hunt with the young men of his village, an old Indian, and one in high standing with his people, was appointed to act in his stead, and commissioned to conclude a peace with the Cherokees, according to the wish they had expressed by their messengers. But what was his surprise, when, on arriving at the spot designated as that at which the council was to be held, instead of a few chiefs and old men, as had been represented, he found himself surrounded by the whole armed force of the Cherokees. He was seized and put to death on the spot. The design of this act of perfidy had been to effect the destruction of Clermont, the bravest and most powerful of the Osages. The Cherokees then proceeded to the attack of the town, where, on account of the absence of the efficient men, they encountered little resistance. A scene of outrage and bloodshed ensued, in which the eleven Americans are said to have acted a conspicuous and a shameful part. They fired the village, destroyed the corn and other provisions, of which the Osages had raised a plentiful crop, killed and took prisoners between fifty and sixty persons, all old men, women, and children. Four of these prisoners, who had been since held in captivity by the Cherokees east of the Mississippi, had been brought to Point Pleasant, by a metiff called Captain Rogers, and a consultation was now to be held, concerning the manner of restoring them to the Osages.

In the winter of 1817-18, some of the leading men of both nations had been summoned to a council at St. Louis, by Governor Clark, for the purpose of negociating a peace. By the treaty then made, the Cherokees had agreed to relinquish the prisoners in question, in consideration of which they were to be allowed the privilege of hunting in the country north of the Arkansa, as high as the Grand river or Six Bulls, and on the south side as high as they pleased. The stipulated surrender of the prisoners not having been made, a party of Osages, who were hunting on Red river, some time in the ensuing winter, fell in with three Cherokee hunters, and whom they murdered by way of retaliation. This circumstance tended to widen the breach between them, till at length both parties were resolved on war, which was for the present prevented by the interference of Governor Miller, and by the check imposed by the presence of an armed force at Belle Point, on the frontiers of the two nations. At the time of our visit, it was hoped the influence of Governor Miller would effect the establishment of a permanent peace. The first of the ensuing month (October) had been appointed for the surrender of the prisoners, and Governor Miller was said to be then on his way to Belle Point, to ensure the fulfilment of the conditions stipulated between the contending parties. The Osages were to give up the men concerned in the murder on Red river, in exchange for the women and children then prisoners with the Cherokees.

The Cherokees were taught the culture of cotton many years since, by Governor Blount of North Carolina, who offered them a stipulated price per pound, for all they would deliver at the trading-house. They were for several years paid regularly for their cotton; but the factor at length refusing any longer to receive it, they complained to Governor Blount, who advised them to manufacture it into clothing for their own use, which they consented to do, on condition of being furnished with a person to give the requisite instruction. They now raise considerable quantities of cotton, and many of them are comfortably clad in garments of their own manufacture.

The introduction of a considerable degree of civilization among the Cherokees, has been attended with the usual consequence of inequality in the distribution of property, and a larger share of the evils resulting from that inequality, than are known among untutored savages. Encroachments upon the newly-established rights of exclusive possession have been frequent, and have rendered the numerous class of the poor among the Cherokees troublesome neighbours, both to the wealthy of their own nation, and to those of the white settlers in their vicinity who had any thing to lose. But wealth seldom finds itself destitute of the means of protection. Three bands of regulators, or troops of light horse, as they are sometimes called, are maintained among the Cherokees, consisting each of ten men well armed and mounted, and invested with an almost unlimited authority. [11] A few days previous to our arrival at Point Pleasant, a young man had been apprehended by one of these bands of regulators, on suspicion of horse-theft. On examination, the supposed delinquent proved stubborn and refractory, whereupon the captain ordered the infliction of fifty lashes; and this not seeming to produce the desired effect, an additional fifty was commenced, when the culprit confessed himself guilty, and disclosed the whole transaction, in which he had been concerned. We were called upon for advice in the case of the Osage prisoners, a young woman and three children labouring under an attack of intermitting fever. The young woman we found sitting upon the floor in a little cabin, near the trading-house, and crying bitterly, not more, as we were informed, on account of ill-health, than of her reluctance to return to the Osages. She had been long among the Cherokees, whose customs she had adopted, and among whom she had formed attachments.

Fikatok's village, which we passed on the 25th, is situated on the Illinois Bayou, about seven miles above Point Pleasant. It consists of no more than five or six cabins, but is the residence of the venerable Fikatok, who, since the death of Fallantusky in 1817, has been considered the principal chief of this portion of the Cherokee nation. He has been a distinguished benefactor to his people, and is familiarly known by the name of " The Beloved." The Cherokees who live at and about this village, and those settled at a distance from the Arkansa, generally are less subject to fevers than those who reside on the river bottoms. At a little distance above the village we left the Illinois, and proceeded across the wilderness towards Little Red river, on our route to Cape Girardeau. Two or three scattered plantations, occupied by Cherokees, occur in the country between Point Pleasant and Little Red river, where we arrived on the 28th. This river has a deep rocky channel, sixty or one hundred yards in width, at the point where we crossed it, which is distant about eighty miles from its confluence with White river. It had at this time scarcely a perceptible current, and in many places might be crossed on foot without wading. It is, however, like most of the rivers of this region, subject to great and sudden floods, which, in several instances, have drowned the cattle, and destroyed and swept away the crops of those who were settled along the banks. From the marks left by the last flood upon the banks, we perceived that the range, from high to low water, could not be less than sixty feet. From Stanley's settlement on Little Red river, it is about thirty-six miles north-east to Harding's ferry on White river. Here are numerous settlements of Whites; but notwithstanding the country is hilly and profusely irrigated with numerous rapid streams, the inhabitants have almost without exception a sickly appearance. Harding's ferry is about four hundred miles distant from the confluence of White river and the Mississippi. White river is navigable for keel-boats at high water to this place, and during a considerable portion of the year, they may ascend one hundred miles farther. It is here about three hundred yards wide. Its water is remarkably clear, and flows with a moderate current over a gravelly or stony-bed.

Near Harding's ferry, on the south side of White river, is the Chattahocchee mountain, of about two thousand feet elevation, somewhat surpassing any other point in its vicinity. The top of this mountain marks the north-eastern angle of the Cherokee boundary, as established by General Jackson's treaty. The eastern boundary of the tract, ceded by that treaty to the Cherokees, runs in a straight line from the top of the Chattahoochee to the mouth of Point Remove or Eddy Point creek, which enters the Arkansa about thirty miles above Cadron. This line coincides nearly with the eastern limit of the mountainous region. Many small portions of valuable land are included in the territory lately ceded to the Cherokees, but by far the greater part is mountainous and barren, and unfit for cultivation. White river has its source in the Ozark mountains, near the 94th degree of west longitude, and about the 36th degree north latitude, in the same district, from which descend, on the south-west the Illinois river of Arkansa, and on the north the Yungar Fork of the Osage. The average direction of its course is nearly due east parallel to the Arkansa, crossing about four degrees of longitude to its confluence with Black river, in latitude 35° 15', then turning abruptly south, it flows through 1° 15' of latitude to its bifarcation, and the confluence of its eastern branch with the Mississippi in 34 degrees north. Below the point where it receives the Black river from the north, and even at the Chattahoochee mountains, near one hundred miles above that point, White river is little inferior, either in the width of its channel, or in its volume of water, to the Arkansa under the same meridian. When we have had occasion to mention among the people of White river, that we had crossed the Arkansa at the Rocky Mountains, more than one thousand miles to the west, the question has been repeatedly put to us, " Where did you cross White river ?" Those who have known only the lower portions of both rivers, consider them as nearly of equal length, and as heading near each other ; whereas the entire extent of country drained by White river, compared to that of the Arkansa, is as one to six nearly. Three miles above its confluence with the Mississippi, White river divides into two branches, the lesser of which, turning off at right angles, flows south-west, with a current sometimes equal to three miles per hour, and falls into the Arkansa at the distance of four miles and a half. It is said the current flows through this communication alternately to and from the Arkansa, according as the water in that river is higher or lower than in White river. Major Long entered the Arkansa through this cut-off on the 13th of October 1817, and it has been passed more recently by Mr. Nuttall*, in 1819. In both these instances the current flowed from White river towards the Arkansa. The mouth of that branch of White river which communicates immediately with the Mississippi is situated fifteen miles above the mouth of the Arkansa [12], and is about two hundred yards wide. The current is very gentle, and the water deep. Though perfectly transparent, it is of a yellowish colour. The banks are low, and subject to periodical inundations. The soil near the mouth of White river is an intermixture of clay and fine sand, the clay predominating, and the whole of a reddish tinge.

Numerous settlements have heretofore been formed on the lands contiguous to White river, and several in the portion above the Chattahoochee mountain on the south side ; but all these lands having by treaty been surrendered to the Cherokees, many whites

---

* Nuttall's Travels, p. 65.

have been compelled to withdraw, and leave their farms to the Indians. The tract of land ceded] to the Indians by the treaty above alluded to, is for the most part rocky and barren. Some of the tributaries of White river have extensive and fertile bottoms, but the greater part of the country watered by this river, is mountainous and unfit for cultivation. At MacNeil's ferry, where the road from Little Rock on the Arkansa to Davidsonville, in Lawrence county, crosses White river, the bottoms are wide, and as fertile as any of those on the Arkansa. Here the miegia and the papaw attain their greatest perfection, and the soil is found well adapted to the culture of corn, cotton, and tobacco. At the point formed by the confluence of White and Black rivers, is a portion of land of a triangular form, and bounded by sides about fifteen miles in extent, which, in the excellence of its soil, as we were informed by the surveyors, is surpassed by none in the western country. There are considerable portions of the upland soil of White river, where the profuse supply of streams and springs of excellent water, the elevation and comparative healthfulness of many situations, and the vicinity of navigable rivers and other local advantages, make amends for the want of exuberant fertility in the soil. The same remark is applicable to the country south of the Arkansa, where are extensive tracts of hilly and rocky soils, which seem admirably adapted to the culture of the vine and the olive. In every part of the Ozark mountains, there are vallies, and small portions of land within the hills, having a deep and fertile soil, covered with heavy forests of oak, ash, hickory, and in some places with the sugar maple, and abounding in excellent water. The labour of a few years will be sufficient to convert these tracts into productive farms, but the inconvenience resulting from the difficulty of communication and access to the different parts of the country, will for a long time retard their settlement.

In several parts of the Arkansa territory we were shewn dollars, which were believed to have been coined in some of the upper settlements of White river; and it has been currently reported, that mines of silver exist, and are wrought there. It appears, however, upon examination, that much spurious coin is here in circulation; and it is probable that the White river country owes its present reputation for mineral wealth to the successful labours of some manufacturer of imitation dollars. Since the time of De Soto, it has been confidently asserted by many who have written concerning Louisiana, that mines of gold and silver exist in that part of the country of which we are speaking. In an old map, by Du Pratz, a gold mine is placed somewhere near the confluence of the Illinois and the Arkansa; a silver mine on the Merameg, and he says, " I myself saw a rivulet whose waters rolled down gold dust." [13] We are informed by Schoolcraft, that granite exists about the sources of the St. Francis, which are near those of White river, p. 213. Of the extent and character of this formation of granite, we have not yet been able to form any very definite ideas; it is, however, by no means improbable, that to its plates of yellow and white mica, we are to look for the origin of the fabulous accounts of the precious metals in those regions. Like the country of the gilded king, the El Dorado of South America, it is probable the gold and silver mines of the Arkansa territory will recede, before the progress of examination, first into the wildest and most inaccessible parts, and at length disappear entirely. We by no means intend to assert, that the region in question will not prove of immense importance, on account of its mineral treasures; valuable mines of lead and iron are certainly frequent in many parts of it. And we can assign no reason why silver and other metals should not be found in the argillite with quartzy veins, and in the other rocks of the transition period, which we know to exist in these mountains. We only intend to give it as our opinion, that there has as yet been no foundation in actual discovery for the belief that such mines do exist.

The bed of White river, at the place where we crossed it, is paved with pebbles and fragments of a yellowish white petiosiliceous stone, intermixed with rounded masses of transparent quartz, and sometimes with pieces of calcedony. Its water is uncommonly transparent, and this, with the whiteness of its bed, and the brisk motion of the current, gives it an aspect of unusual beauty. The banks are high, and in many places not exposed to inundation. Dense and heavy forests of sycamore and cotton-wood stretch along the river, disclosing here and there, at distant intervals, the solitary hut and the circumscribed *clearing* of the recent settler. Some who have been no more than two or three years resident upon their present farms, and who commenced in the unbroken forests, have now abundant crops of corn and pumpkins, with large fields of cotton, which is said to equal in quality that of the uplands of Georgia and Carolina. Few attempts have hitherto been made to cultivate any grain, except Indian corn, though the soil is thought to be in many places well adapted to wheat, barley, oats, &c. The maize cultivated in the Arkansa territory, and in the southern and western states, generally is the variety called the ground seed, having a long and compressed kernel, shrivelled at the end when fully ripe; and crops are not uncommon yielding from sixty to ninety bushels per acre. In all the uplands, the prevailing growth is oak. At the time of our journey, the acorns were falling in such quantities, that the ground for an extent of many acres was often seen almost covered with them. Many recent settlers, indulging the disposition to indolence which seizes upon almost every man who fixes his residence in these remote forests, place as much dependence upon the crop of mast as on the products of their own industry. Vast numbers of swine are suffered to range at large in the forests, and in the fall of the year, when they have become fat by feeding on the acorns, they are hunted and killed like wild animals, affording to the inhabitants a very important article of subsistence. It is remarked also, that the venison becomes fat somewhat in proportion as acorns are abundant. Turkies, which are still vastly numerous in the settlements of White river, feed upon them, but are said to grow poor in consequence.

Sweet potatoes* are produced in great perfection in many parts of the Arkansa territory, and are but too much cultivated and eaten, their constant use as an article of food being little beneficial to health. The common or *Irish potatoe*, as it is here universally called, succeeds but indifferently, and few attempts are made to cultivate it.

A few of the roads which traverse the country from the Mississippi to the upper settlements of Red river and the Arkansa, have been sufficiently opened to admit the passage of waggons. On these are seen many families migrating from Missouri to Red river, and from Red river to Missouri. The first settlements in the wilderness are most commonly made by persons to whom hardihood and adventure have become confirmed and almost indispensable habits, and who choose to depend upon the chase, and the spontaneous products of the unreclaimed forest, rather than submit to the confinement and monotony of an agricultural life. They are therefore, of necessity, kept somewhat in advance of those settlers who intend a permanent residence in the situations they first occupy. Removing from place to place with their cattle, horses, and swine, they confine them-

---

* The tuberous roots of the convolvulus batatas of Linnæus.

selves to one spot no longer than *the range* continues to afford a sufficient supply of the articles most necessary to life. When the canes are fed down and destroyed, and the acorns become scarce, the small corn-field and the rude cabin are abandoned, and the *squatter* goes in search of a place where all the original wealth of the forest is yet undiminished. Here he again builds his hut, removes the trees from a few acres of land, which supplies its annual crop of corn, while the neighbouring woods, for an extent of several miles, are used both as pasture and hunting grounds. Though there is in this way of life an evident tendency to bring men back to a state of barbarism, we have often met among the rudest of the squatters with much hospitality and kindness. Near White river, we called at a house to purchase food for ourselves and our horses, but having no silver money, our request was refused, although we offered the notes of the bank of Missouri, then in good credit. In a few miles we arrived at another cabin, where we found every member of the numerous family sick with the ague and fever, except one young girl. But here they were willing to furnish every refreshment their house afforded. There were at this time very few houses, particularly in the settlements about White river, which did not exhibit scenes of suffering similar to those in the one of which we were now the reluctant guests. We have seen some instances, where, of a family of eight or ten, not a single individual was capable of attending to the services of the household, or of administering to the wants of his suffering relatives. In these instances we thought it better to pitch our tents at a little distance, and intrude ourselves no farther than was necessary to procure corn and other indispensable supplies.

On the evening of September 30th, we halted at a little rivulet called Bayou Curæ. The dwelling of our landlord consisted, as is commonly the case in the new settlements, of a single room, with beds in two or three of the corners. We were cordially invited to make use of the beds, though it would have been at the expence of rendering it necessary for our host, his wife, and daughters, to sleep upon the floor of the same room. We accordingly spread our blankets, and deposited ourselves around the hearth, while the family occupied their usual stations. On the first of October we arrived at the ford of Strawberry river, a tributary entering the Big Black, not far from the confluence of the latter with White river, and about fourteen miles beyond, at the ford of Spring river, a parallel stream. Both of these are rapid and beautiful rivers, possessing all the peculiarities, as to the abundance, transparency, and purity of their waters, usually observed in those rivers which traverse elevated and mountainous districts. The entire length of Spring river is said to be but about one hundred and forty miles; yet in the quantity of water which it discharges, it more than twice exceeds the Canadian, having a course of more than nine hundred miles. It is said to have its principal source in a spring of uncommon magnitude. Spring river unites with another, called Eleven Point, near the little town of Davidsonville, the seat of justice for Lawrence county, and flows thence nearly due east, two or three miles to its junction with Big Black. The country around Davidsonville is hilly, having a deep and fertile primary soil, and abounding in heavy forests. The sources of Eleven Point, we have been told, are in eleven large springs, and are near those of Spring river.

To those who have been long accustomed to the thirsty regions of the Missouri, the Platte, and the Upper Arkansa, it is somewhat surprising to meet in tracts, having nearly the same elevation, and resting to a great extent on rocks of a similar character, so great a number of large streams crowded into such narrow compass.

Is it not probable, that a large portion of the water falling in rains upon the extensive plains at the eastern side of the Rocky Mountains, may sink through the loose and porous soil, till at length, meeting with some compact stratum, it may be collected into rills, and even considerable streams, which, descending along the surface of this stratum in the direction of the general inclination of the country, at length meet with the nucleus of the Ozark mountains, traversing the secondary strata like a mineral dike, and are consequently made to appear in the form of large springs? Whether any course of this kind operates to supply the unusual profusion of water with which this hilly tract is irrigated, must be for others to decide. The fact is an established one.

Black river originates in an elevated part of the Ozark mountains, between 37° and 38° north latitude, and between 90° and 91° west longitude. From the same tract descend, on the north, the waters of the Merameg; on the north-east, those of Big river; on the east and south, those of the St. Francis and Black river; and on the west, those of the Osage and the Gasconade. By an examination of the map which accompanies this work, it will be seen that the direction of the watercourses clearly indicates the existence of an elevated ridge, running from the confluence of the Missouri and Mississippi, on the north-east, to the junction of the Arkansa and the Canadian on the south-west. On the north-western side of this ridge, we observed the Osage, the Grand river, the Verdigrise, and even the Arkansa, inflected from that due eastern course, which the tributaries of the Mississippi and Missouri on the west incline to pursue; and coming near its base, we find the Illinois river of the Arkansa, and the Yungar Fork of Osage, running in opposite directions, and nearly at right angles to the general course of the Canadian, the Arkansa, the Main Osage, and Konzas. The Illinois, and the great eastern tributary of the Osage, receive numerous streams from the western slope of the Ozark mountains, but they traverse a region hitherto very imperfectly known. It appears, however, that these two rivers drain all the north-western side of the mountainous range in question. Black river runs nearly parallel, that is, from north-east to south-west, along the south-eastern side of the range. Its sources are in the district of the lead mines, and at no great distance from those of the Merameg and the St. Francis. Its course is at first south-east, about sixty or one hundred miles; then turning to the southwest, it receives in succession from the south-eastern side of the mountains, the Little Black, the currents Tourche, De Thomas, Eleven Point spring, and Strawberry rivers, uniting at length with White river, in latitude 35° 15′. As far as hitherto known, it receives no considerable tributary from the east. About the sources of Black river reside the Peola or Peoria Indians, who are said to number about fifty warriors. Parallel to this river, and from twenty to sixty miles distant on the east, is the St. Francis, a larger river, but one in many respects resembling Black river. It rises in the high lands, about one hundred miles to the westward of St. Genevieve in Missouri, and receiving, before it leaves the hills, Bear Creek, Castor White water, and numerous other streams, it descends toward the south-east, soon entering the extensive swamp which stretches from New Madrid on the Mississippi, along the base of the mountains, to the Arkansa. We have been informed by some of the inhabitants of the countries of Cape Girardeau and Madison, that in this swamp the St. Francis is so much obstructed with rafts, and so lost among islands, that its course can with difficulty be traced. It is well known that in the lower part of its course it is so obstructed by a large raft, as not to admit the passage of the smallest boats. Its confluence with the Mississippi is about three hundred and five miles below the Ohio, and eighty above the mouth of White river. Running parallel both to the Mississippi and White river, and at no great distance from either, the St. Francis can have no very large tributaries; indeed we know of none on either side which deserve the name of rivers. We have no very definite information respecting the great swamp in which the St. Francis is said to lose itself soon after leaving the hills; the accounts of the hunters, and of some settlers who have seen it, agree in representing it as almost impassable, covered with heavy forests of cypress, and wholly unfit to become the residence of men. This swamp, and the country about the sources of Black river and the St. Francis, appear to be near the centre of the region so powerfully affected by earthquakes in the year 1811. The fertile lands, on the upper branches of the St. Francis, are not very extensive, and are all more or less subject to inundation by the sudden overflowing of the streams. On this account they cannot be considered as of great value for agriculture; but the wealth which this region possesses in its mines, renders it one of the most important parts of ancient Louisiana.

On the 8th October we arrived at Jackson, the seat of justice for the county of Cape Girardeau, and, after St. Louis and St. Charles, one of the largest towns in Missouri. It lies about eleven or twelve miles north-west of the old town of Cape Girardeau, on the Mississippi, and is surrounded by a hilly and fertile tract of country, at this time rapidly increasing in wealth and population. Jackson is what is called a thriving village, and contains at present more than fifty houses, which, though built of logs, seem to aspire to a degree of importance unknown to the humble dwellings of the scattered and solitary settlers, assuming an appearance of consequence and superiority similar to that we immediately distinguished in the appearance and manners of the people. Our horses, having never been accustomed to such displays of magnificence, signified great reluctance to enter the village. Whips and heels were exercised with unusual animation, but in a great measure without effect, until we dismounted; when by dint of coaxing, pushing, kicking, and whipping, we at length urged our clownish animals up to the door of the inn.

Fifteen miles north of Jackson, on a little stream called Apple creek, reside about four hundred Indians, mostly Delawares and Shawnees. At the time of our visit the head of a Shawnee, who had been concerned in the murder of a white woman, was to be seen elevated on a pole by the side of the road leading from Jackson to the Indian settlement of Apple creek. It was related to us that the crime, for which this punishment had been inflicted, was committed at the instigation of a white man. The murderer was demanded of the Shawnees by the people of Jackson, and being at length discovered by the Indians, and refusing to surrender himself, he was shot by his own people, and his head delivered up, agreeable to the demand.

It is painful to witness the degradation and misery of this people, once powerful and independent; still more so to see them submitting to the unnecessary cruelties of their oppressors. We have not been informed by what authority the punishment above mentioned was inflicted upon a whole community for the crime of one of its members, and we are sorry to have occasion to record a circumstance so little honourable to the people of Missouri.

A miserable remnant of the Shawnee, Delaware, and Peola tribes, with a few Chickasaws and Cherokees, were at this time scattered through the country, from the Mississippi at the mouth of Apple creek westward to the sources of Black river. They were, however, about to remove farther west, and many of them were already on their way to the country about the upper branches of White river, where, by becoming intruders upon the territories of the Cherokees, it may be expected their speedy and entire extinction will be insured.

The road from White river joins that from the upper settlements on the St. Francis. At some distance beyond Jackson, Castor and White water are two beautiful streams, traversing the country west of Jackson. They run towards the south, and soon after their confluence enter the great swamp through which they find their way to the St. Francis.

The district of the lead mines, situated near the sources of the Merameg, the Gasconade, and the St. Francis, has been repeatedly described. The best accounts of it are in the works of Bradbury, Brackenridge, Stoddart, and Schoolcraft. * To those accounts we have to add a few observations respecting the rocks and soils of the region, a considerable part of which we have seen and examined as attentively as circumstances would admit. But as discussions of this kind have little interest for the general reader, we propose to give at the end of the work such remarks as we have had the opportunity to make connected with the mineralogy of this interesting territory.

* Bradbury's Travels in the Interior of America, p. 258, 2d edition. Brackenridge's Views of Louisiana, p. 390. Stoddart's Sketches of Louisiana, p. 390.

CHAPTER X.

HOT SPRINGS OF THE WASHITA.—GRANITE OF THE COVE.—
SALINE RIVER.

WE return to give a hasty account of an excursion from Point Pleasant, in the country of the Cherokees, to the hot springs of the Washita.

On the morning of the 25th, our little party, consisting of Captain Kearney, Lieutenant Swift, and myself, having taken leave of our companions, recrossed the Arkansa from Webber's, and proceeded on our journey without a guide.

Having mistaken the route we had been directed to follow, we were bewildered during a considerable part of the day, wandering about through a fertile country without settlements, and so covered with dense forests as to render the travelling exceedingly harassing. Towards evening we arrived at a settlement of Cherokees, where we engaged a guide to conduct us to the trace leading to the springs. For this service we paid him two dollars. At night we encamped in an open forest of oak, where we found a sufficient supply of grass for our horses. The hills south of the Arkansa range from N. E. to S. W., their sides are sometimes nearly naked, but more commonly covered with small and scattered trees. Several kinds of oak, and the chinquapin (castanea pumila, Ph.) attaining the dimensions of a tree, are met with in the sandstone tracts. We distinguished here, in the uplands, two separate varieties of soil. That just mentioned, based upon a compact hard sandstone, and bearing forests of oak, and another resting upon a white petrosiliceous rock, with fragments of which it is much intermixed. This latter is often covered with pine forests. The most common species, yellow pine (P. resinosa,) attains unusual magnitude. The rigida, and some other species occur, but are not frequent. We also observed several species of vaucinum, the mitchella, the kalmia latifolia, hamamelis virginica? cunila mariana, and many other plants common to this region and the Alleghany mountains.

There are no settlements between those of the Cherokees about Derdonai on the Arkansa and the hot springs. The blind path which we followed traverses a rugged and mountainous region, having considerable resemblance, except in the want of parallelism in the ranges, to the sandstone portions of the Alleghanies. As the weather was rainy we felt the inconvenience of travelling in the wilderness and encamping without tents. On the 28th we arrived at the hot springs. The country near these, on the north and north-west, is high and rocky. The sandstone, which extends from the Arkansa to within a few miles to the springs, becomes, as you go south, something inclined, and apparently of a more ancient deposition, until it is succeeded by a highly inclined primitive argillite. Both these rocks are traversed by large veins of white quartz. They are inclined towards the south, and the argillite at a great angle. In some localities it is but indistinctly slaty in its structure, and its laminæ are nearly perpendicular.

It contains extensive beds of a yellowish white siliceous stone, which is often somewhat translucent, and resembles some varieties of hornstone. Its fracture is a little splintery, and sometimes largely conchoidal; it is of a close texture, but the recent surface is generally destitute of lustre. It is this rock which affords the stones called Washita oilstones. It may, with propriety, be denominated petrosilex. This name is, however, to be understood as having the application given it by Kirwan, who uses it to designate the fusible varieties of the hornstone of

Werner, and not the several varieties of compact felspar to which it has been sometimes applied. In passing from the hot springs, north-east to the lead-mine country, about the sources of the Merimeg, this rock is found to be intimately connected, and to pass by minute and imperceptible gradations, into the flint rock of that district, which is decidedly secondary, and of contemporaneous origin with the compact limestone which it accompanies. About the hot springs it is not distinctly stratified, but occurs in very extensive masses, sometimes forming the body of large hills, and is marked by perpendicular seams and fissures, often placed very near each other.

The hot springs of the Washita are in north latitude 34° 31′, and west longitude 92° 50′ 45″ *, near the base of the south-eastern slope of the Ozark mountains, and six miles north of the Washita. They have been erroneously represented as the principal sources of that river, which are more than one hundred miles distant.

We have been informed that these remarkable springs were unknown, even to the American hunters, until the year 1779. At that time, it is said, there was but one spring discharging heated water. This is described as a circular orifice, about six inches in diameter, pouring out a stream of water of the same size, from the side of a perpendicular cliff, about eight feet from its base. This cliff was situate then, as it is now, along the eastern side of a small creek, but was at a greater distance from the stream than at present. At another place, near the top of the mountain, which rises abruptly towards the east, the heated water is said to have made its appearance near the surface of the ground, in a state of ebullition, and to have sunk and disappeared again upon the same spot. It is probable these representations

* Hunter and Dunbar.

are in a great measure fabulous; all we are to understand by them is, that the gradual augmentation of the thermal rocks, which are constantly forming about the springs, has changed the position, and perhaps increased the number of the orifices. [14]

These springs were visited by Hunter and Dunbar in 1804, and the information communicated by them, as well as much derived from other sources, together with an analysis of the waters, has been placed before the public by Dr. Mitchell.* They have been subsequently examined by Major Long, in January 1818, from whose notes we derive much of the information we have to communicate respecting them. They are about seventy in number, occupying situations at the bottom and along one side of a narrow ravine, separating two considerable hills of clay-slate. A small creek enters the ravine from the north by two branches, one from the north-west, and the other from the north-east, flowing after their union nearly due south, and blending with the water of the springs, increasing rapidly in size, and acquiring so high a temperature, that at the time of our visit the hand could not be borne immersed in it. After traversing from north to south the narrow valley containing the springs, this creek meanders away to the south-east, and enters the Washita at the distance of eight or ten miles. All the springs are within a distance of six hundred yards below the junction of the two brooks, and all, except one, on the east side of the creek.

We subjoin a note, containing some particulars observed by Major Long at the time of his visit in 1818. [15] During the winter the steam which rises from the springs is condensed to a white vapour, which is often visible at a great distance.

The water of the springs is limpid and colourless, and destitute, when cooled, of either taste or smell,

* See the New York Medical Repository.

and, according to the analysis of Dr. Mitchell, purer than ordinary spring water. It however deposits, as it comes in contact with the air, a copious sediment, which has gradually accumulated until it has become an independent rock formation of considerable extent. This rock appears to consist of flint, lime, and a little oxide of iron. It is often of a porous or vasicular texture, and the amygdaloidal cavities are sometimes empty and sometimes contain very delicate stalactites. Hæmatitic iron ore occurs disseminated in very part. Also extensive caverns, sometimes filled with a bright red metallic oxide. Dr. Wilson, who has been some time resident at the springs, informed us, that the continued use of the water occasions salivation, from which it has been commonly inferred that mercury exists in the water in solution.

The time of our visit to the springs being one of very unusual drought, the quantity of water was somewhat less and the temperature higher than ordinary. The time required to boil eggs, as much as they usually are for the table, was fifteen minutes. In the same time a cup of coffee was made by immersing our kettle in one of the springs. [16]

A number of baths have been made, by hollowing out excavations in the rock, to which the hot water is constantly flowing. By cutting off or increasing the supply the temperature can be regulated at pleasure; over some of these are built small log cabins, and in the neighbourhood are twenty or thirty huts, occupied at some seasons of the year by persons who resort hither for the benefit of the waters.

Three miles north-east from the hot springs is a large fountain of water, of the ordinary temperature, forming the source of the small stream already mentioned as flowing down from that direction. It rises from the summit of a little knoll, six or eight feet in diameter, and divides into two streams, one of which flows towards the east, the other towards the west. Both, however, unite at the base of the knoll, and the brook flows thence south-west, between two petrosiliceous hills, to its confluence with another from the north-west, to form the hot spring creek. The quantity of water discharged by this spring can scarcely be less than from eighty to one hundred gallons per minute. Immediately on the south rises a large hill, and the elevation of the spring itself, above the level of the highest of the thermal springs, is thought to be not less than one hundred and fifty feet. The water is transparent, but has a perceptible metallic taste, and deposits upon the stones over which it flows a copious rust-like sediment. The spring is known in the neighbouring settlements as the "poison spring," a name which we were told it had received from the following circumstance, said to have taken place many years since. A hunter who had been pursuing a bear, and was much exhausted with heat and fatigue, arrived at this spring in the middle of the day, and finding the water cool, and not unpleasant to the taste, drank freely of it, but immediately afterwards sickened and died. His death was occasioned, probably, not by any deleterious quality in the water, but by the disease commonly induced by drinking too largely of cold water when the body is heated. The neighbouring inhabitants, however, imputed the hunter's death to some supposed poisonous property in the spring. Not long afterwards a discontented invalid, residing at the hot springs, came to a resolution of putting a period to his own life. This he concluded to bring about by drinking the water of the poison spring. He accordingly repaired to it, and after drinking as much as he could, filled his bottle, and returned home. Instead of dying, as he had expected, he found himself greatly benefited by his potation. Notwithstanding this discovery of the sanative quality of the water the spring still retained its former name. It is however used without apprehension, and is much resorted to by people who visit the warm springs.

About two miles to the north-east of this spring, a little to the left of the road leading to the settlement of Derdonai, is the principal quarry from which the Washita oilstones are procured. It is near the summit of a high and steep hill of the petrosiliceous rock already mentioned. The oilstones are found in the perpendicular seams or fissures of the rock, from which they are detached with little difficulty, having, as they are dug from the quarry, nearly the requisite shape and size. They are then carried by hand, or thrown to the foot of the precipice, whence there is an easy transportation of ten or twelve miles to the Washita. By this river they descend to New Orleans, and some have been carried thence to New York, where they are known as the Missouri oilstones. These stones are said not to be inferior in quality to the oilstones from Turkey.

In the immediate neighbourhood of the hot springs we observed a number of interesting plants. The American holly (ilex opaca) is a conspicuous and beautiful tree in the narrow vallies within the mountains. The leaves of another species of ilex (I. cassine), the celebrated cassine naupon frequent about the springs, are there used as a substitute for tea. The angelica tree (aralia spinosa, Ph.) is common along the banks of the creek, rising to the height of twelve to fifteen feet, and bending beneath its heavy clusters or purple fruit. The pteris atropurpurea, asplenium melanoraulon, A. ebeneum, and other filices are found adhering to the rocks. In the open pine woods the germandia pectinata, considered as a variety of G. pedicularia, is one of the most conspicuous objects.

The sources of the Washita are in a high and broken part of the Ozark mountains, in north latitude 34° 15′, and between 93° and 94° west longitude, and sixty or an hundred miles south-west of the settlement of Cadron on the Arkansa. From the same mountainous district descend towards the north-east the Petit Jean and Le Fevre, tributaries to the Arkansa; on the north-west the upper branches of the Poteau; on the south-west the Kiamesha; and on the south-east the Mountain, Cossetot, Rolling Forks, and other streams, discharging into Little river of Red river. The principal source of the Washita is said to be very near that of the Fourche Le Fevre, and to descend towards the west from the same hill, out of which flow the upper branches of the Le Fevre towards the east. These particulars are, however, of little importance, except as serving to illustrate the character of that portion of the country. The whole of that region is strictly mountainous, and its numerous streams are rapid and circuitous, winding their way among abrupt and craggy hills, so thinly covered with pine and post oak, that the sober gray of the sandstone is often the prevailing colour of the landscape. The hills, at the sources of the Poteau and the Kiamesha, abound in clay-slate, and a slaty petrosilex destitute of organic remains. * It is remarked by hunters, that the most remote and elevated sources of all the rivers of this region are joined in or near extensive woodless plains. As far as this is the case, it would seem to prove that the existing inequalities of the surface have been produced almost entirely by the currents of water wearing down and removing extensive portions of the horizontally stratified rocks. In districts where secondary rocks only are found, as in the country of the Ohio, there appears little difficulty in attributing this origin to all the hills; and even in the mountainous district under consideration, as the most recent rocks, and those of horizontal stratification, occupy the highest portions of the hills, we may perhaps be allowed to suppose they formerly covered a much greater extent of country than at present, overlaying those strata of more ancient deposition, which now appear upon the declivities of the mountains. It cannot escape

* Nuttall's Travels, p. 150.

the remark of any person who shall visit the range of country, which we call the Ozark mountains, that the direction of the ridges, (particularly of those where sandstone is the prevailing rock,) conforms to the course of the principal streams.

None of the tributaries to the Washita, above the hot springs, have hitherto been explored. The Little Missouri and the Fourche-au-Cadeau, enter it in succession from the west, in the course of a considerable bend which it makes to the south, after receiving the waters of Hot Spring creek. These two streams run mostly in a mountainous country, though some fertile lands and some settlements occur on each. On the Little Missouri, Hunter and Dunbar found the maclura, a tree confined to fertile soils. The first considerable stream entering the Washita from the north is the Saline, rising in three principal branches, twenty or thirty miles north-west of the hot springs. The road from Derdonai to the springs crosses these streams near their sources, in an extremely rugged and mountainous region. The Saline, like the Washita itself in this part, and the other tributaries already enumerated, is liable to great and sudden floods, and also to great depression in seasons of drought. Originating in a mountainous tract, and in the continuation of the range so profusely supplied with springs in the country about the sources of White river, we might expect that the Washita would be fed by numerous and unfailing fountains. It appears, however, to derive the greater part of its supplies from the water of rains, and consequently to rise and fall according to the time of year and the state of the weather. Where Major Long crossed the Washita, on the 31st December 1817, six miles south-west of the hot springs, the river was one hundred and fifty yards wide, about four feet deep, and extremely rapid.

In the latter part of October 1820, at the time of our journey, the Washita at Keisler's settlement, about fifteen miles below the springs, was something less than one hundred yards in width, flowing in a deep and unequal channel over a bed of clay-slate. The water is here ten or fifteen feet deep in many places, and the currents scarce perceptible; as we looked down upon the river from the elevated banks it appeared like a quiet lake, and the unusual blackness of the waters suggested the idea of its great depth. Little groups of naked rocky islands were disclosed here and there in different parts of the channel. On examination we found the apparent dark colour of the water to depend upon the complexion of the rocks which form the bottom and sides of the bed, they being principally of a dark-coloured argillite; and not only these, but the small fragments of quartz and other whitish stones, had acquired, from lying in the water, a peculiar tinge of dark brown. We expected to find an incrustation covering the surfaces of these stones, but upon examination the colouring matter seemed inseparably blended with the rock itself. The water, seen by transmitted light, was entirely transparent, and had no perceptible saltness.

At the distance of five or six miles south-east from the hot springs, on the road leading towards the town of Little Rock, on the Arkansa, commences a tract of land, having a fertile soil and a beautiful situation, and extending to the Washita. Some parts of this region afford exceptions to the remark generally applicable to Arkansa territory, that the best soils are found in the alluvion of the rivers. Some extensive districts of primary soil along the base of the mountains are of a quality rarely surpassed in fertility, bearing heavy forests of oak, ash, and sugar maple, which attain here to greater size than we have seen in other parts of the United States.

We arrived about sunset on the 28th at Keisler's plantation, where we made application for permission to spend the night. This was readily granted, though, as is often the case in such remote and solitary habitations, the house was not in the most complete readiness for the accommodation of travellers. A quantity of Indian corn was immediately gathered in the adjoining field, a part of it given to our horses, and a part prepared for our own supper. During the green-corn season, which is a time of jubilee and rejoicing among the agricultural Indians, and scarcely less so with many of the white settlers, those who live remote from corn mills use no other bread than such as we now saw prepared, within the space of an hour, from the standing corn. Such ears are selected as are fit for roasting, and the corn grated from the cob by means of the side of a tin lanthorn, or some portion of an old coffee-pot, perforated with several holes. In this state it forms a soft paste, which, with the addition of a little salt, is spread upon a heated stone or an iron pan, and baked before the fire. Our supper consisted of bread of this sort, bear's meat, and coffee — a treat worthy the attention of an epicure.

The Cove is a valley commencing among the mountains at no great distance to the east of the hot springs, and containing a small rivulet which enters the Washita six or eight miles below Keisler's. This valley is bounded towards the west by loamy hills, disclosing at intervals cliffs and ledges of clay-slate and petrosilex. In the lowest part of this valley, at a place called Roark's settlement, we discovered a bed of granite forming the basis of a broad hill, which rose by a very gradual ascent towards the east. We were directed to the examination which brought us acquainted with the existence of this rock by the representation of Roark, that in his corn field, not far from the house, was a bed of plaister of Paris. Being conducted to the spot, we found a quantity of loose granitic soil, that had been raised from a shallow excavation, and was intermixed with numerous large scales of talc. The examination had been carried a few feet below the surface, and had terminated upon the granite in question. Having collected several beautiful masses of an aggregate of felspar, talc and quartz, we returned to the house where our breakfast was in preparation. Being informed by our landlord that blue vitriol, native copper, and other interesting minerals, had been formerly discovered near the sources of the little brook that ran past the house, we delayed our journey some time, that we might continue our examination. In following the brook towards its sources, we were much gratified in finding an extensive bed of native magnet, which seemed to be embraced in the granite. Not far distant the same rock contained large masses of pyrites and of bluish green mica. In these we readily perceived the blue vitriol and native copper mentioned by our host. In some places we found the bed of the brook paved almost exclusively with detached schorls. We collected also several other interesting imbedded minerals. More extensive examinations will hereafter show this spot to be one among the most interesting in America to a mineralogist. The great depth of soil resting upon this formation of granite prevented our examining it at as many points as we could wish; also from ascertaining to our satisfaction its extent, and its connexion with the neighbouring rocks. It appears, however, at several points in an area of fifteen or twenty acres, and always in place. We saw not a single detached mass at any distance. This may be owing in part to the perishable structure of the granite, and in part to its being surrounded on all sides by more elevated rocks of slate or sandstone. On the summit of the hill a grave had recently been dug. In the granitic soil which lay about it we saw many fragments of pyrites, also uncommonly large and beautiful laminæ of talc intermixed with scales of mica. These two minerals are, we think, rarely found in such intimate connexion, yet retaining so perfectly their distinctive characters, as in the instance under consideration. The talc in some instances forms an integrant part of the granite, and we have seen it blended with mica in the same specimen.

The road, leading towards the Little Rock on the Arkansa, passes from the granite of the Cove over a coarse hard sandstone, embracing beds of conglomeratic or pudding-stone, and in many respects closely resembling some of the varieties of the old red sandstone of the Alleghany mountains. Towards the east the surface of the country rises gradually, and the sandstone, without giving place to any other stratum, becomes more micaceous and slaty, and at length assumes all the characters of a sandstone accompanying coal.

In the afternoon of the 29th we arrived at Lockhart's settlement, on the Saline Fork of the Washita. The soil of some of the bottom lands along this stream is not inferior to any we have seen west of the Mississippi. It is well watered, and abounds in excellent timber. Pine and oak are intermixed with the ash, hickory, and sugar maple. Here are some well cultivated gardens, and extensive plantations of corn, cotton, and tobacco. Mr. Lockhart and his family, who are emigrants from North Carolina, consider the climate more agreeable than that of the country they came from, and have continued, during a residence of several years, to enjoy good health. We could not fail to attribute this remarkable exemption from disease, in a great measure, to the regularity, neatness, and good order of their domestic economy.

October 30th. In crossing some broken ridges of sandstone, which occupy the high and uninhabited tract between the vallies of the Arkansa and Washita, we followed the obscure path communicating between the settlements on the Saline and the town of Little Rock. As we were descending from one of these ridges our attention was called to an unusual noise, proceeding from a copse of low bushes on our right, at a few rods from the path. On arriving at the spot we found two buck deer, their horns fast interlocked with each other, and both much spent with fatigue, one, in particular, being so much exhausted as to be unable to stand. As we perceived it would be impossible they should extricate themselves, and must either linger in their present situation until they died of hunger, or were destroyed by the wolves, we despatched them with our knives, not without having first made an unavailing attempt to disentangle their antlers. Leaving their bodies in the place where we had killed them, we called at the cabin of a settler, which we found within a few miles, and requested him to go back and fetch the venison for the use of his family.

From the occasional occurrence of the skulls of deer and elk with the horns interlocked with each other, and from the fact above mentioned, it appears that the contests of these animals at the rutting season often prove fatal to both parties. From the form of the horns, and the manner of fighting, it seems probable they must often be entangled with each other, and when this is the case both fall an easy prey to the wolves.

The Saline has an entire length of about one hundred and fifty miles, running all the way nearly parallel to the Washita, to its confluence near the latitude 33° north. After entering the state of Louisiana, the Washita receives from the east the Barthelemi, the Boeuf, the Macon, and the Tensa, all of which, having their sources near the west bank of the Mississippi, may be considered as inosculating branches of that river, since at times of high floods they are fed from the Mississippi. The western tributaries are the Saluder, Derbane, and Ocatahoola, deriving their sources from a spur of the Ozark mountains, which, in the northern part of Louisiana, divides the broad alluvial valley of Red river from that of the Mississippi. About twenty miles south-west from the confluence of the Tensa, Washita, and Ocatahoola, the latter expands into a considerable lake, and sends off a branch to Red river. Indeed the Washita might, without great impropriety, be considered as entering the Mississippi at the point where its waters unite with those of the Ocatahoola and Tensa. The periodical inundations cover the country westward to this point, and even in times of low water the channels communicating with the Mississippi are numerous. From this point there is an uninterrupted connexion, through a system of lakes and watercourses, stretching along parallel to the Mississippi, about thirty miles distant, and communicating, through the river and lake Atchofalaya, with the gulf of Mexico, at a point more than one hundred and fifty miles west of the principal debouchure of the Mississippi.

CHAPTER XI.

RED RIVER. — EXPLORING EXPEDITION OF 1806. — RETURN TO THE ARKANSA. — EARTHQUAKES.

The Red river of Louisiana enters the Mississippi from the west, in north latitude 31° 5′*, and in 16° 35′ west longitude from Philadelphia. From the Mississippi to the mouth of Black river (as the Washita is called below the confluence of the Ocatahoola and Tensa) is twenty-six miles by water. The aggregate width of Red river, for this distance, is from three hundred to three hundred and fifty yards. The depth of the water in summer varies, according to the actual measurement of Messrs. Freeman and Humphrey, from eighty-four to forty-two feet, the range from extreme high to low-water is from twenty-five to thirty feet, and the banks are elevated from fourteen to twenty-five feet above the surface of the river at low-water. At no great distance, on each side, is a second alluvial bank, rising a few feet higher than the immediate bank of the river. Back of this the surface is elevated nearly to high-water mark, but descends gradually towards the lakes and swamps, which occur along both sides of the valley of the river. In the wet season the lower part of Red and Black rivers are lost in an extensive lake, covering the country from the Mississippi westward near one hundred miles to the settlement of the Avoyelles.

The distinction made by Du Pratz, between the country on the south and that on the north side of Red river, appears to be strictly applicable only to

* Ellicott; 31° 1′ 15″, according to M. de Ferrer.

the part lying below the point where Red river enters the immediate valley of the Mississippi. [17]

Above the confluence of Black river the bed of Red river immediately contracts to one hundred and twenty yards, which is its average width from this point to the rapids seventy-two miles above: the current becomes in a corresponding degree more rapid, running with a velocity of from two and a half to three miles per hour, at a moderate stage of water, in the early part of summer. The average depth in this section is stated at from eighteen to twenty feet, at a time when the water is twenty-one feet below its maximum of elevation. The banks are generally bold and steep on one side or the other, and often on both. The bottom lands are level and exceedingly fertile, but bear the marks of periodical inundation. The forests of the lower section of Red river differ little from those of the Mississippi and the Arkansa. White gum, cotton-wood, pecan, locusts, white oak, mulberry, sycamore, hackberry, and cypress occupy the low grounds, while the low and scattered hills are covered with pine, intermixed with a small proportion of oak and hickory. The only portion of the low lands in any sort fit for cultivation is a narrow strip immediately on each bank, commencing a little above the mouth of Black river, and enlarging upwards; but even here the settler is not secure, as uncommon swellings of the river sometimes lay the whole under water. Aside from this, the extreme insalubrity of the air, occasioned by the vicinity of extensive swamps, stagnant ponds, and lagoons, tends to retard the progress of settlements in this quarter.

At the rapids the river spreads to three hundred yards in width. The banks are thirty feet high, and never overflowed. Here has for many years been a settlement. The soil of the neighbouring country is extremely fertile. A bed of soft sandstone, or indurated clay, crosses the river, causing a fall of ten feet in fifty yards. " This stone, when exposed to the air, becomes as hard as free-stone; but under water it is found as soft as chalk. A channel could, with very little labour or expense, be cut through any part of the bed of the river, and need not be extended more than two hundred yards. It appears to me that twenty men, in ten days, with mattocks only, could at low water open a channel sufficiently wide and deep for all the barges that trade in this river to pass with safety and ease." * Three quarters of a mile above this rapid is another, very similar in extent and magnitude.

Thirty miles above the rapids we find the river divided into two beds, each having a high bold bank. The right-hand channel contains about one third of the volume of water of the whole river. They separate from each other four or five miles below Natchitoches, and unite again here, forming an island sixty miles long and five wide.

The right-hand branch is called by the French Rigollé Bon Dieu, and the other Old river. Another island, commencing one-fourth of a mile below Natchitoches, extends parallel to that above mentioned, thirty-four miles and a half; this is about four miles wide. The current, in all the branches which lie between these islands and the main-shore, is rapid, but not equally so. The description already given of the valley of the river is applicable to this portion; on each side the surface descends from the river, terminating in a line of pools and cypress swamps, which extend along the base of the bluff. Settlements were here somewhat numerous in 1806. The small cottages are placed near the bank of the river, and the cultivated lands extend back but a little distance. " The inhabitants," says Freeman " are a mixture of French, Spanish, Indian, and Negro blood, the latter often predominating."

* Freeman's MS. Report to W. Dunbar, esq.

The separation of the water of the river into three distinct branches, each confined within high and steep banks, raised twenty and even thirty feet above the medium elevation of the water, and their reunion, after traversing severally an extent of sixty and thirty miles, might at first view appear a matter of curious inquiry; but upon the slightest investigation it will be discovered that this whole country adjacent to the river has been made or raised to its present elevated position by frequent inundation and depositions from the water. This evidently appears from the great quantities of timber frequently seen as you ascend the river, deposited as low as low-water mark, under steep banks of different heights from twelve to thirty feet.

Red river takes its name from the colour of its water, which is in time of floods of a bright red, and partakes more or less of this colour throughout the year. There can be no doubt the colouring matter on which this tinge depends is derived from the red sandstone of the salt formation already described when speaking of the sources of the Canadian river of Arkansa, although no person qualified to give a satisfactory account of the country has hitherto traced Red river to that formation. We propose to add some brief notices of this important river, derived from the unpublished materials of the exploring party sent out by the government of the United States in 1806; also from the notes of Major Long, who visited the upper settlements in 1817; not neglecting such additional information from the works of Darby, Nuttall, and others who have written of Louisiana, as may appear deserving of confidence.

Red river was explored at a very early period by the French, but their examinations appear to have extended no farther than to the country of the Natchitoches and the Cadoes*; and although subsequent

* In 1700 M. de Bienville ascended the Red river to the country of the Natchitoches and Yatassee Indians, but could find no Spanish

examinations have a little enlarged our acquaintance with its upper branches, we are still unfortunately ignorant of the position of its sources. Three years after the cession of Louisiana to the United States, a small party, known by the name of the " Exploring Expedition of Red river," and consisting of Captain Sparks, Mr. Freeman, Lieut. Humphrey, and Dr. Custis, with seventeen private soldiers, two non-commissioned officers, and a black servant, embarked from St. Catherine's landing, near Natchez, on board several barges and small boats, with instructions to ascend Red river to its sources. On the 3d of May 1806 they entered Red river, expecting to be able to ascend with their boats to the country of the Pawnee Piqua Indians. Here it was their intention to leave their boats, and packing their provision on horses which they should purchase of the Pawnees, they were to " proceed to the top of the mountains," the distance being, as they believed, about three hundred miles.

On the 19th of May they arrived at Natchitoches, distant from the Mississippi 184 miles 266 perches, measured by log-line and time. At this place they delayed some days; and having received information that their progress would be opposed by the Spaniards, they resolved to increase the strength of their party by retaining a detachment which had been ordered by the secretary at war to join them at Natchitoches, " for the purpose of assisting the exploring party to ascend the river to the upper end of the Great Raft, and to continue as far afterwards as might appear necessary to repel by force any opposition they might meet with." Accordingly, twenty men were selected from the garrison at Natchitoches, and, under the command of Lieutenant Duforest, joined the explor-

---

establishments in that quarter. The Yatassee village was about forty miles north-west of the present town of Natchitoches, in the settlement of Bayou Pierre.

Darby, on the Authority of La Harpe.

ing party. They were now thirty-seven in number aside from the officers, and were furnished with a supply of flour sufficient for nine months' provision. On the 2d of June they left Natchitoches, and proceeded towards their destination. The journal of their tour by Mr. Freeman, which has been obligingly put into our hands by General D. Parker, is extremely circumstantial, and embraces much valuable information. We make use of it, without particular reference, whenever we have occasion to speak of that part of Red river visited by the expedition. On the 7th of June the party were overtaken, near a small village of Natchitoches and Paskagoulas, by an Indian guide and interpreter, whom they had hired at Natchitoches. He brought a letter from Dr. Sibley, the Indian agent, giving information that a detachment of Spanish troops were already on their march from Nacogdoches, with a design to intercept the exploring party. At the distance of one hundred and two miles above Natchitoches they left the bed of the river, turning out through one of those numerous communications called Bayous, which connect the principal channel with those lateral chains of lakes, pools, swamps, and marshes, which extend along the sides of the valley. Their design in leaving the river was to avoid that singular obstruction to the navigation called the Great Raft, having been informed by Mr. Toolan, an old and respectable French inhabitant, that it would be impossible for them to pass through it. They had already encountered three similar obstructions, through which they had made their way with extreme toil, by loosening and floating out the logs and trunks of trees, that had been piled upon each other in such numbers as to fill the bed of the river from the bottom, usually at the depth of thirty feet, and rising three or four feet above the surface of the water.

The Bayou Datche, as the part of the river is called into which they entered, conducted them to a beautiful lake called Big Broth.* It is thus described by Mr. Freeman. " This beautiful sheet of water extends, from the place we first entered it, seventy miles in a north-westerly direction; and, as far as we saw it, is beautifully variegated with handsome clumps of cypress trees thinly scattered in it; on the right-hand side it is bounded by high land, which ascends from the surface of the water, and at the distance of one hundred yards is elevated about forty feet, and covered with forests of black oak, hickory, dog-wood, &c.; soil good second-rate. It is bounded on the left by a low plain covered with cypress trees and bushes. The depth of water is from two to six feet. High-water mark ten feet above the present surface. It is called by the Indians *Big Broth*, from the vast quantities of froth seen floating on its surface at high water. The passage out of this lake is by a very difficult communication, through bayous, into another very handsome lake of about one mile wide called Swan lake, and so on, through long crooked bayous, lakes, and swamps, full of dead standing timber." Having made their way for many days along this chain of lakes, they were at length anxious to return to the river. After searching several days for a passage, and finding their pilot incapable to direct them, they resolved to wait while they could send messengers by land to the Coashatay village †, and procure a guide. The return of this messenger brought them some information calculated to aid in extricating themselves from the labyrinth of lakes in which they were bewildered, also the promise of the Coashatay chief, that he would join the party himself, and conduct them to the river. This promise, however, it was not his intention to fulfil. The party therefore, on the 20th of June, resumed their search for a passage, returning some distance on their route.

* Lake Bistineau. † Coshatta, *Darby*, &c.

On the 25th they discovered a narrow and obstructed channel, through which, after removing several rafts, trees, &c. they found their way into the river. "Thus," says the journal of the expedition, "after fourteen days of incessant fatigue, toil and danger, doubt and uncertainty, we at length gained the river above the Great Raft, contrary to the decided opinion of every person who had any knowledge of the difficulties we had to encounter."

The distance from Natchitoches to the point where the party entered Red river, above the Great Raft, is two hundred and one miles by the meanders of their route. Above the Raft the river is two hundred and thirty yards wide, thirty-four feet deep, and has a very gentle current. The banks are ten or twelve feet high. On the north side the lands rise considerably at a little distance, and are covered with heavy forests of oak, poplar, and red cedar. At the Coashatay village, about twenty miles above the Great Raft, the commander of the exploring party received information, by an express, from the chief of the principal village of the Cadoes, which is thirty miles farther to the west, " that about three hundred Spanish dragoons, with four or five hundred horses and mules, were encamped near that village, with the design to prevent the further progress of the Americans." The Coashatay and Cadoe Indians of this part of Red river are an agricultural half-civilized people, like the Cherokees.

On the 1st of July a messenger arrived at the encampment of the party, near the Coashatay village, giving information of the near approach of the Cadoe chief, with forty young men and warriors of his village. About noon they made their appearance on the opposite bank of the river, and kept up, for a few minutes, an irregular firing by way of salute. This was returned both from the camp and the village, in a manner highly gratifying to the Cadoe party. The customary ceremonies used in meeting Indians being past, an exchange of complimentary speeches followed.

The Cadoe chief expressed great uneasiness on account of the Spaniards who were encamped near his village. Their commandant, he said, had come to see him, had taken him by the hand, and asked him, if he loved the Americans; he answered, he did not know what to say, but if the Spaniards wished to fight the Americans, they might go down to Natchitoches, and fight them there; but they should not shed blood in his territories. He said he was pleased with what he had heard respecting the designs of the exploring party; he wished them to go on and see all his country, and all his neighbours. "You have far to go, and will meet with many difficulties, but I wish you to go on. My friends, the Pawnees, will be glad to see you, and will take you by the hand. If you meet with any of the Huzaa's (Osages), and kill them, I will dance for a month. If they kill any of your party, I will go with my young men and warriors, and we will be avenged for you." The soldiers belonging to the expedition having paraded in open order and single file, the forty young Cadoes commenced on the right of the line, and marching towards the left, shook each man by the hand in the most earnest manner. When their leader had reached the other extremity of the line, they instantly placed themselves in a corresponding line, about three paces distant, and their partizan or principal warrior delivered a short address to the serjeant.

"Here we are," said he, "all men and warriors shaking hands together, let us hold fast, and be friends for ever." It was said by the interpreter he prefaced his observation by saying, he was glad to see that his new brothers had the faces of men, and looked like men and warriors.

After a delay of a few days the Cadoe chief, professing the most friendly disposition towards the exploring party, withdrew with his young men to his own village. On the 11th of July the officers of the party, having as yet no certain knowledge of the designs of the Spaniards, re-embarked on board their little fleet, and began to ascend Red river from the Coashatay village, having engaged the Cadoe chief to watch the motions of the Spanish troops, and to give timely notice of any thing interesting to the expedition. The river, above the Coashatay village, became very crooked and wide, and the water was so low that the boats were often aground, though they drew no more than from sixteen to twenty inches of water.

On the 26th of July, in the afternoon, three Indians appeared on the sand-beach, who were found to be the runners sent from the Cadoe chief, agreeable to previous engagement. They brought information that the Spaniards had returned to Nacogdoches, for a reinforcement and new instructions; that six days since they had arrived at the Cadoe village, about one thousand strong; that they had cut down the United States' flag in the Cadoe village, and had said, it was their intention to destroy the exploring party. They had taken from the Cadoe village two young men to conduct them to a handsome bluff, a few miles above where they were now encamped, to await the arrival of the party. The Indian messengers, and the Cadoes who had remained with the party, appeared much alarmed, and intreated the commanding officer to return, saying, if they met the Spaniards, not one would come back alive. The distance to the Spanish camp was three days' journey. On the following day the party made a deposit of some of their most important papers, with a small stock of ammunition, provisions, and astronomical instruments in a retired place, that they might not be entirely destitute of resources after the contemplated rencontre with the Spaniards should have taken place. At sunset, on the 28th of July, as they were about to encamp, they heard several guns a-head of them, which left no doubt that they had arrived near the Spanish camp. On the ensuing morning Captain Sparks, Mr. Freeman, and a favourite Indian, walked a-head of the boats, along the sand-beach, with their guns in their hands. The Indian soon discovered some tracks, ran hastily up among the bushes on the bank, and then returning, made signs that the Spaniards were there. The party was now halted, the arms examined, and put in readiness for immediate action; then all went on board the boats, and they continued their ascent, as if they had known nothing of the Spanish troops. The advanced guard which the Indian had discovered consisted of twenty-two men, stationed a mile and a half below the encampment of the main body. On seeing the boats they fled instantly, and hid themselves in the woods, leaving behind their clothes and provisions.

On turning the next bend they commanded a beautiful view of the river, extending about a mile, with steep banks on both sides, and level sand beaches, occupying more than half the bed of the river. On one of these, at the distance of half a mile, they discovered a sentinel, and soon afterwards saw a detachment of horse gallop from thence through the small cotton-wood bushes near the next bend of the river, and shortly after return to their former station. As it was now the middle of the day, the exploring party halted according to custom, and kindled fires to prepare their dinner.

About half an hour after they had halted, a large detachment from the Spanish camp were seen riding down the sand-beach, enveloped in such a cloud of dust that their numbers could not be accurately estimated. The soldiers belonging to the exploring party were sent to take possession of a thick cane brake on the immediate bank of the river, at a short distance above the boats, to be in readiness, should there be occasion, to attack the advancing party on their flank. A non-commissioned officer and six men were sent still farther up the river, and ordered to be in readiness to assail the Spaniards in the rear.

The advancing party of horse came on at full speed, and neglecting the first challenge of the two sentinels stationed at some distance in advance of the boats. When the sentinels cried "halt" the second time, they cocked their pieces, and were in the act of presenting them to fire, when the Spanish squadron halted, and displayed on the beach about one hundred and fifty yards distant. Their officers moved slowly forward, and were met by Captain Sparks, whom the Spanish commandant politely saluted, and a parley ensued, which continued about three-quarters of an hour. The Spaniards being greatly superior in numbers, and expressing a determined resolution to fulfil their orders, which were to prevent, at all hazards, the farther progress of the exploring expedition, the officers of that party reluctantly consented to relinquish their undertaking. The spot where this interruption took place is two hundred and thirty miles by water above the Coashatay village, consequently six hundred and thirty-five miles above the mouth of Red river.

Below this point it appears the river and the country lose, in a great measure, the peculiar characters which belong to the region of recent alluvial lands near the mouth of the river. Swamps, bayous, and lagoons, are less frequent; the forests are more open, the trees smaller, and the soil less fertile and open; meadows more frequent here than below. A portion of Red river above, between this point and the upper settlements, is but imperfectly known.

The average direction of Red river, as far as it has been hitherto explored, from the confluence of the Kiamesha, in latitude 33° 30', to its junction with the Mississippi in 31° 5', is from north-west to south-east. Above the Kiamesha it is supposed to flow more directly from west to east. The streams tributary to Red river are comparatively small and few in number. Above the Washita the principal are the Little river of the south and the Little river of the north, both entering near the north-western angle of the state of Louisiana, and both hitherto little known. The next in order is the Kiamesha, rising in the Ozark mountains, opposite the Poteau, and entering Red river about one thousand miles from the Mississippi. The Kiamesha has been explored from its sources to its confluence by Major Long, who first visited it in 1817. The country about the sources of this river is mountainous, being broken into numerous irregular peaks and ridges, of an old ferruginous sandstone, with its stratifications highly inclined towards the south. The timber in the mountainous country is the yellow pine, intermixed with red, white, and mountain oak, the small chesnut, the American box or hop hornbeam (ostrya virginica), the red cedar, &c.

In the low lands, towards Red river, all the forest trees common to the valley of the Arkansa are found, with the addition of the maclura, which is now so rare about the Arkansa that it can scarcely be said to make a part of the forests there. Extensive prairies exist on the lower part of the Kiamesha, some of which command delightful views of the surrounding country. Before you lies the great valley of Red river, exhibiting a pleasing variety of forests and lawns; beyond rises the gentle slope of the Ozark mountains, imprinting the broad outline of their azure summits upon the margin of the sky. At the mouth of the Kiamesha, Red river is about two hundred yards wide. Its course is meandering, forming points alternately on the right and left, terminating in sandbars, covered with red mud or clay, deposited from the water of the river. In its lowest stage the river may be forded at any place, so that a person may pass along the bed, as in the Canadian, by travelling on the sand-bars, and occasionally crossing the water between them. The soil and climate of Red river are said to be peculiarly adapted to the culture of cotton. The crop sometimes yields twenty-five hundred pounds of seed-cotton per acre, and this of a quality inferior to none, except the Sea island.

Of the Vaseau, or Boggy Bayou, and the Blue river, two considerable streams tributary to Red river, next above the Kiamesha, we have little information. They appear to enter like what are called the north and south forks of the Canadian, near the foot of the western slope of the Ozark mountains. Above these the principal tributary is the Faux Onachitta, or False Washita, from the north, which has been described to us (by Mr. Findlay, an enterprising hunter, whose pursuits often led him to visit its banks), as bearing a very near resemblance to the Canadian river of Arkansa.

We are as yet ignorant of the true position of the sources of Red river; but we are well assured the long received opinion, that its principal branch rises " about thirty or forty miles east of Santa Fé," is erroneous.

Several persons have recently arrived at St. Louis in Missouri, from Santa Fé, and, among others, the brother of Captain Shreeves, who gives information of a large and frequented road, which runs nearly due east from that place, and strikes one of the branches of the Canadian, that at a considerable distance to the south of this point in the high plain is the principal source of Red river. His account confirms an opinion we had previously formed, namely, that the branch of the Canadian explored by Major Long's party, in August 1820, has its sources near those of some stream which descends towards the west into the Rio Del Norte, and consequently that some other region must contain the head of Red river. From a careful comparison of all the information we have been able to collect, we are satisfied that the stream on which we encamped on the 31st of August is the Rio Raijo of Humboldt, long mistaken for the source of the Red river of Natchitoches, and that our camp of September 2d was within forty or fifty miles east from Santa Fé. In a region of red clay and sand, where all the streams have nearly the colour of arterial blood, it is not surprising that several rivers should have received the same name; nor is it surprising that so accurate a topographer as the Baron Humboldt, having learned that a Red river rises forty or fifty miles east of Santa Fé, and runs to the east, should conjecture it might be the source of the Red river of Natchitoches. This conjecture (for it is no more) we believe to have been adopted by our geographers, who have with much confidence made their delineations and their accounts correspond to it.

In relation to the climate of the country on Red river we have received little definite information. The journal of the Exploring Expedition contains a record of thermometric observations for thirty-six days, commencing with June 1st, 1806, and extending to July 6th. These were made between Natchitoches and the Coashatay village; and the temperature, both of the air and the water of the river, are noted three times per day, at 6 A.M. and 3 and 9 P.M. They indicate a climate extremely mild and equable. The range of atmospheric temperature is from 72° to 93° Fah. that of the water from 79° to 92°. The daily oscillations are nearly equal, and the aggregate temperature rises slowly and uniformly towards midsummer.

From Lockhart's settlement on the Saline river of Washita to Little Rock on the Arkansa, is a distance about twenty-five miles. As we approached the Arkansa, we found the country less broken and rocky than above. The soil of the uplands is gravelly and comparatively barren, producing almost exclusively scattered forests of oak, while along the streams are small tracts of extremely fertile bottom lands. In some of the vallies, however, the cypress appears filling extensive swamps, and imparting a gloomy and unpromising aspect to the country. This tree is well known in all the southern section of the United States, to indicate a low and marshy soil, but not universally one which is irreclaimable. It is rarely if ever met with north of the latitude of 38°. In many respects, particularly in the texture, firmness, and durability of its wood, and in its choice of situation, it resembles the white cedar * of the northern states, but far surpasses it in size, being one of the largest trees in North America. "There is," says Du Pratz, " a cypress tree at Baton Rouge, which measures twelve yards round, and is of prodigious height." In the cypress swamps, few other trees, and no bushes are to be seen, and the innumerable conic excrescences called knees, which spring up from the roots, resembling the monuments in a church-yard, give a gloomy and peculiar aspect to the scenery of those cypress swamps. The old error of Du Pratz, with regard to the manner of the reproduction of the cypress, is still maintained by great numbers of people who never heard of his book. " It renews itself," says he, "in a most extraordinary manner :— A short time after it is cut down a shoot is observed to grow from one of its roots, exactly in the form of a sugarloaf, and this sometimes rises ten feet high before any leaf appears; the branches at length rise from the head of this conical shoot." p. 239. We have often been reminded of this account of Du Pratz, by hearing the assertion among the settlers, that the cypress never grows from the seed; it would appear, however, that he could have been little acquainted with the tree, or he would have been aware that the conic excrescences in question spring up and grow during the life-time of the tree, but never after it is cut down.

At Little Rock, a village of six or eight houses, we found several of the members of a missionary family

* Thuja occidentalis.

destined to the Osages. They had exposed themselves during the heat of summer to the pestilential atmosphere of the Lower Mississippi and Arkansa; and we were not surprised, when we considered their former habits, to find they had suffered most severely from their imprudence. They had all been sick, and two or three of their number had died; the survivors, we understood, were on the recovery. They had been some time at Little Rock, the water in the Arkansa having fallen so low as to render their further ascent impracticable.

The village of Little Rock occupies the summit of a high bank of clay-slate on the south-west side of the Arkansa. Its site is elevated, and the country immediately adjoining, in a great measure, exempt from the operation of those causes which produce a state of the atmosphere unfavourable to health. It is near the commencement of the hilly country, and for a part of the year will be at the head of steamboat navigation on the Arkansa. The country in the rear of the projected town is high, and covered for the most part with open oak forests.

October 3d. We left Little Rock at an early hour, taking the road towards Davidsonville. This led us for about four miles through the deep and gloomy forests of the Arkansa bottoms. Here we saw the ricinus palma christi growing spontaneously by the road side, and rising to the height of twelve or fourteen feet. We arrived at Little Red river by about nine o'clock, the distance from the Arkansa being not more than eight or nine miles. In the high and rocky country about White river, we fell in with the route which had been pursued by Major Long and his party, and following this, we reached Cape Girardeau a few days after their arrival. The distance from Belle Point to Little Rock by the way of the hot springs is two hundred and ten miles, from Little Rock to Cape Girardeau three hundred; in the whole, five hundred and ten miles.

Major Long's notes of a tour in the Arkansa territory contain tables of meteorological observations, showing the variations of temperature from September 30th, 1817, to January 31st, 1818. The country in which these observations were made, is that between the Arkansa at Fort Smith, and the Red river at the mouth of the Kiamesha, about the hot springs of the Washita, the settlement of Cadron, &c. Here we find in the month of January the mercury at zero, and shortly after at 58°, a degree of cold that would not discredit the climate of Moscow, and a rapidity of change and violence of vicissitude to compare with the ever-varying temperature of the Atlantic states. We might expect in the latitude of 34°, and in a region placed along the south-eastern slope of a moderately elevated range of mountains, a mild and equable climate. But almost every portion of the territory of the United States seems alike exposed to the influence of the western and north-western winds, refrigerated in their passage over the wide and frozen regions of the Rocky Mountains, and rushing down unobstructed across the naked plains of the great desert, penetrating with almost unmitigated rigour to the Atlantic coast. It is proper to remark, that the winter of 1817-18 was considered one of unusual severity in the Arkansa territory. From the accounts of Hunter and Dunbar, it appears, that in December 1804 the weather was much milder in the same portion of country. An alligator was seen in December many miles above the confluence of the Saline Fork, and even at the hot springs many plants were in flower, and the ground in the woods had considerable appearance of verdure. We have been assured by emigrants from North Carolina, that the winter temperature of the country, about the upper branches of the Washita, is more mild and equable than that of the corresponding latitudes on the Atlantic coast.

On the 12th October the exploring party were all assembled at Cape Girardeau. Lieutenant Graham, with the steam-boat Western Engineer, had arrived a day or two before from St. Louis; having delayed there some time subsequent to his return from the Upper Mississippi. In the discharge of the duties on which he had been ordered, Lieutenant G. and all his party had suffered severely from bilious and intermitting fever.

A few days subsequent to our arrival at Cape Girardeau, the greater number of those who had been of the party by land, experienced severe attacks of intermitting fever; none escaped, except Captain Bell, Mr. Peale, and Lieutenant Swift. Major Long and Captain Kearney, who had continued their journey immediately towards St. Louis, were taken ill at St. Genevieve, and the latter confined some weeks. The attack was almost simultaneous in the cases of those of the party who remained at Cape Girardeau; and it is highly probable we had all received the impression which produced the disease nearly at the same time. The interruption of accustomed habits, and the discontinuance of the excitement afforded by travelling, may have somewhat accelerated the attack. We had observed that we had felt somewhat less than the usual degree of health, since breathing the impure and offensive atmosphere of the Arkansa bottoms about Belle Point, and there we have no doubt the disease fastened upon us. In every instance, we had the opportunity of observing, the attack assumed the form of a daily intermittent. The cold stage commenced with a sensation of languor and depression, attended with almost incessant yawning, and a disinclination to motion, soon followed by shivering, and a distressing sensation of cold. These symptoms pass off gradually, and the hot stage succeeds. The degree of fever is usually somewhat proportioned to the violence of the cold fit, the respiration becomes full and frequent, the face flushed, the skin moist, and the patient falls into a heavy slumber; on awaking, after some time, extreme languor and exhaustion are felt, though few symptoms of fever remain. This routine of most uncomfortable feelings, commencing at nine or ten in the morning, occupied for some time the greater part of our days. Late at evening, and during the night, we suffered less. Intermitting fevers are of such universal occurrence in every part of the newly-settled country to the west, that every person is well acquainted with the symptoms, and has some favourite method of treatment. A very common practice, and one productive of much mischief, is that of administering large draughts of whiskey and black pepper previous to the accession of the cold stage. Applications of this kind may sometimes shorten the cold fit, but the consequent fever is comparatively increased, and the disease rendered more obstinate. The Peruvian bark is much used, but often so injudiciously as to occasion great mischief.

Cape Girardeau, formerly the seat of justice for a county of the same name, is one of the oldest settlements in Upper Louisiana, having been for a long time the residence of a Spanish intendant or governor. Occupying the first considerable elevation on the western bank of the Mississippi, above the mouth of Ohio, and affording a convenient landing for boats, it promises to become a place of some little importance, as it must be the depôt of a fertile district of country, extending from the commencement of the great swamp on the south-east to the upper branches of the St. Francis. The advantages of its situation must be considered greater than those of the settlements of Ynwapatia and New Madrid, which are not sufficiently elevated. It is at the commencement of the hilly country, extending up the Mississippi to the confluence of the Missouri, north-west of the Gasconade and Osage rivers, and south-west to the province of Texas. Two or three miles below Cape

Girardeau the cypress swamps commence, extending with little interruption far to the south.

The town comprises at this time about twenty log-cabins, several of them in ruins, a log-jail no longer occupied, a large unfinished brick dwelling, falling rapidly to decay, and a small one finished and occupied. It stands on the slope, and part of the summit of a broad hill, elevated about one hundred and fifty feet above the Mississippi, and having a deep primary soil resting on horizontal strata of compact and sparry limestone. Near the place where boats usually land is a point of white rocks, jutting into the Mississippi, and at a very low stage of water producing a perceptible rapid. These are of a white sparry limestone, abounding in remains of encrini and other marine animals. If traced some distance, they will be found to alternate with the common blue compact limestone, so frequently seen in secondary districts. Though the stratifications of this sparry limestone are horizontal, the rock is little divided by seams and fissures, and would undoubtedly afford a valuable marble, not unlike the Darling marble quarried on the Hudson.

The streets of Cape Girardeau are marked out with formal regularity, intersecting each other at right angles; but they are now in some parts so gullied and torn by the rains, as to be impassable; in others, overgrown with such thickets of gigantic vernonias and urticas, as to resemble small forests. The country, back of the town, is hilly, covered with heavy forests of oak, tulip-tree, and nyssa, intermixed in the vallies with the sugar-tree and the fagus sylvatica, and on the hills, with an undergrowth of the American hazel, and the shot-bush or angelica tree. Settlements are considerably advanced, and many well-cultivated farms occur in various directions.

Two or three weeks elapsed previous to Major Long's return from St. Louis; when, notwithstanding his ill health, he left Cape Girardeau immediately, as did Captain Bell, both intending to prosecute, without delay, their journey to the seat of government.

About the 1st of November, Messrs. Say, Graham, and Seymour had so far recovered their health, as to venture on undertaking a voyage to New Orleans on their way home. They left Cape Girardeau in a small boat, which they exchanged at the mouth of the Ohio for a steam-boat about to descend the Mississippi. Mr. Peale, who had escaped the prevailing sickness, accompanied them, leaving only Dr. James and Lieut. Swift with the steam-boat Western Engineer at Cape Girardeau. Lieut. Swift had received instructions, as soon as the water should rise sufficiently, to proceed with the boat to the Falls of Ohio, where it was to remain during the winter.

Early in November, the frosts had been so severe at Cape Girardeau, that the leaves were fallen, and the country had assumed the aspect of winter. On the 9th, at four P. M. the shock of an earthquake was felt. The agitation was such as to cause considerable motion in the furniture and other loose articles in the room where we were sitting. Before we had time to collect our thoughts and run out of the house, it had ceased entirely; we had therefore no opportunity to form an opinion of its direction. Several others occurred in the time of our stay at the Cape, but they all happened at night, and were all of short duration. "Shakes," as these concussions are called by the inhabitants, are in this part of the country extremely frequent, and are spoken of as matters of every day occurrence. [18] Several houses in and about Cape Girardeau have formerly been shaken down, forests have been overthrown *, and other considerable changes produced by their

* The forest adjoining the settlement of Little Prairie, below New Madrid, presents a singular scene of confusion; the trees standing inclined in every direction, and many having their trunks and branches broken.

agency. Their effect upon the constantly varying channels and bars in the bed of the Mississippi must doubtless be very important.

These concussions are felt through a great extent of country, from the settlements on Red river and the Washita to the falls of Ohio, and from the mouth of the Missouri to New Orleans. Their great extent, and the very considerable degree of violence with which they affect not only a large portion of the valley of the Mississippi, but of the adjacent hilly and mountainous country, appear to us most clearly to indicate that they are produced by causes far more efficient and deep-seated than " the decomposition of beds of lignite or wood-coal situated near the level of the river, and filled with pyrites," according to the suggestion of Mr. Nuttall.* It has been repeatedly asserted, that volcanic appearances exist in the mountainous country between Cape Girardeau and the hot springs of the Washita, particularly at the latter place; but our observation has not tended to confirm these accounts; and Hunter and Dunbar, who spent some time at the hot springs, confidently deny the existence of any such appearances in that quarter. Reports have been often circulated, principally on the authority of hunters, of explosions, subterraneous fires, blowings and bellowings of the mountains, and many other singular phenomena, said to exist on the Little Missouri of Washita, and other parts of the region of the hot springs; but it is easy to see that the combustion of a coal-bed, or some other affair of equal insignificance, may have afforded all the foundation on which these reports ever rested. But though no traces of existing or of extinct volcanoes should be found in any part of the country affected by these earthquakes, it is not therefore necessary to go in search of some cause unlike those which in

* See Mississippi Navigator, p. 180.

other parts of the earth are believed to produce similar effects.

On the morning following the earthquake above mentioned, a fall of snow commenced, and continued during the day; towards evening it fell mixed with hail and rain, and covered the ground to the depth of about six inches.

The rain continued for some days, the mercury ranging from 40° to 48° and 50°, a temperature and state of weather as little grateful to an ague-shaken invalid as any weather can be. The snow which fell on the 10th remained on the ground until the 15th, when it had nearly disappeared, and a succession of bright days followed. The air was now filled with countless flocks of geese, sand-hill cranes, and other migratory birds on their passage to the south. The migrations of the ardea canadensis afford one of the most beautiful instances of animal motion we can any where meet with. These birds fly at a great height, and never in a direct line, but wheeling in circles, they appear to float without effort on the surface of an aerial current, by whose eddies they are borne about in an endless series of revolutions. Though larger than a goose, they rise to so great an elevation as to appear like points, sometimes luminous, and sometimes opaque, as they happen to intercept or reflect the rays of the sun; but never so high but their shrill and incessant clamours may be heard.

While at Cape Girardeau we were induced, from motives of curiosity, to attend at the performance of some ceremonies by the negroes, over the grave of one of their friends, who had been buried a month since. They were assembled round the grave, where several hymns were sung. An exhortation was pronounced by one, who officiated as minister of the gospel, who also made a prayer for the welfare of the soul of the deceased. This ceremony, we are told, is common among the negroes in many parts of the

United States: the dead are buried privately, and with few marks of attention ; a month afterwards the friends assemble at the grave, where they indulge their grief, and signify their sorrow for the deceased, by the performance of numerous religious rites.

On the 22d of November, having been informed the Ohio had risen several inches, Lieut. Swift determined to leave Cape Girardeau with the steam-boat on the following day. Dr. James had so far recovered as to be able to travel on horseback ; and immediately set forward on the journey to the Falls of Ohio, intending to proceed by the nearest route across the interior of Illinois.

The immediate valley of the Mississippi, opposite the little village of Bainbridge, ten miles above Cape Girardeau, is four miles wide, and exclusive of the river, which washes the bluffs along the western side. Upwards, it expands into the broad fertile and anciently populous valley, called the American bottom; on the east, it is bounded by abrupt hills of a deep argillaceous loam, disclosing no rocks, and rather infertile, bearing forests of oak, sweet gum, tupelo, &c. The road crossing the hilly country between the Mississippi and the village of Golconda on the Ohio passes several precocious little towns, which appear, as is often the case in a recently settled country, to have outgrown their permanent resources. The lands, however, are not entirely worthless ; and on some of the upper branches of the Cacha, a river of the Ohio, we passed some fertile bottoms, though they are not entirely exempt from inundation at the periodical floods. The compact limestone about Golconda, near the sources of Grand Pierre creek, and near Covedown rock, contains beautiful crystals of Derbyshire spar ; sulphuret of lead also occurs in that vicinity, as we have been informed, in veins accompanying the fluate of lime.

On arriving at Golconda, Dr. James had become so much indisposed, by a recurrence of fever and ague, as to be unable to proceed. This circumstance, with others, induced Lieut. Swift to leave the steamboat, for the winter, at the mouth of Cumberland river. After a delay of a few days, he continued his journey towards Philadelphia on horseback.*

HAVING thus traced the progress of the exploring party to their final separation, we shall add some discussions concerning the countries west of the Alleghany mountains, of a more general description than deemed compatible with the humble style of a diary, which we thought convenient to be retained in our narrative.

The following paper, from Major Long, comprises, moreover, the results of many observations made on various journies previous to those detailed in the foregoing account, and in parts of the country remote from those traversed by the expedition.

* Most of the collections made on this expedition have arrived at Philadelphia, and are in good preservation; they comprise, among other things, more than sixty prepared skins of new or rare animals. Several thousand insects, seven or eight hundred of which are probably new; five hundred have already been ascertained to be so, and have been described. The herbarium contains between four and five hundred species of plants new to the Flora of the United States, and many of them supposed to be undescribed.

Many of the minerals collected by Mr. Jessup were left at Smithland, Kentucky. A suit of small specimens, adapted to the illustration of the geology of the country from the Alleghanies to the Rocky Mountains, has been received.

A collection of terrestrial and fluviatile shells was also made. Of these more than twenty new species have already been described and published. The organic reliquiæ collected on the voyage from Pittsburgh to St. Louis have not as yet been received in Philadelphia, but are daily expected.

The sketches, executed by Mr. Peale, amounted to one hundred and twenty-two. Of these, twenty-one only were finished; the residue being merely outlines of quadrupeds, birds, insects, &c.

The landscape-views, by Mr. Seymour, are one hundred and fifty in number; of these, sixty have been finished.

A GENERAL DESCRIPTION OF

THE COUNTRY

TRAVERSED BY THE EXPLORING EXPEDITION,

BEING THE

Copy of a Report of Major Long to the Hon. J. C. Calhoun, Secretary of War,

Dated Philadelphia, Jan. 20. 1821.

Sir,

In obedience to your order of the 28th of November, I have the honour to submit the following report, embracing a concise account of the movements of the exploring expedition under my command, and a general description of the country explored by them. Although there may be no very striking incidents to embellish the narration, yet the diversity of scenery presented to the view, the changes in the character and aspect of the country, and the variety of other interesting matter in the several departments of natural science, which have been subjects of particular attention, cannot fail to awaken a lively interest in the minds of an enlightened community, inasmuch as a discussion of them must lead to a knowledge of the condition and natural resources of a large portion of the United States' territory. But as the principal object contemplated in this report is a general view of the topography of the country, the subjects of description will be such only as are thought to be illustrative of such a view.

Movements of the Expedition.

The expedition embarked on board of the United States' steam-boat, Western Engineer, at Pittsburg, on the 4th of May, 1819. Their outfit consisted of such books, instruments, stationery, &c. (a return of which is on file in the engineer department), together with such provisions, &c. as were deemed requisite at the commencement of their voyage. They proceeded down the Ohio river, making such observations and surveys along its banks as are calculated to augment the stock of intelligence already acquired in relation to that part of the country. This part of their route having been previously traversed by gentlemen of science, who have judiciously arranged and generously promulgated the intelligence they have collected, but little matter of a novel or interesting character could be expected. Yet an investigation of the numerous organic remains, and mineral productions, discoverable on the Ohio throughout its whole extent, together with such an examination of the country as is requisite to a general description of its aspect, soil, and vegetable productions, were considered as objects meriting their attention in the discharge of their several duties.

On arriving at the confluence of the Ohio and Mississippi, they proceeded up the latter to the Missouri, and thence up the river last mentioned to the Council Bluffs, improving every opportunity of extending their researches in the various branches of natural science. At the time of their arrival at the Council Bluffs, the season was so far spent, that it was deemed inexpedient to proceed further till the ensuing season; and the boat was accordingly dismantled, and moored in a safe harbour, and quarters constructed for the accommodation of the party during the then approaching winter. Being located in a situation central to a variety of Indian tribes and nations, inhabiting the neighbouring country, they were enabled to acquire a pretty extensive acquaintance with the manners, customs, and character of the natives in that quarter. Surveys of the surrounding country were made; observations for determining the latitude, longitude, magnetic variation, dip, &c. were taken; the changes of the weather, and other meteorologic phenomena were recorded; and such other duties performed, as pertained to the pursuits of the expedition.

On the voyage up the Missouri, a party was detached from the steam-boat at Fort Osage, with instructions to proceed across the country by land, to the Konzas village, and thence to the villages of the Pawnees, on the river Platte, and to return on board again at the Council Bluffs. This excursion was undertaken with a view of prosecuting the business of the expedition. The party had accomplished part of the duties assigned them, when they were met near the Konzas village by a war-party of the Republican Pawnees, and robbed of their horses, baggage, &c., which compelled them to give up the further prosecution of their enterprize. This misfortune rendered it necessary for them to change their route, and shape their course for the Missouri, which they reached at Cow Island, having obtained much useful information concerning the country through which they passed, and the natives inhabiting it.

On my return to the wintering post of the expedition, to which we had given the name of Engineer Cantonment, I pursued a course north of the Missouri, from near its mouth to that place, taking sketches of the country, preparatory to a topographical delineation. The observance of courses, distances, magnetic variations, &c. were objects of our particular care and attention in all the movements of the expedition.

On my arrival at the cantonment, which I reached on the 27th of May last, preparations were made, with all convenient despatch, for reconnoitring the country westward to the Rocky Mountains, in conformity to your order of the 28th of February, 1820. The steam-boat was ordered on topographical duties under the command of Lieut. Graham, who proceeded with her down the Missouri to St. Louis, thence up the Mississippi to the De Moyen rapids, and thence down the river to Cape Girardeau, taking such observations and sketches on the voyage as are requisite in constructing a chart of that part of the river and the adjacent country.

Having made the necessary arrangements, and rendered our outfit, for the western tour, as complete as circumstances would permit, we commenced our march on the 6th of June, all in good health, except Mr. Say, the zoologist for the expedition. It may not be improper here to give a list, exhibiting the names of the persons composing the party, and the several capacities in which they served.

S. H. Long, Major I. Engineers, commanding Expedition.
J. R. Bell, Capt. Lieut. Artillery, Journalist.
W. H. Swift, Lieut. Artillery, Assistant Topographer and Commanding Guard.
T. Say, Zoologist, &c.
E. James, Botanist, Mineralogist, and Surgeon.
T. R. Peale, Assistant Naturalist.
S. Seymour, Landscape-painter, &c.
Joseph Bijeau, Guide and Interpreter.
Abraam Ledoux, Farrier and Hunter.
Stephen Julien, Interpreter.
H. Dougherty, Hunter.
Zachariah Wilson, Baggage Master.
J. Duncan, J. Oakley, and D. Adams, Engagees.
John Sweney, Private of the Corps of Artillery.
Joseph Verplank, William Parish, Robert Foster, Mordecai Nowland, Peter Barnard, and Charles Myers, Privates of the Rifle Regiment, Packhorse-men and Hunters.

The number of horses and mules, provided for the use of the party, was thirty-four, including several that were the property of individuals; so that we were able to have all of the party mounted, and also a sufficient number of horses besides, for the transportation of baggage. In addition to arms, ammunition, a small quantity of provisions and other necessaries for the tour, our outfit embraced a small supply of Indian goods for presents, not exceeding £150 in value.

The instruments for astronomical and other observations, comprehended in our outfit, were very limited, both in number and variety. The mode of transporting them that we were compelled to adopt was by no means suited to the conveyance of delicate instruments, or such as required much space in packing. We, however, took all [belonging to the expedition that were in good repair and of a portable construction. The principal were the following: one sextant of five inches radius; one snuff box sextant; one mercurial horizon with a glass frame; one patent lever watch of an excellent quality; three travelling compasses; one measuring tape; two thermometers; and some few articles of apparatus for the use of the naturalists.

Every man being accoutred with a gun, shot-pouch, and powder-horn, and most of them with pistols, the exploring party proceeded westwardly to the Pawnee villages, situated on a branch of the Platte called the Loup Fork, thence southwardly to the Platte, and thence westwardly along the valley of the Platte, to the place where it issues from the Rocky Mountains. Having examined the mountains at that place, and finding the country too hilly and broken to penetrate with horses within their range, we shaped our course southwardly along their base, taking occasion to ascend the peaks and spurs of the mountains whenever a favourable opportunity presented, for the purpose of ascertaining their geological character, and that of the vegetables growing upon them.

On arriving at the Arkansa Captain Bell was detached with a small party to ascend along the river as far as it was practicable to travel with horses, and was able to ascend nearly thirty miles, when his further progress was intercepted by the proximity of the hills to the river.

Having descended the Arkansa about one hundred miles to the point whence it was judged expedient to strike upon a southwardly course in quest of the source of the Red river, the party was formed into two detachments; the one to proceed down the Arkansa, under the direction of Captain Bell, and the other to accompany me, with the view of exploring the country southwardly to Red river, and thence down its valley to the upper settlements thereon.

Captain Bell's party, with the exception of three soldiers last mentioned in the foregoing list, who deserted on the march, arrived in safety at Belle Point, their place of destination, having performed the duties assigned them.

On separating from Captain Bell, the detachment under my direction proceeded southwardly in view of the mountains about one hundred and fifty miles, and arrived at a creek, having a southwardly course, which we took to be tributary to Red river. Having travelled down its valley about two hundred miles, we fell in with a party of Indians of the nation of Kaskaias, or Bad-hearts, who gave us to understand that the stream along which we were travelling was Red river. We accordingly continued our march down the river several hundred miles further; when, to our no small disappointment, we discovered that it was the Canadian of the Arkansa, instead of Red river, that we had been exploring. Our horses being nearly worn out with the fatigue of our long journey, which they had to perform bare-footed, and the season being too far advanced to admit of retracing our steps and going again in quest of the source of Red river with the possibility of exploring it before the commencement of winter, it was deemed advisable to give over the enterprise for the present, and make our way to the settlements on the Arkansa. We were led to the commission of this mistake in consequence of our not having been able to procure a guide acquainted with this part of the country. Our only dependence, in this respect, was upon Pike's map, which assigns to the head-waters of the Red river the apparent locality of those of the Canadian. We continued our march, therefore, and arrived at Belle Point on the Arkansa on the 13th September, four days after the arrival of Captain Bell and his party.

Both parties suffered occasionally for the want of food and water; but in general the game of the country yielded us an ample supply of the former, and the watercourses, along which we for the most part travelled, satisfied our demands for the latter. In regard to health we were all highly favoured, except Mr. Say, who was more or less indisposed throughout the tour. Some of the rest were occasionally affected with slight indisposition.

It is a source of much regret that we had the misfortune to lose some of our most valuable manuscripts by the desertion of three soldiers of Captain Bell's party before mentioned. They deserted on the head-waters of the Verdigrise river, within about two hundred miles of the upper settlements of the Arkansa, taking with them three horses, the best belonging to the party, four saddle-bags, containing wearing apparel and other things belonging to the gentlemen of the party, besides the following manuscripts: viz. Journal of the Tour, one number; Manners and Customs of the Indians, one number; Zoological Description and Remarks, one number; Vocabularies of Indian Languages, two numbers; all by Mr. Say; and one number, containing Topographical Notes and Sketches, by Lieutenant Swift. In addition to the above, the loss of a few horses that died on the march was the only accident or misfortune worthy of notice that befel the expedition.

From Belle Point the exploring party proceeded across the country in a north-eastwardly direction to Cape Girardeau, where they arrived on the 10th October, having been occupied a little more than four months in the performance of the tour from the Council Bluff.

Throughout the whole excursion the attention of the gentlemen of the expedition was constantly occupied upon the several subjects of investigation which were deemed essential to a topographical and scientific description of the country. In the discharge of our duties, however, we laboured under many disadvantages for want of a sufficient variety of instruments to furnish all the data proper and desirable in giving an account of the geology and meteorology of the country. A barometer would have been particularly useful; but out of three belonging to the expedition two were rendered completely unfit for use, partly by accident and partly by defects in their construction, and the third was in such a condition that it was not deemed advisable to take it with us, as it was not likely to remain fit for service but for a short time only. In ascertaining the humidity of the atmosphere a hygrometer would have been particularly useful, but it has never been in my power to procure one that had any claim to being accurate. In taking the various observations, however, that could be effected by means of the few instruments we had with us, no pains were spared, and no opportunities lost; those in particular, for the calculation of latitude and longitude, were taken as often as it was thought necessary, and with the utmost care and precision that circumstances would permit.

On our arrival at Cape Girardeau we had contemplated to embark on board of the Western Engineer, which was at that port ready for our accommodation, and sail for Louisville; but, learning that the water of the Ohio was at that time too low to admit even the passage of a boat drawing no more than fifteen or sixteen inches of water, we were compelled to seek another mode of conveyance. Those of the expedition who had been on duty during the two last seasons, being very anxious to visit their homes, arrangements were accordingly made for their return to Philadelphia, when they would be enabled to complete and report the intelligence they had collected. Messrs. Say, Peale, Seymour, and Lieut. Graham, being desirous to return by water, waited the opportunity of taking a passage to New Orleans, and thence to Philadelphia. Most of the curiosities collected by the expedition were placed in the charge of Mr. Say, to be shipped for this place.

Lieut. Swift was left in command of the steam-boat and crew, with instructions to proceed with them to Louisville as soon as the water would permit. He was instructed to leave the boat in the care of the pilot employed on board of her, — order her crew of United States' soldiers to Newport, Kentucky, for winter quarters and subsistence, and report in person at Philadelphia, for topographical duty.

GENERAL DESCRIPTION OF THE COUNTRY TRAVERSED BY THE EXPLORING EXPEDITION.

Having given the foregoing brief account of the movements of the expedition, we next proceed to a consideration of the region explored by them, which embraces a very considerable portion of the immense valley situated between the Alleghany and Rocky Mountains. The portion of this valley to which their attention has been more particularly directed, and relative to which intelligence has been collected, is situated between thirty-five and forty-two degrees of north latitude, and eighty and one hundred and six degrees of west longitude, embracing an extent of about five hundred miles in width from north to south, and thirteen hundred miles in length from east to west. As might be expected in a region of this extent, a great diversity of surface is presented to view, exhibiting all the varieties, from the most level and unbroken to the most rugged and mountainous aspect. The most broken parts of this region are those situated along the Ohio, from its source to its confluence with the Mississippi, and on the west of the Mississippi, between Red river and the Arkansa, and between the latter and the Missouri, extending westward about four hundred miles from the Mississippi. The whole region, in a geological point of view, is constituted of three varieties of formations, which characterize the surface throughout; viz. transition, secondary, and alluvial. A tract, however, of considerable extent, including the hot springs of the Washita, and extending northwardly to the lead mines back of St. Genevieve, has, by some, been considered as possessing a primitive character; but it is believed that the rocks discoverable therein are not sufficiently uniform to warrant such a decision. Moreover, an insulated tract of primitive country, surrounded by others exhibiting the most unequivocal marks of their being secondary, and at the same time presenting a similar conformation in their general aspect, is such an anomaly in natural science as requires more than ordinary proof to be admitted. The particular tract under consideration is probably analogous to other tracts within the region above specified, exhibiting a surface characterized by primitive formation superincumbent upon others of a secondary character.

In order to give a more distinct conception of the country or region under consideration, it may be regarded as divisible into the following sections: viz. 1st, the country situated between the Ohio river and the Alleghany mountains; 2d, the country situated between the Ohio, Mississippi, and the Lakes;

3d, the country situated between the Mississippi and Missouri rivers; 4th, the country situated between the Red and Missouri rivers, west of the Mississippi and east of the meridian of the Council Bluff; and 5th, the country between the proposed meridian and the Rocky Mountains.

Of the country situated between the Ohio river and the Alleghany mountains.

The country on the south side of the Ohio, including the northerly parts of Pennsylvania, Virginia, and Tennessee, together with the whole of Kentucky, abounds in hills elevated, in the vicinity of the Ohio, from four to eight hundred or a thousand feet above the water-table of the river, and rising many hundred feet higher in the neighbourhood of the Alleghany mountains. This section is watered by many streams of considerable magnitude tributary to the Ohio, the most important of which are the Monongahela, Kenhawa, Great Sandy, Licking, Kentucky, Salt, Green, Cumberland, and Tennessee. These rivers are all navigable for keel-boats, and many of them for steam-boats, some hundreds of miles, during the boating season, which generally commences about the 20th February and terminates early in June. Occasional freshets contribute to render them navigable during short portions of the other months of the year; but no reliance can be placed in periodical returns of freshets, excepting those of the spring season. Upon these rivers are extensive and valuable tracts of bottom land covered with deep and heavy forests, and possessed of a soil adapted to the cultivation of all the variety of vegetable products common to the various climates in which they are situated. The highlands, back of the bottoms, although variegated with hills and vallies alternating with each other in quick succession, are generally possessed of a surface susceptible of being tilled, and in many instances of a soil equally rich and prolific with that of the bottoms.

In many parts of the country, however, the hills are abrupt and stony to such a degree as renders them unfit for tillage. The average produce per acre, upon the farming lands of this section, may be estimated at the following rates: viz. Indian corn or maize, forty bushels; wheat, twenty-two; rye, twenty-six; oats, thirty-five; barley, thirty; tobacco, from twelve to fifteen cwt., and cotton from five to seven cwt. In regard to the products last mentioned, viz. cotton and tobacco, it should be observed, that they are cultivated only in the south-westerly parts of this section, and that oats and barley are seldom cultivated except in the upper or north-easterly parts.

Of the population of this section, if we except the towns and villages and their immediate vicinities, as also a large portion of country surrounding Lexington, Kentucky, and another of considerable extent, including Nashville, Tennessee, it is yet but thinly inhabited, affording room for a population far more numerous and more widely diffused. There are extensive tracts of country between the Alleghany mountains and the Ohio as yet almost entirely destitute of inhabitants, the most considerable of which are situated in the vicinity of the mountains, also the country generally between Tennessee river and the Mississippi. As this section of country is pretty generally well known, the foregoing outline of its topography will suffice.

Of the country situated between the Ohio, Mississippi, and the Lakes.

The section of country next in the order proposed is situated north of the Ohio river, and comprehends the states of Ohio, Indiana, and Illinois. This section may be subdivided into three orders or varieties of country, which merit a separate consideration, viz. the hilly, the plain or rolling, and the valley country.

The hilly country, like that south of the Ohio, exhibits a very uneven surface, variegated with hills and dales irregularly distributed, and occupying about one third part of the section under consideration. This portion of the country is of an oblong shape, bounded on the south-east by the Ohio river, and on the north-west by an imaginary line, commencing on the Mississippi near the grand tower, and running in a direction nearly E. N. E., till it approaches the easterly part of Lake Erie. On the east it mingles with the hilly country, comprehending the back parts of Pennsylvania and New York. In short, the whole region situated between the Alleghany mountains and the imaginary line above specified, or in other words, the country through which the Ohio and its tributaries, except the Wabash, have their courses, may be arranged under this head. The hills throughout the whole are very similar in respect to their altitudes, multiplicity and conformation.

Although the hilly country north of the Ohio is in many places rugged and broken, yet a large proportion of it is susceptible of cultivation. No high mountains are to be seen; the hills usually rise from six to eight hundred feet above the common level, or about one thousand feet above the water-tables of the principal rivers, and invariably present rounded summits. Interspersed among the hills are numerous fine tracts of arable land, which may in general be alleged of the valleys of the numerous rivers and creeks by which the country is watered. The soil upon the hills is generally productive, except where the surface is rocky and the declivities abrupt, which is more particularly the case in the vicinity of rivers, where the high lands are divided into numerous knobs, being cut by deep ravines with abrupt and precipitous banks.

The hilly country, having been generally esteemed more healthy than either of the other varieties above mentioned, has acquired a more numerous population than the latter. As yet, however, no part of this section has its full complement of inhabitants, if we except, as before, the numerous towns and villages and their immediate neighbourhoods. In regard to the products of agriculture, the same remarks that have been made concerning the section south of the Ohio are equally applicable to the country under consideration, with the exception that cotton is cultivated only in the south-westerly extreme of this section, and tobacco is raised for domestic uses only.

The most considerable rivers intersecting this section of country are the Muskingum, Sciota, Big Miami, and Wabash, all of which, in the spring season, are navigable two or three hundred miles from their mouths.

The valleys of these rivers give place to many extensive and fertile bottoms well adapted to cultivation, and producing the necessaries of life in great abundance and variety.

The plain, or rolling country, is separated from that last under consideration by the imaginary line above mentioned. It is not to be inferred, however, that the junction of these two regions is distinctly marked by any characters whatever by which the line can be traced with precision, but that a gradual change of aspect is observable in travelling from one variety of country to the other, and that the general direction of the line indicated by this change is that specified above. The other boundaries of this variety are the Mississippi on the west, and the Lakes Erie and Michigan, and the Fox and Wisconsan rivers on the north and east. This variety of country, although not entirely destitute of hills, is almost throughout its whole extent possessed of an undulating or rolling surface, rising into broad and gentle swells in some parts, and subsiding into extensive flats or plains in others. The valleys of numberless watercourses, bounded by abrupt bluffs or banks, afford some diversity to its aspect; and the bluffs in particular of the principal streams, being cut by numerous ravines, contribute in many places to give the surface a hilly and broken appearance. Although no part of this region can with propriety be denominated hilly, especially when compared with the portions of country above considered, yet upon the Wisconsan, Fox, the headwaters of Rock and Melwakee rivers, the country is considerably diversified with hills, or rather swells, and valleys. The only hills worthy of particular notice, not only in this variety, but in the whole section under consideration, are the Ocooch and Smokey mountains, which are broad and elevated ridges rather than mountains. The former is situated about twelve miles north of the Wisconsan, one hundred miles above its mouth, and the latter about forty miles south of the portage between the river just mentioned and Fox river of Green Bay. The rivers of most note within this region are, the Wabash, above the hilly country before described, the Kaskaskias, Illinois, Rock and Wisconsan, tributary to the Mississippi; the Fox of Green Bay, the St. Joseph of Lake Michigan, and the Maumee and Sandusky, tributary to Lake Erie. These rivers are all navigable for boats of ten or fifteen tons burden when swollen by spring freshets; but, during the greater part of the summer and fall, they have not a sufficient depth of water for boats of burden, and in winter their navigation is entirely obstructed by ice. The spring freshets, consequent to the melting of the snow and ice, usually take place in the month of March, the southerly streams being open for navigation much earlier than those in the north.

The prairies, or champaigns, east of the Mississippi, are mostly situated in this particular region, occupying at least three fourths of it. These are waving or flat tracts of country, of greater or less extent, separated from each other by narrow skirts of woodland situated upon the margins of rivers and creeks. They are generally possessed of a rich soil, yielding a spontaneous growth of grass and herbage of a luxuriant appearance. They are well adapted to the cultivation of corn, wheat, rye, barley, oats, &c. of which they yield plentiful crops.

The prevailing opinion in regard to this portion of the country, viz. that it is unhealthy, appears too well founded to admit of refutation. The causes that contribute to render it so are very obvious: a large proportion of the prairies are so flat that much of the water deposited upon them by showers remains stagnant upon the surface till it is carried off gradually by evaporation, which renders the atmosphere humid and unhealthy. The vegetable mould of which the immediate surface is composed, and the abundance of vegetables that spring and decay upon the ground, contribute largely to render these exhalations more deleterious. Although there are but few swamps or marshes, and very rarely pools of stagnant water, to be met with in this region, still the general water-table of the country is so little inclined, that the streams, having but a moderate descent, are uniformly sluggish, often exhibiting the appearance of a succession of stagnant pools. The consequence is, that the vegetable matter they contain, instead of being carried away by the strength of the current, is deposited upon the bottoms and sides of the channels, and, while in its putrescent state, serves to augment the quantity of noxious effluvia with which the atmosphere is charged.

The population of this region, compared with its extent, is very limited; and with the exception of a few villages the settlements are very scattering. Large portions of it, embracing the northerly parts of Indiana and Illinois, are almost entirely destitute of inhabitants. Many parts of the country must remain uninhabited for many years to come, on account of the scarcity of timber and other deficiencies, such as the want of mill-seats, springs of water, &c. which are serious blemishes in the character of a large proportion of the country. There are, however, numerous and extensive tracts within this region possessed of a rich soil, and in other respects well adapted for settlements, and presenting the strongest inducements for emigrants to occupy them.

The country of the third order, agreeably to the subdivision above given, viz. the valley country, is situated upon the rivers, and is included within the hilly and plain country above described. The tracts belonging to this order, usually denominated bottoms, are altogether alluvial, being composed of alternate layers of sand and soil deposited from the water of the rivers upon which they are respectively situated. The alluvion thus deposited, having once constituted a part of the surface of the countries drained by the watercourses tributary to the rivers along which the deposit has been made, it will readily be inferred that the fecundity of the valleys will in some measure correspond with that of the countries whence their alluvion was derived. Accordingly we find the bottoms more or less productive in proportion to the fertility of the regions in which the rivers take their rise and through which they flow. In the valley of the Ohio the quality of the soil appears to improve from its source downwards. The alluvion, of which it is composed is supplied by the Alleghany and Monongahela rivers, which have their origin and courses in a hilly and mountainous country, possessed in general of a sandy surface. The alluvion, supplied by other tributaries entering the Ohio at various points between its source and its mouth, is of a better quality, being composed principally of argillaceous and calcareous earth, which are prevailing ingredients in the soil of the country drained by those tributaries.

It should be remarked, however, in relation to all the varieties of alluvia, that they are partially composed of the fine particles of decayed vegetable matter with which the water drained from the surface of the ground is invariably charged. This property in alluvial deposits often prevails to such a degree as to render soils, apparently sandy and steril, remarkably productive. The alluvial bottoms throughout the United States afford innumerable examples of this fact. The fertilizing matter often exhibits itself in the slimy deposits left upon the surface of the ground after an inundation.

The most extensive tract of valley country east of the Mississippi is that situated within the bluffs of this river, usually denominated the American Bottom, extending from the mouth of the Ocoa, or Kaskaskias river, northwardly to that of the Missouri. This spacious bottom, although at present elevated much above the range of the highest freshets, is nevertheless alluvial. Its length along the Mississippi is about eighty, and its average breadth about four miles. It is generally destitute of a timber growth, except along the margin of the river, upon which there is a skirt of woodland extending almost from one end of the tract to the other. The alluvion of the American Bottom is composed of the rich mud brought down by the turbid Missouri, united with an abundance of vegetable matter yielded by the waters of the upper Mississippi, which also characterizes the bottoms of this extensive river from the Missouri downward to its mouth. Upon this bottom are situated the town of Kaskaskias, the villages of Prairie de Rocher, Harrison, Prairie de Pont, Cahokia and Illinois, together with many other settlements.

On the same side of the river another large tract of valley land, called the Mississippi Bottom, commences a few miles below the mouth of the river Kaskaskias, and extends downwards along the Mississippi, between fifty and sixty miles, having an average width of about three miles. This tract, in regard to soil and aspect, is of a character similar to that of the American Bottom, except that the former is more plentifully stocked with timber.

Besides these, there are numerous other bottoms on the Mississippi, within the limits prescribed for this report, all of which are composed of a rich alluvion. Those in particular situated below the confluence of the Mississippi and Missouri are possessed of a soil exceedingly luxuriant, being composed, as before observed, of the rich and fertilizing mud deposited from the water of the Missouri. Most of them are covered with deep and heavy forests of timber, accompanied with a luxuriant undergrowth of vines, shrubs, grass and other herbage.

The bottoms of the Wabash, Kaskaskias, Illinois, and Rock rivers, are also made up of a rich alluvion of sand and loam, containing a large proportion of vegetable mould. Their surfaces, like those of the Mississippi bottoms, are generally flat, exhibiting tabular elevations or benches, formed by the washing of their rivers at different periods. Large tracts of prairie land are to be met with upon them; but for the most part the proportion of woodland is amply sufficient to supply the adjacent country with timber and fuel.

The valleys of these rivers differ from that of the Ohio, not only in having a greater width, but also in being limited on both sides by bluffs stretching along their whole length, and maintaining nearly a parallel direction; whereas the valley of the Ohio is bounded by abrupt hills irregularly disposed, in some instances protruding far into the valley like promontories, and in others retiring from the river, and affording room for bottoms of pretty large extent. The Ohio bottoms are uniformly clad in deep forests, except where they have been removed by settlers; no prairies worthy of notice making their appearance.

The valley country, from the circumstances already detailed in allusion to the country constituting the second variety, is almost without exception unhealthy. But at the same time it appears evident, that this evil gradually decreases in proportion to the increase of population, and the consequent advancement of agriculture; for the products of the soil, which the bottoms yield in the greatest profusion, instead of being left to wither and decay upon the surface, are necessarily consumed in the subsistence of man and beast; in consequence of which, one of the most fruitful causes of pestilential effluvia, viz. vegetable putrefaction, is in a very considerable degree removed.

The prevailing timber growth of the region comprehending the two sections of country already described, is exhibited in the following list of trees: viz. cotton-wood, willow, sycamore, black walnut, pecan, coffee-tree, sweet and sour or black gum, red and water elm, hackberrry, blue and white ash, linden, yellow and white poplar, catalpa, black and honey locust, buck-eye, bur oak, white and black oak, mulberry, box, elder, white dogwood, sugar-tree, white maple, wild cherry, red oak, hickory, ironwood, and hop hornbeam. The foregoing constitute the principal timber growth of the valley country, and are to be met with more or less frequently throughout the whole of it. Red beech is abundant in some parts of the valley of the Ohio, and in those of many of its tributaries; it abounds also in the northerly parts of the States of Ohio and Indiana. Post oak, black jack, and several other varieties of the oak, also chesnut, white and shell bark, hickory, persimmon, &c. are sometimes found in the bottoms, but are more prevalent upon the hills and highlands. Pitch pine abounds in many parts of Ohio and Indiana, and generally in the neighbourhood of the Alleghany mountains. White pine occasionally makes its appearance in the northerly parts of Ohio. Red cedar is found in a great variety of places throughout the country, but no where in great abundance.

The under-growth of the several tracts of country above considered includes a great variety of shrubs, vines, brambles, grass and other herbage, to be enumerated in a botanical catalogue daily expected from Dr. James.

The most valuable timber trees are the white, post, and bur oaks, the white and blue ash, the shell bark hickory, the black walnut, the cherry, the locust, chesnut, poplar, mulberry, beach, cotton-wood and linden. The two last mentioned are seldom used where other kinds of timber are to be had. The cotton-wood is not only the most abundant timber-growth upon the bottoms, but is more widely diffused than any other, and in many places is the only variety of forest trees that make their appearance; which, however, is more particularly the case westward of the Mississippi.

Of the country situated between the Mississippi and Missouri rivers.

We next proceed to a consideration of the country west of the Mississippi, and shall begin with that situated between this river and the Missouri. This section contains no mountains, or indeed hills, of any considerable magnitude. The term *rolling* appears to be peculiarly applicable in conveying an idea of the surface of this region, although it is not entirely destitute of abrupt hills and precipices. The aspect of the whole is variegated with the broad valleys of rivers and creeks, and intervening tracts of undulating upland, united to the valleys by gentle slopes. Its surface is chequered with stripes of woodland situated upon the margins of the watercourses, and dividing the whole into extensive parterres. If we except those parts of the section that are contiguous to the Mississippi and Missouri, at least nineteen-twentieths of the country are completely destitute of a timber-growth.

Within the valleys of these two rivers are extensive tracts of alluvial bottom possessed of a rich soil. The bottoms of the Missouri in particular are probably inferior to none within the limits of the United States in point of fertility. Those of the Mississippi are very rich, but do not exhibit symptoms of so great fecundity as the former. The bottoms of both, on ascending the rivers, become more sandy, and apparently less productive.

The bottoms of the Missouri are for the most part clad in a deep and heavy growth of timber and underbrush, to the distance of about three hundred and fifty miles above its mouth. There are, however, prairies of considerable extent occasionally to be met with on this part of the river. Higher up, the prairies within the river valley become more numerous and extensive, till at length no woodlands appear, except tracts of small size, situated at the points formed by the meanders of the river.

The bottoms on the Upper Mississippi (that part of the Mississippi situated above its confluence with the Missouri being distinguished by this appellation) contain less woodland, in proportion to their extent, than those of the Missouri. The prairies upon this river also become more numerous and extensive as we proceed upward.

The interior of the country, situated between the valleys of these rivers, presents, as before remarked, a rolling aspect, inclining to hilly, and broken in some parts, but generally variegated with gentle swells and broad valleys. Within this section are numerous small rivers and creeks, with valleys of a character similar to those of the Mississippi or Missouri, but not so fertile. These valleys expand to a great width, compared with the magnitude of the streams upon which they are situated, but are not bounded by abrupt bluffs, like those of the two rivers just mentioned. They are generally covered with a luxuriant growth of grass and other herbage, and occasionally present copses of woodland of moderate extent. The timber-growth of the bottoms is similar to that of the Mississippi bottoms; cotton-wood, blue and white ash, hackberry, black walnut, cherry, mulberry, hickory, and several varieties of the oak, being the prevailing timber trees. The hills or high lands are in some instances covered with a scrubby growth of timber and furze, consisting of post oak, black jack, hazel, green brier, &c.

The soil of this section is probably equal, if not superior, to that of any other tract of upland of equal extent within our territory. But the scarcity of timber, mill-seats, and springs of water, —defects that are almost uniformly prevalent, — must for a long time prove serious impediments in the way of settling the country.

The population of this section of country is located almost exclusively within the valleys of the Mississippi and Missouri, and in their immediate neighbourhood, extending upwards along the former about one hundred and sixty, and along the latter about three hundred and twenty miles above their confluence. The most populous parts of the country are the county of St. Charles, situated near the junction of these two rivers; Cote Sans Dessein and its vicinity; that part usually denominated the Boon's Lick country, extending from the mouth of Osage river upward along the Miami to the river Charaton; and the country on the Mississippi, including the Salt river settlements, which have become numerous and pretty widely diffused.

Along the valleys, both of the Mississippi and Missouri, there are still innumerable vacancies for settlement, holding forth inducements for emigrants to occupy them, equally as strong as any of the positions already occupied. The inhabitants of this section have frequently been visited by the prevailing epidemics of the western country, which may be attributed, in all probability, to the same causes that have been herein assigned in relation to the country east of the Mississippi, which operate with equal force and effect upon the inhabitants of this section.

Of the country situated between the Missouri and Red rivers, west of the Mississippi and east of the meridian of the Council Bluff.

Although no precise limits can be assigned as the western boundary of this section, yet the meridian above proposed may be regarded as a line of division between two regions differing in their general character and aspect. It is not pretended that the immediate course of the line is marked by any distinct features of the country, but that a gradual change is observable in the general aspect of the two regions, which takes place in the vicinity of the proposed line. The assumed meridian is in longitude ninety-six degrees west nearly, and crosses the Platte a few miles above its mouth, the Konzas near the junction of the principal forks, the Arkansa about one hundred miles above the Verdigrise, or seven hundred miles from its mouth, the Canadian about one hundred and fifty miles from its mouth, and the Red river about one hundred and fifty miles above the Kiamesha river.

The section of country under consideration exhibits a great variety of aspect, the surface being diversified by mountains, hills, valleys, and occasional tracts of rolling country; within the section, is an extensive tract of bottom land deserving of a particular consideration. It is situated on the Mississippi, commencing a few miles below the Ohio, and extending downward to Red river, uninterrupted by hills or high lands, and subject in many places to inundation from the freshets of the Mississippi. The bottoms contain many large swamps, rendered almost impenetrable by a dense growth of cypress and cypress-knees (the latter of which are conical excrescences springing from the roots of the cypress, and shooting up in profusion to the height of from one to eight or ten feet). The most extensive of these swamps commences near the head of the bottom, and passes south-westwardly back of New Madrid, the Little Prairie, St.Francisville, &c., and terminates near the village of the Port of Arkansa. The Great Swamp, the name by which this extensive morass is designated, is about two hundred miles in length, and is of a variable width, from five to twenty or thirty miles. The timber-growth of this and of the other swamps, which are of a similar character, but inferior in magnitude, consist principally of cypress of a superior quality. But the difficulty of removing it renders it of little value to the country. Within the bottom are also numerous lakes, lagoons, and marshes, once, no doubt, parts of the bed of the Mississippi, or of some of its tributaries that have their courses through the bottom. Notwithstanding the general depression of this bottom, it contains many insulated tracts of considerable extent, elevated above the range of the highest floods. The bottom, almost throughout its whole extent, supports a dense and heavy growth of timber, of an excellent quality, together with a luxuriant under-growth of cane brake, vines, &c.

It may not be improper to remark in this place, that great havoc is annually made amongst the timber of this tract, by lumber and fuel mongers, who furnish the New Orleans market with large supplies of these articles, particularly of the former.

The bottom is bounded on the west by a chain of heights, corresponding to the river bluffs on other parts of the Mississippi, but not arranged in so regular a manner. These are the commencement of a part of the hilly country hereafter to be considered. The most considerable rivers that flow through the bottoms, and pour their tribute into the Mississippi, are the St. Francis, the Big Black and White rivers, which are confluent, the Washita and Red river.

There are also a few other bottoms on the west side of the Mississippi of moderate size. The largest of these are Tywapata and Bois Broulè, situated a little above the mouth of the Ohio.

The hilly and mountainous country commences immediately west of the Mississippi bottoms, and extends westwardly about four hundred miles. Although the terms *hilly* and *mountainous* are expressive of the general character of the country, yet the following portions of this section may be enumerated as exceptions, viz. a tract of country comprehending St. Louis, Belle Fontain, Florissant, and extending south-westwardly so as to include the lead mine tract, Belle View, &c. This tract (which embraces the most populous part of the Missouri territory) may be denominated rolling, or moderately hilly. Considerable portions of the country situated between the Arkansa and Red rivers, particularly in the vicinity of the latter, are also of this character. On the Arkansa, above Belle Point, is an extensive tract of a similar description; as also many tracts of inferior size, on the north side of the Arkansa, between the villages of the Port and the Cadron settlements. On the south side of the Missouri is also an extensive tract of rolling country, commencing at the river Le Mine, six miles above Franklin, and extending upward along the Missouri, with occasional interruptions, to the Council Bluff. Such is the extent of this tract, that it comprises almost the whole of the country situated between the assumed meridian line and the Missouri, from Fort Osage upward. On the head waters of the Osage river, and on those of its principal tributaries, the country is said to be of a similar character also. To these may be added large portions of country situated on the Verdigrise river, upon the Arkansa, above Grand river, and upon the

Canadian, from its mouth upwards to the distance of about two hundred miles. The tracts here designated, exhibit broad and elevated swells of land, separated from each other by deep and spacious valleys.

These portions of country are chequered with woodlands and prairies, in many instances alternating with each other in due proportion, for the accommodation of settlers with farming and woodlands. On the Missouri above Fort Osage, and on the Osage river, however, the proportion of woodland is very inconsiderable, and the timber it affords of a scrubby character. The prairies here, as on the north of the Missouri, occupy at least nineteen-twentieths of the whole surface. Some portions of the Red river country are also deficient in the quantum of woodlands allotted to them; but in general it may be observed, that the more southerly regions are better supplied with timber than those farther north. The growth of the woodlands interspersed amongst the prairies is mostly post oak, hickory, black jack, and white oak upon the high lands; and cotton-wood, sycamore, black and white walnut, maple, bur oak, and several other trees common to the western bottoms, in the valleys. The bow wood, or, as it is sometimes called, the Osage orange, is found upon the southerly tributaries of the Arkansa, and upon the Red river and its tributaries. This tree is deserving of particular notice, inasmuch as it affords a timber extremely compact and elastic; its trunk and roots may prove very useful in dying yellow, and its fruit of importance in medicine.

The residue of this section, with the exception of the river bottoms, and tracts of valley land scattered in various directions throughout the whole, is extremely hilly, broken, and mountainous, the hills and mountains rising from five to fifteen hundred feet above the water-table of the country in which they are situated. They are exceedingly numerous, and are divided into a multiplicity of knobs and peaks, having rounded summits, and presenting perpendicular cliffs and abrupt precipices of sandstone. Their surfaces generally are covered with rocks of this description, or flinty fragments strewed in profusion upon them. The growth upon them is, almost exclusively, pitch pine, cedar, scrubby oaks, hickory, haw and bramble; the poverty of the soil in some instances, and the scarcity of it in others, excluding the more luxuriant vegetable productions common to the more level country in their vicinity.

The range of mountains situated between the Arkansa and Red rivers gives rise to the following streams, all of which are sufficiently copious for millseats, and abound in cascades and falls, well adapted to such purposes; viz. the Blue Water, Kiamesha and Little rivers; the Mountain, Rolling, Cossetot and Saline forks of Little river, all of which are tributary to Red river; the Little Missouri, Cadeau, Washita, and the Saline, all confluent; the Mamelle, Le Fevre, Petit Jean and Poteau, tributary to the Arkansa, besides numerous creeks of less note.

The hills and mountains between the Arkansa and Missouri are equally prolific in watercourses. The most considerable of these are the Verdigrise, Neosho or Grand river, Illinois; together with the Frogs, Mulberry, White Oak, Spadra, Pine, Illinois, Point Remove and Cadron creeks, tributary to the Arkansa; the Little Red and White rivers, confluent streams; the Strawberry, Spring, Eleven Point, Currant, Little and Big Black, all confluent, and tributary to White river, which enters the Mississippi about thirty miles above the mouth of the Arkansa. The St. Francis and the Merameg have their sources in this broken region also, and discharge themselves into the Mississippi. Of the valleys of the rivers last enumerated, viz. those north of the Arkansa and tributary to the Mississippi, it is observable that they are uniformly possessed of a rich soil, but owing to the excessive floods occasionally brought down through them from the hills and mountains, their cultivation is very precarious. The valley of White river, and those of some few others, are in many places elevated above the reach of the highest freshets, and are not altogether subject to this inconvenience. But for the most part they are liable to being swept by overwhelming freshets, which prostrate fences, buildings, and every artificial structure that opposes their march. Even a fall freshet has been known to inundate plantations situated within the valleys, to the depth of eight or ten feet. These floods are generally very sudden, as well as excessive, to such a degree, that on some occasions the water has risen, in the course of one night, more than twenty feet. By these sudden rises of the water, the planter that in the evening thought his family and possessions secure from harm, has been compelled the next morning to embark with his family in a canoe, to save themselves from impending destruction, while his habitation, fields, cattle, and all his effects, are abandoned to the fury of the torrent.

The streams rising in the same hilly country, and tributary to the Missouri, are the following, viz. the Bon Homme creek, the Gasconade, the Osage and its tributaries, the Le Mine, the Blue Water, and several streams tributary to the Konzas river. Upon some of these, as the Bon Homme, Gasconade, and some few creeks besides, mills have been constructed, at which much of the timber of the St. Louis market is sawed.

This section, as yet, is but very partially populated, although the inhabitants in some portions of it are considerably numerous. The most populous part of the section is the country situated immediately below the mouth of the Missouri, including the town of St. Louis and the villages of Florissant and Carondelet, Herculaneum, St. Genevieve, Bainbridge, Cape Girardeau, Jackson, St. Michael's, and the country in their vicinity; the lead mine tract, including Mima Berton, Potosi, and Belle View, are considerably populous. The settlements in these places, however, if we except the scites occupied by the towns and villages just enumerated, are still very scattering, and but a small proportion of the land susceptible of agriculture is yet under cultivation. Besides these, there are numerous other settlements and several small villages within this part of the Missouri territory, distributed in various directions, and constituting but a very scanty population. They are scattered along the Missouri from its mouth to Fort Osage, a distance of more than three hundred miles, on the Gasconade, Merameg, St. Francis, Big Black, and several of its tributaries.

Within the Arkansa territory, there are but few villages, and the settlements are as yet very scattering. The principal villages are the Port of Arkansa, situated about sixty miles above the mouth of the river; Davidsonville, on Big Black river; a small village at the commencement of the high lands on the Arkansa, at a place called the Little Rock, about two hundred miles from the mouth of the river, selected as the seat of government for the territory. Besides these, there are a few other inconsiderable villages on the Arkansa river, as also several of small size, situated in the country between the river just mentioned and the Red river, the most considerable of which are at Pecan Point, Mount Prairie, Prairie de Inde, &c. These villages contain but very few houses, and those generally of a rude structure, a circumstance attributable only to the infancy of the territory. The settlements of the territory are scattered along the Arkansa, from the White river cut off (a channel uniting these two rivers at the distance of thirty miles above the mouth of the former, and three miles above that of the latter) to Belle Point, a distance of about four hundred miles. On Little Red, White, and Strawberry rivers, are many scattering settlements, as also on the Washita, Cadeau, Little Missouri, and the several forks of Little river. The settlements upon Red river extend upward to the Kiamesha, a distance of about nine hundred miles from its mouth, following the meanders of the river.

The settlements of the section under consideration are most numerous in those parts represented, in the foregoing description, as being variegated with prairies and woodlands alternating with each other. In the valley of the Arkansa, however, which is generally clad in rich forests and luxuriant cane brakes, prairies are seldom to be met with, and settlers have had recourse to clearing the land necessary for their plantations.

In addition to the white settlements above pointed out, there are numerous villages and settlements of the Cherokee Indians extending along the Arkansa, from the mouth of Point Remove creek upward to Mulberry river, a distance of about one hundred miles. These settlements, in respect to the comforts and conveniences of life they afford, appear to vie with, and in many instances even surpass, those of the Americans in that part of the country.

There are a few villages of the Quawpaws or Arkansas, and Choctaws, situated on the south side of the Arkansa river, below the high lands. They are not numerous, subsist principally upon game and Indian corn of their own raising, and have ever been friendly to the whites. Upon the river St. Francis are a few settlements of the Delawares and Shawnees, dispersed remnants of those unfortunate nations. The several bands of the Osage nation resident upon the Verdigrise, and upon the head waters of Osage river, also the Konzas Indians living upon the river bearing their name, are included within this section of the country.

In regard to climate, this region, as it expands through more than eight degrees of latitude, may be expected to afford a considerable variety; and the position is sufficiently verified by the commencement and progress of annual vegetation. The change of climate is also indicated by certain peculiarities observable in the vegetable products of different parts of the country. For example, vegetation begins at least a month earlier in the southern than in the northern extreme of the region. The Spanish moss disappears northwardly of the 33d degree of north latitude; cotton and indigo cannot be cultivated to advantage in a latitude higher than 36 or 37 degrees; and the cane brake is seldom found north of $37\frac{1}{2}$ degrees.

In regard to the salubrity of the climate, there is also a diversity, depending upon local circumstances rather than upon the temperature of the weather. A luxuriant soil yielding its products to decay and putrefy upon the ground, also stagnant waters, flat lands and marshes in which the river valleys of this region abound, cannot fail to load the atmosphere with pestilential miasmata, and render the country unhealthy, wherever these occurrences are to be met with. But it is presumed that the causes of disease will gradually be exterminated as the population of the country increases.

Of the rivers of this region there are many that are navigable for keel-boats of several tons burden, but all of them have more or less obstructions from shoals and frosts at different periods. The Arkansa, which, in point of magnitude and extent, deservedly ranks second amongst the tributaries of the Mississippi (the Missouri being the first), is navigable to the mouth of the Neosho, or Grand river, a distance of about six hundred miles. In this part of the river, however, the navigation is liable to obstructions, for want of a sufficient depth of water, during a period of two and a half or three months, commencing in July. Occasional obstructions are also imposed by ice forming in the river during the winter season, but these are seldom of long continuance, the winters being usually short and mild. As the freshets of the river seldom prevail more than a few days at a time, and are usually attended by sudden rises and falls of the water, boats of moderate draft and burden only are suited to its navigation. The Arkansa is navigable at all seasons for boats of this description about two hundred miles, which comprehends the distance by the meanders of the river from the Mississippi to the commencement of the high lands. Above the mouth of the Neosho it spreads to a much greater width than below, and the water is more extensively diffused over its bed, which renders the shoals more numerous and the navigation more precarious. This part of the Arkansa cannot indeed be considered navigable, even for perogues of a large size, except during the short period of a freshet, which is seldom long enough to complete a voyage of one hundred miles ascending and descending.

The Red river is navigable, during most of the year, to the Great Raft, about five hundred miles from its mouth. At this place its navigation is effectually obstructed, except in a high stage of water, when keel-boats of ten or fifteen tons burden may pass around it and ascend several hundred miles above. That part of the river situated above the Raft, however, like the upper part of the Arkansa, is rendered impassable for boats of burden, by shoals and sandbars.

The Washita, tributary to Red river, is navigable many miles. That part of it particularly situated within the valley of the Mississippi, and denominated Black river, admits of constant navigation for boats of considerable burden. The Little river, which is also tributary to Red river, together with its forks, heretofore enumerated, is navigable in high water. White river is navigable in a moderate stage of water between three and four hundred miles. Also the Big Black, its principal tributary, and several branches of the river last mentioned, viz. the Strawberry, Currant, Eleven Point, and Spring rivers. The navigation of the St. Francis is blocked up near its mouth, and rendered impassable for boats of every description, by rafts of logs and drift-wood, completely choking the channel of the river, and in many places occupying the whole of its bed for the distance of several miles together. The Merameg is also navigable in a moderate stage of water for many miles.

The Gasconade, Osage, and Konzas rivers are navigable in the spring season, but their navigation seldom extends far inland from their mouths, being obstructed by shoals or rapids.

Of the rivers tributary to the Missouri, it is remarkable that their mouths are generally blocked up with mud, consequent to the subsidence of the summer freshet of that river, which usually takes place in the month of July. The reason is obvious; the freshets of the more southerly tributaries are discharged early in the season, and wash from their mouths the sand and mud previously deposited therein, leaving them free from obstructions. These freshets having subsided, the more northerly branches discharge their floods, formed by the melting of the snow at a later period. The Missouri being swollen thereby, backs its waters, charged with mud, considerable distances up the mouths of the tributaries before alluded to. The water here becoming stagnant, deposits its mud; and the tributaries, having no more freshets to expel it, remain with their mouths thus obstructed till the ensuing spring.

The lower part of the Canadian river, although it is included within the section under consideration, will be described in the sequel of the report, in connexion with the rest of that river.

Of the animals found in the several sections of country above described, there are a great variety in almost every department of zoology. But as most of them are common in other parts of the United States, they need not to be enumerated here.

Of the country situated between the meridian of the Council Bluff and the Rocky Mountains.

We next proceed to a description of the country westward of the assumed meridian, and extending to the Rocky Mountains, which are its western boundary. This section embraces an extent of about four hundred miles square, lying between 96 and 105 degrees of west longitude, and between 35 and 42 degrees of north latitude.

Proceeding westwardly across the meridian above specified, the hilly country gradually subsides, giving place to a region of vast extent, spreading towards the north and south, and presenting an undulating surface, with nothing to limit the view or variegate the prospect, but here and there a hill, knob, or insulated tract of table-land. At length the Rocky Mountains break upon the view, towering abruptly from the plains, and mingling their snow-capped summits with the clouds.

On approaching the mountains, no other change is observable in the general aspect of the country, except that the isolated knobs and table-lands above alluded to become more frequent and more distinctly marked, the bluffs by which the valleys of watercourses are bounded present a greater abundance of rocks, stones lie in greater profusion upon the surface, and the soil becomes more sandy and sterile. If, to the characteristics above intimated, we add that of an almost complete destitution of woodland (for not more than one thousandth part of the section can be said to possess a timber-growth) we shall have a pretty correct idea of the general aspect of the whole country.

The insulated tracts herein alluded to as table-lands, are scattered throughout the section, and give to the country a very remarkable appearance. They rise from six to eight hundred feet above the common level, and are surrounded in many instances by rugged slopes and perpendicular precipices, rendering their summits almost inaccessible. Many of them are in this manner completely insulated, while others are connected with the plains below by gentle acclivities, leading from their basis to their summits, upon one side or other of each eminence. These tracts, as before intimated, are more numerous, but less extensive in the vicinity of the Rocky Mountains than they are farther eastward; and in the former situations, they are more strikingly characterized by the marks above specified than in the latter.

The geological formations that present themselves along the declivities of those heights are principally horizontal strata of secondary sandstones, and breccia or puddingstone, alternating with each other. Clinkstone prevails upon the surface of them in many places, but in general the superior strata are rocks of the description just before mentioned. These tracts are denominated tabular, not from any flatness of surface by which they are characterized, but from their appearance at a distant view, and from the horizontal disposition of the stratifications imbedded in them. Their surfaces are usually waving, and in some instances rise into knobs and ridges of several hundred feet high; many of them are clad in a scanty growth of pitch. pine, red cedar, scrubby oaks, &c., while others exhibit a bald or prairie surface.

By far the greater proportion of this section of country is characterized by a rolling and plain surface, which may be alleged not only of the space included within the limits above assigned, but of extensive portions of country north and south of it. Although the elevated table-lands, a description of which has just been given, are situated within this region, they occupy but a small proportion of it. In addition to these inequalities in the surface of the country, there are numerous mounds or knobs of different magnitude, and occasionally swells of greater or less extent, which contribute to give a pleasing variety to the prospect. The country is also divided into extensive parterres by the valleys of rivers and creeks, which are usually sunk 150 or 200 feet below the common level, and bounded in some places by perpendicular precipices, and in others by bluffs, or banks of gentle slopes.

Immediately at the base of the mountains, and also at those of some of the insular table-lands, are situated many remarkable ridges, rising in the form of parapets, to the height of between fifty and one hundred and fifty feet. These appear to have been attached to the neighbouring heights, of which they once constituted a part, but have, at some remote period, been cleft asunder from them by some extraordinary convulsion of nature, which has prostrated them in their present condition.

The rocky stratifications, of which these ridges are principally composed, and which are exactly similar to those of the insulated table-lands, are variously inclined, having various dips, from forty-five to eighty degrees.

Throughout this section of country the surface is occasionally characterized by water-worn pebbles, and gravel of granite, gneiss, and quartz, but the predominant characteristic is sand, which in many instances prevails almost to the entire exclusion of vegetable mould. Large tracts are often to be met with, exhibiting scarcely a trace of vegetation. The whole region, as before hinted, is almost entirely destitute of a timber-growth of any description. In some few instances, however, sandy knobs and ridges make their appearance, thickly covered with red cedars of a dwarfish growth. There are also some few tracts clad in a growth of pitch pine and scrubby oaks; but, in general, nothing of vegetation appears upon the uplands but withered grass of a stinted growth, no more than two or three inches high, prickly pears profusely covering extensive tracts, and weeds of a few varieties, which, like the prickly pear, seem to thrive best in the most arid and sterile soil.

In the vicinity of the Rocky Mountains, southwardly of the Arkansa river, the surface of the country, in many places, is profusely covered with loose fragments of volcanic rocks. On some occasions, stones of this description are so numerous as almost to exclude vegetation. A multiplicity of ridges and knobs of various sizes, containing rocks of this character, also make their appearance. All these formations seem to be superincumbent upon horizontal strata of secondary sandstone. But the volcanoes whence they originated have left no vestiges by which their exact locality can be determined. In all probability, they were extinguished previously to the recession of the waters that once inundated the vast region between the Alleghany and Rocky Mountains.

Of the rivers that have their courses through this section, those of most note are the Platte, the Konzas and its forks, the Arkansa, and the Canadian tributary to the Arkansa. The Platte rises in the Rocky Mountains, and after an easterly course of about eight hundred miles, falls into the Missouri, at the distance of about seven hundred miles from the Mississippi. It derives its name from the circumstance of its being broad and shoal; its average width being about twelve hundred yards, exclusive of the islands it embosoms; and its depth, in a moderate stage of water, so inconsiderable, that the river is fordable in almost every place. The main Platte is formed of two confluent tributaries of nearly equal size, called the North and South forks, both of which have their sources considerably within the range of the Rocky Mountains. They unite about four hundred miles westward from the mouth of the Platte, having meandered about the same distance eastwardly from the mountains. Besides these, the Platte has two considerable tributaries, the one called the Elk Horn, entering a few miles above its mouth, and the other the Loup Fork, entering about ninety miles above the same place. The valleys of the Platte and its several tributaries are extremely broad, and in many places considerably fertile. They gradually become less fertile on ascending from the mouths of the rivers on which they are situated, till at length they exhibit an arid and sterile appearance. The alluvion of which the bottoms are composed contains a large proportion of sand, which, added to the nitrous and saline matter blended with it, occasions frequent appearances of complete barrenness. Magnesia also appears to be a component part of the soil, a quality invariably derogatory to the fertility of any soil. The valley of the Platte, from its mouths to its constituent forks, spreads to the width of ten or twelve miles, and forms a most beautiful expanse of level country. It is bounded on both sides by high lands, elevated twenty-five or thirty feet above the valley, and connected therewith by gentle slopes.

The river in several places expands to the width of many miles, embosoming numerous islands, some of which are broad and considerably extensive, and all of them covered with a growth of cotton-wood and willows. These are the only woodlands that make their appearance along the river, and in travelling westward these become less numerous and extensive, till at length they entirely disappear. Copses and skirts of woodland again present themselves in the neighbourhood of the mountains, but they are of small magnitude, and the trees they furnish are of a dwarfish growth. For a distance of nearly two hundred miles, commencing at the confluence of the North and South forks, and extending westwardly towards the mountains, the country is almost entirely destitute of woodland, scarcely a tree, bush, or even a shrub, making its appearance.

The Platte is seldom navigable, except for skin canoes, requiring but a moderate depth of water, and for these only when a freshet prevails in the river. No attempts have ever been made to ascend the river in canoes for any great distance; the prevalence of shoals, and the rapidity of the current, discouraging such an undertaking. The bed of the Platte is seldom depressed more than six or eight feet below the surface of the bottoms, and in many places even less; and spreads to such a width, that the highest freshets pass off without inundating the bottoms, except in their lowest parts; the rise of the water, on such occasions, being no more than five or six feet.

In order to account in some measure for the diversity of soil observable in the vallies of most of our western rivers, it may not be improper in this place to assign one of the principal causes that operate in producing this effect. The alluvial deposits of which the river bottoms are formed, consist of particles of mud and sand, more or less minute. The coarser and more ponderous particles are of course soonest deposited, while the finer are transported by the current to a greater distance, and deposited near the mouths of the rivers. Thus it happens, that the bottoms situated nearest to the sources of the western rivers, are sandy, and contain but a small proportion of vegetable mould, while those nearer their mouths are generally furnished with a rich and fertile loam.

The Konzas, or Konzays, as it is pronounced by the Indians, is made up of two considerable streams, heading in the plains between the Platte and Arkansa rivers, called the Republican and Smoky-hill forks; tributary to the former of these, are the Solomon's and Salim forks, of less magnitude, rising also in the same plains. The Konzas is navigable only in high freshets for boats of burden, and on such occasions not more than one hundred and fifty or two hundred miles, the navigation being obstructed by shoals.

The character of this river and its several branches is similar to that of the Platte and its tributaries. Woodlands are seldom to be met with, except in narrow skirts and small copses along the watercourses. Much of the country situated upon its forks is said to be possessed of a good soil, but is rendered uninhabitable for want of timber and water. The bottoms are possessed of a light sandy soil, and the uplands are in many places characterized by aridity and barrenness. The surface for the most part is rolling, but in some instances inclines to hilly.

That portion of the Arkansa included within the section under consideration has a bed or channel varying in width from four hundred yards to more than a mile, exclusively of islands. In the neighbourhood of the mountains, its width does not exceed fifty or sixty yards, gradually growing wider in its progress downward. Its valley, for a distance of more than one hundred miles from the place where it issues from the mountains, contains a considerable timber-growth, principally of cotton-wood, in skirts bordering upon the river, which occasionally embosoms islands clad in the same kind of growth. Every appearance of timber, however, is lost on a further progress eastward, and nothing is presented to variegate or adorn the prospect inland, but a broad expanse of waving prairies.

Proceeding eastward along the river, its valley gradually widens, and the bluffs or banks by which it is bounded become less elevated and abrupt. The bottoms rise but a few feet above the water-level of the river, but the freshets, having a broad bed like that of the Platte to expand upon, seldom rise so high as to inundate the bottoms. This part of the Arkansa, as before hinted, cannot be considered as navigable, except for boats of light burden during the prevalence of a freshet. In a very low stage, the river is said to disappear in many places, the whole of its water passing off through the immense body of sand of which its bed is composed.

The Arkansa, having a direction nearly east and west, has no great variety of climate to traverse in its course from the mountains to the Mississippi; consequently there is no succession of thaws taking place upon the river, calculated to maintain a freshet for any considerable length of time. The freshets are occasioned by a simultaneous melting of the snow throughout the whole extent of the river, and by showers of rain, which, falling upon a rolling surface, is quickly drained off, and causes sudden, but seldom excessive rises in the river. I have witnessed, in the Arkansa, no less than three considerable rises and falls of the water in the course of two weeks.

The most considerable streams tributary to this part of the Arkansa are the Negracka or Red Fork, and the Newsewketongu, or Grand Salim, on the south, and the Little Arkansa and Stinking Fork on the north side. The Negracka rises within fifty or sixty miles of the mountains, and after meandering eastwardly between four and five hundred miles, unites with the Arkansa at the distance of about nine hundred miles from the mouth of the latter. The Newsewketongu has its source in the plains between the Arkansa and Canadian rivers, and unites with the former about one hundred and fifty miles below the Negracka. The head waters of the Little Arkansa interlock with those of the Smoky-hill Fork of the Konzas, and are discharged into the Arkansa, about fifteen hundred miles above its mouth. The Stinking Fork rises amongst the head-waters of the Neosho, and enters the Arkansa about eight hundred miles from its mouth. Besides these, there are many other streams of smaller size entering on both sides of the river.

The Canadian rises at the base of the Rocky Mountains, and after a meandering course of about one thousand miles, enters the Arkansa at the distance of about five hundred and fifty miles from the mouth of the latter. This river has generally been represented, upon the maps of the country, as having a north-easterly course; whereas its source is nearly in the same latitude as its confluence with the Arkansa, consequently its general course is nearly east. In its course, it forms an extensive curve to the southward, leaving a broad space between it and the Arkansa, in which several streams, many hundred miles in length, tributary to both of these rivers, have their origin and course.

This river has a broad valley, bounded by bluffs from two to five hundred feet high, faced with rocky precipices near its source, and presenting abrupt declivities, intersected by numerous ravines lower down. It has a spacious bed, depressed but a few feet below the bottoms, and exhibiting one continued stratum of sand through the greater part of its length. It is the channel through which the water of a vast extent of country is carried off, yet, during most of the summer season, it is entirely destitute of running water throughout a large proportion of its extent, a circumstance in proof of the aridity of region drained by it. Fifty miles above its mouth, it receives at least two-thirds of its water from its principal tributary, denominated the North Fork. This fork rises between the Arkansa and Canadian, and has a meandering course of about seven hundred miles. Six miles above the fork just mentioned, another tributary enters the Canadian called the South Fork, about half as large as the other. Notwithstanding the supplies afforded by these two tributaries, the Canadian has not a sufficiency of water in summer to render it navigable even to their mouths. At the distance of twenty miles above its mouth, a chain of rocks (slaty sandstone) extends across the bed of the river, but occasions no considerable fall. A little above the entrance of the South Fork, is another of the same description, forming rapids of moderate descent, not more than four hundred yards in length. With these exceptions, the bed of the river presents no rocky formations in place, for more than four hundred miles from its confluence with the Arkansa. About three hundred and fifty miles from that point, beds of gypsum, or plaster of Paris, begin to make their appearance in the bluffs fronting upon the river, and upon the declivities of the highland knobs. A great abundance of this article is to be met with, not only upon the Canadian, but also upon the upper part of the Arkansa. The hills, in which it is imbedded, are composed of ferruginous clay and fine sand of a deep red complexion. Hence the Arkansa derives the colouring matter that gives to its waters their reddish hue.

The bottoms of the Canadian, in the neighbourhood of its mouth, are possessed of a soil exceedingly prolific; but, like those of the other rivers of this region, the more remote their situation from the mouth of the river, the more sandy and sterile is their appearance. Its valley is plentifully supplied with timber of an excellent quality, for a distance of about two hundred miles on the lower part of the river; and the high lands, for nearly the same distance, are agreeably diversified with prairies and woodlands. This portion of the river is situated eastward of the assumed meridian, and the country upon it has already been partially described in a former part of this report.

The woodland growth, upon the lower part of the Canadian, consists of cotton-wood, sycamore, white, blue, and black ash, swamp cedar, red elm, coffee tree, yellow wood, sugar tree, box elder, white and black walnut, wild cherry, mulberry, &c. in the river valley; and hickory, white and post oak, black jack, black oak, &c. upon the adjacent uplands. On a progress westward, the most valuable of the timber trees above enumerated disappear, till at length occasional groves of cotton-wood, mingled with mulberry, red elm, and stunted shrubbery of various kinds, constitute the only woodlands of the country. On this occasion, it may be observed, that the cane or reed, the pea-vine, pawpaw, spice-wood, hop-vine, and several other varieties of shrubs and vines common only to rich soils, are no where to be found within this section, or westward of the proposed meridian.

The country of the Canadian above that last considered, or that portion of it west of the assumed meridian, appears to be possessed of a soil somewhat richer than the more northerly parts of the section, but exhibits no indications of extraordinary fecundity in any part of it. Proceeding westward, a very gradual change is observable in the apparent fertility of the soil, the surface becoming more sandy and sterile, and the vegetation less vigorous and luxuriant. The bottoms appear to be composed, in many places, almost exclusively of loose sand, exhibiting but few signs of vegetation. Knobs and drifts of sand, driven from the bed of the river by the violence of the wind, are piled in profusion along the margin of the river throughout the greater part of its length. It is remarkable, that these drifts are in many instances covered with grape vines of a scrubby appearance, bearing fruit in the greatest abundance and perfection. The vines grow to various heights, from eighteen inches to four feet, unaccompanied, in some instances, by any other vegetable, and bear a grape of a dark purple or black colour, of a delicious flavour, and of the size of a large pea or common gooseberry.

The waters of this section, almost in every part of it, appear to hold in solution a greater or less proportion of common salt and sulphate of magnesia, which, in many instances, render them too brackish or bitter for use. Saline and nitrous efflorescences frequently occur upon the surface, in various parts of the country, and incrustations of salt, of considerable thickness, are to be found in some few places south of the Arkansa river. As to the existence of rock salt in a mineral state some doubts are to be entertained, if the decision is to rest upon the character of the specimens exhibited as proofs of the fact. The several examples of this formation that we have witnessed, are evidently crystalline salt deposited by a regular process of evaporation and crystallization, and formed into concrete masses or crusts upon the surface of the ground.

Indications of coal are occasionally to be seen, but this mineral does not probably occur in large quantities. The geological character of this section is not such as to encourage the search for valuable minerals. A deep crust of secondary sandstone, occasionally alternating with breccia, with here and there a superstratum of rocks of a primitive type, are the principal formations that present themselves.

Of the animals of this region, the buffaloe or bison ranks first in importance, inasmuch as it supplies multitudes of savages not only with the principal part of their necessary food, but also contributes to furnish them with warm clothing. The flesh of this animal is equal, if not superior, to beef, and affords not only a savoury but a wholesome diet. A large proportion of this section, commencing at the assumed meridian, and extending westward to within one hundred miles of the Rocky Mountains, constitutes a part only of their pasture ground, over which they roam in numbers to an incredible amount. Their range extends northwardly and southwardly of the section, as far as we have any particular account of the country. The animal next in importance is the wild horse, a descendant, no doubt, of the Spanish breed of horses, to which its size, form and variety of colours, show that it is nearly allied. In regard to their contour, symmetry, &c. they afford all the varieties common to that breed of horses. They are considerably numerous in some parts of the country, but not abundant. They are generally collected in gangs, but are sometimes solitary.

Grizzly or white bears are frequently to be seen in the vicinity of the mountains. They are much larger than the common bear, endowed with great strength, and are said to be exceedingly ferocious. The black or common bears are numerous in some parts of the country, but none of these animals are found remote from woodlands, upon the products of which they in a great measure depend for their subsistence.

The common deer are to be met with in every part of this section, but are most numerous in the vicinity of woodlands. The black-tailed or mule deer is found only in the neighbourhood of the mountains; hilly and broken lands seem to afford them their favourite pasture ground. The elk is also an inhabitant of this section, but is not to be found remote from woodlands. The cabric wild goat, or, as it is more frequently called, the antelope, is common. They are numerous, and with the buffaloe are the common occupants of the plains, from which they retire only in quest of water.

Wolves are exceedingly numerous, particularly within the immediate range of the buffaloe. Of these there are many varieties, distinguishable by their shape, size and colour.

The marmot, commonly called the prairie dog, is more abundant throughout this section than any other quadruped. They live in villages scattered in every direction, and thickly inhabited; a single village in some instances occupying a tract of ground three or four miles in extent. Their habitations are burrows three or four inches in diameter, situated at the distance of fifteen or twenty paces asunder. Their habits and manners in other respects are peculiarly interesting. They subsist on vegetables; their flesh is similar to that of the ground hog, and their hair equally as coarse.

The beaver, otter, mink, and muskrat, are numerous upon the rivers, creeks, and rivulets issuing from the mountains, and generally upon those whose valleys are supplied with woodland.

Badgers, raccoons, hares, polecats, porcupines, many varieties of squirrels, panthers, wild cats, lynxes and foxes of several species, are also inhabitants of this section. Besides these, the country affords a great variety and abundance of reptiles and insects, both venomous and harmless.

Of the feathered tribes, no very considerable variety is observable. The turtle-dove, the jay, the barn swallow, the quail (partridge of the Middle States), the owl, whip-poor-will, and lark, which seem more widely distributed over the territory of the United States than any other birds, are found here. Several varieties of the hawk, containing some new species, the bald and gray eagle, the buzzard, raven, crow, jackdaw, magpie, turkey, two or three varieties of the grouse, pheasant, pigeon, many varieties of the sparrow and fly-catcher, the whooping or sandhill crane, curlew, sandpiper, together with a variety of other land and water fowls, are more or less numerous in this region. It is remarkable that birds of various kinds common to the sea-coast, and seldom found far in the interior, pervade the valley of the Mississippi to a great distance from the gulf of Mexico, and frequent the regions adjacent to the Rocky Mountains.

In regard to this extensive section of country, I do not hesitate in giving the opinion, that it is almost wholly unfit for cultivation, and of course uninhabitable by a people depending upon agriculture for their subsistence. Although tracts of fertile land considerably extensive are occasionally to be met with, yet the scarcity of wood and water, almost uniformly prevalent, will prove an insuperable obstacle in the way of settling the country. This objection rests not only against the section immediately under consideration, but applies with equal propriety to a much larger portion of the country. Agreeably to the best intelligence that can be had, concerning the country both northward and southward of the section, and especially to the inferences deducible from the account given by Lewis and Clarke of the country situated between the Missouri and the Rocky Mountains above the river Platte, the vast region commencing near the sources of the Sabine, Trinity, Brases, and Colorado, and extending northwardly to the forty-ninth degree of north latitude, by which the United States' territory is limited in that direction, is throughout of a similar character. The whole of this region seems peculiarly adapted as a range for buffaloes, wild goats, and other wild game; incalculable multitudes of which find ample pasturage and subsistence upon it.

This region, however, viewed as a frontier, may prove of infinite importance to the United States, inasmuch as it is calculated to serve as a barrier to prevent too great an extension of our population westward, and secure us against the machinations or incursions of an enemy that might otherwise be disposed to annoy us in that part of our frontier.

The Indians of the section last described, whose numbers are very limited compared with the extent of country they inhabit, will be considered in the sequel of this report.

Of the Rocky Mountains.

This range of mountains has been distinguished by a variety of appellations, amongst which the following are the most common, viz. Rocky, Shining, Mexican, Chippewyan, Andes, &c. The general course of the range is about N.N.W. or S.S.E. Its breadth varies from fifty to one hundred miles. They rise abruptly out of the plains, which lie extended at their base on the east side, towering into peaks of great height, which renders them visible at the distance of more than one hundred miles eastward from their base. They consist of ridges, knobs, and peaks, variously disposed, among which are interspersed many broad and fertile valleys. The more elevated parts of the mountains are covered with perpetual snows, which contribute to give them a luminous and at a great distance even a brilliant appearance, whence they have derived the name of Shining Mountains.

Between the Arkansa and Platte, on a small creek tributary to the former, is situated a high part of the mountains, denominated the "Highest Peak" on many maps of the country, and said to be more elevated than any other part within the distance of one hundred and fifty or two hundred miles. This peak, whose summit has been accounted inaccessible, was ascended by a detachment of the expedition conducted by Dr. James, from which circumstance it has been called James's Peak. Its elevation above the common level, ascertained by a trigonometrical measurement, is about eight thousand five hundred feet. But the correctness of the statement, that it is higher than any other parts of the mountains within the distance above mentioned, is questionable. Judging from the position of the snow near the summits of other peaks and ridges at no great distance from it, a much greater elevation is apparent.

The mountains are clad in a scattering growth of scrubby pines, oak, cedar, and furze, and exhibit a very rugged and broken aspect. The rocky formations embodied in them, contrary to the opinion generally received, are of a primitive character, consisting of granite, gneiss, quartz rocks, &c. It should be remarked, however, that a deep crust of secondary rocks, the same as the stratifications of the plains before mentioned, appears to recline against the east side of the mountains, extending upward from their base many hundred feet.

At the base of James's Peak above designated, are two remarkable springs of water, considerably copious, and strongly impregnated with fixed air. At the place also where the Arkansa issues from the mountains, are several medicinal springs on the north side of the river, rising in a small area at the base of the mountain. These springs were discovered by Captain Bell, and, in consequence, I have taken the liberty to call them Bell's Springs. They are six in number, one of which is strongly impregnated with fixed air, another with sulphurated hydrogen, and the rest with salt and sulphur; the water of all being more or less chalybeate.

Of the Indians inhabiting the section of country last described.

This country is exclusively inhabited by savages, no other beings of the human family having fixed their abode within it. They consist of the following tribes and nations, whose numbers, places of residence, and mode of life, will be subjects of consideration as far as our knowledge of them extends.

The Otoes, or as they are called in their own language, the Wahtooh-tah-tah, reside in a permanent village of dirt or earthen lodges, on the south bank of the river Platte, about fifty miles from its confluence with the Missouri, and thirty miles southwestwardly from the Council Bluff. The principal remnant of the old Missouries, who have become extinct as a nation, have their residence with the Otoes. In the course of the last winter, whilst these Indians were absent from their village on their winter-hunt, their town was partly burnt by the

Sauks, which misfortune induced them to take up a temporary abode upon Salt river, a few miles from their former residence. But it was generally supposed that they would return again, and rebuild their town. The name of their principal chief is Shongotongo, or Big Horse. Probable number of lodges 100, of persons 1400. The Otoes and Missouries are esteemed a brave people, and are friendly towards the Americans. They are at war with the Sauks, Foxes, Sioux, Osages, Ietans, and other Indians west of the Missouri. A small band of the Ioways resided for some time with these Indians, but not being able to harmonize with them, lately returned to their old village on the river De Moyen of the Mississippi. Their principal chief, usually called Hard Heart, being dissatisfied with the conduct of his tribe, remains with the Otoes.

The Omawhaw, or as it is commonly written the Maha nation, exultingly boast that they have never killed an American. On the contrary, they have ever been friendly, and still hold the Americans in the highest estimation. Under the influence of their present principal chief, Ongpatonga, or the Big Elk, they never go to war except in the pursuit of a predatory war-party, in consequence of which the traders have given them the reputation of being cowardly. But the history of this people shows that they have been as ambitious of martial renown, and have acquired as large a share of it, as any of their neighbours. They formerly resided in a village of dirt lodges upon Omawhaw creek, a small stream entering the Missouri about two hundred miles above the Council Bluff; but they have recently abandoned it, and are about building a town on Elk Horn river. Their number of souls is about 1500.

The Puncahs have their residence in a small village of dirt lodges, about one hundred and eighty miles above Omawhaw creek. This tribe have a common origin with the Omawhaws, and speak the same language.

Their principal chief is called Smoke Maker. Their number is about 200 souls.

The tribes above enumerated evidently sprung from the same common stock, the language of all being radically the same. They have a tradition that their fathers came from beyond the Lakes.

The Pawnees are a race of Indians distinct from the preceding, their language differing radically from that of the Indians alluded to. The Pawnees consist of three distinct bands, that have their residence at present on a branch of the river Platte called the Loup Fork, about sixty miles from the mouth of the latter, and between 100 and 115 miles westward from the Council Bluff. The three bands are distinguished by the appellation of the Grand, the Republican, and the Loup Pawnees. The two former acknowledge a common origin, but the latter deny having any natural affinity with them, though their habits, language, &c. indicate the same ancestry. They live in three villages, included within an extent of about seven miles on the north bank of the Loup Fork, all compactly built.

The village of the Grand Pawnees is situated immediately on the bank of the river, and contains about 180 earthen lodges, 900 families, or 3500 souls. The name of the principal chief of this village is Tarrarecawaho, or Long Hair.

The village of the Republican Pawnees is situated about three miles above that of the Grand Pawnees, contains about 50 lodges, 250 families, or 1000 souls. The name of their principal chief is Fool Robe, who is very much under the influence of Long Hair. This band separated many years since from the Grand Pawnees, and established themselves upon the Republican fork of Konzas river, where they were visited by Pike on his tour westward. They seem to be gradually amalgamating with the present stock, and their village wears a declining aspect.

The village of the Loup Pawnees, or Skeree, as they call themselves, is situated four miles above that last mentioned, immediately on the bank of the river; it contains about 100 dirt lodges, 500 families, or 2000 souls, making an aggregate of 6500 souls belonging to the three villages. The name of their principal chief is the Knife Chief. A few years since the Loup Pawnees had a custom of annually sacrificing a human victim to the Great Star, but this was abolished by their present chief, aided by the noble daring of his gallant son. They appear unwilling to acknowledge their affinity with the other Pawnees; but their language being very nearly the same, proves them to be of the same origin.

Although these bands are independent of each other in all their domestic concerns, government, &c., yet in their military operations they generally unite, and warfare becomes a common cause with them. Their arms are principally bows and arrows, lances, war-clubs, and shields, with some few fire-arms. They are expert horsemen, but generally fight on foot. They are more numerous, and accounted more formidable in warfare, than any other combination of savages on the Missouri. Their confidence in their own strength gives them a disposition to domineer over their weaker neighbours. They are at war with the Osages, Konzas, Sioux, Ietans, Kaskaias, Kiaways, Shiennes, Crows, &c.

The several tribes above described cultivate maize or Indian corn, pumpkins, beans, watermelons, and squashes. They hunt the bison or buffaloe, elk, deer, beaver, otter; the skins of which they exchange with the traders for fusees, powder, and lead, kettles, knives, strouding, blankets, beads, vermilion, silver ornaments, and other trinkets. They prefer the Mackinaw guns, blankets, &c., and will give a higher price for them, knowing that they are greatly superior to those furnished by American traders.

The Konzas and Osages, both of which reside in the vicinity of the meridian assumed as the eastern boundary of this section, may here be admitted to a more particular consideration than that already allowed them in this report. The Konzas Indians reside in a village of earthen lodges, situated on the north side of the river bearing their name, about one hundred miles from its mouth. Their village consists of about 130 lodges, and contains about 1500 souls. This tribe was formerly very troublesome to our traders, frequently robbing them of their goods, but since the establishment of the upper posts on the Missouri they have become very friendly. They are at war with most of the other tribes and nations herein enumerated, except the Osages and Otoes, with the last of whom they have lately made peace, through the agency of Major O'Fallon, Indian agent for the Missouri. Several Indians of the Missouri tribe reside with them.

The Osages are divided into three bands or tribes, called the Grand Osage, the Little Osage, and Clermont's band; the two former of which reside in permanent villages, situated on the head-waters of Osage river, and the last upon the Verdigrise, about sixty miles from its confluence with the Arkansa. According to Pike, whose estimate of their numbers is probably near the truth, the Grand Osage band amounts to 1695, the Little Osage to 824, and Clermont's to 1500 souls, making an aggregate of about 4000. These Indians are not accounted brave by those inhabiting the country to the north and east of them, but are the dread of those west and south of them. Although they have occasionally been chargeable with depredations committed against the whites, they have been provoked to the perpetration of them by aggressions or trespasses on the part of the latter, or else the depredations have been committed by malcontents of the nation, who will not be governed by the counsel of their chiefs. These Indians hold the people and government of the United States in the highest estimation, and have repeatedly signified their strong desire to be instructed by them in the arts of civilization. The United States have purchased from them large and valuable tracts of country for mere trifles, which the Osages have been the more willing to relinquish, under the prospect and encouragement given them, that the Americans would become their neighbours and instructors. They are in a state of warfare with all the surrounding tribes and nations of Indians, except the Konzas. It is said, that they are about forming an alliance with the Sauks and Fox Indians of the Mississippi, and that the latter are preparing to remove to their country. They have recently driven the Pawnees of Red river from their place of residence, and compelled them to seek an abode upon the head waters either of the Brases or Colorado.

The Konzas and Osages are descendants from the same common origin with the Otoes, Missouries, Ioways, Omawhaws, and Puncahs, to which may be added the Quawpaws, and several other tribes, not mentioned in this report. The languages of all of them are radically the same, but are now distinguished by a variety of dialects.

Of the Arrapahoes, Kaskaias, Kiaways, Ietans, and Shiennes.

These nations have no permanent residences or villages, but roam, sometimes in society and sometimes separately, over the tract of country constituting the section last described. They hunt the bison principally, and migrate from place to place in the pursuit of the herds of that animal, upon the flesh of which they chiefly subsist. Being thus accustomed to a roving life, they neglect the cultivation of the soil, and are compelled to subsist almost exclusively upon animal food. They formerly carried on a limited trade with the Spaniards of Mexico, with whom they exchanged dressed bison-skins for blankets, wheat, flour, maize, &c.; but their supplies of these articles are now cut off by a war, which they at present are waging against that people. They also, at distant periods, held a kind of fair on a tributary of the

Platte, near the mountains (hence called Grand Camp creek), at which they obtained British merchandize from the Shiennes of Shienne river, who obtained the same at the Mandan village from the British traders that frequent that part of our territory. Last winter they traded a great number of horses and mules with a party of white men, who had ascended Red river, but whence the party came from could not be ascertained; it however appeared probable that they were citizens of the United States, or possibly freebooters from Barataria.

The Shiennes associated with these wandering tribes are a small band of seceders from the nation of the same name residing upon Shienne river. They are said to be daring and ferocious. They are however kept under restraint by the energy and firmness of their chief. The Bear Tooth, who is the principal chief of the Arrapahoes, and the head chief of all these nations, possesses great influence over the whole. His mandates, which are uniformly characterized by discretion and propriety, are regarded by his subjects as inviolable laws.

The Kaskaia and Kiaway languages are very difficult to acquire a knowledge of. Our interpreter, who had lived several years with them, could only make himself understood by the language of signs, with the aid of a very few words of the Crow language, which many of them appeared to understand. Indeed many of the individuals of these different nations seemed to be ignorant of each other's language; for when they met, they would communicate by means of signs, with now and then an oral interjection, and would thus maintain a conversation, apparently without the least difficulty or misapprehension.

These nations are at war with all the Missouri Indians, as far down as the Osages, who are also included amongst their enemies; and it was rumoured that hostilities had recently commenced between them and the Shiennes, upon the river of the same name.

Their implements of war consist of the bow and arrow, the lance, war-club, and shield. They usually fight on horseback, and as horsemen display great skill and activity. Their habitations are leather lodges, which serve them as tents on the march, and dwellings at the places of their encampment.

Widely diffused as these Indians are, and never embodied, it is impracticable even to conjecture their numbers with any degree of probable accuracy. They rove not only throughout the section above specified, but extensively within the range of the Rocky Mountains.

The foregoing remarks concerning the Indians of this part of the country have been made for the most part agreeably to the suggestions of Mr. Say, whose attention was particularly directed to researches of this nature. But having been robbed of his notes upon the customs, manners, traditions, &c. of the western Indians, by the men who deserted from Captain Bell's party, he could give no farther account of them than what his recollection could supply. Of the Konzas, Otoes, Pawnees, and other Indians near the Council Bluff, his notes are considerably extensive; but the vessel on board of which they, with other articles, were shipped from New Orleans, having been obstructed in her passage up the Delaware by ice, we have not yet received them.

Observations embracing several traits of character common to the Indians of the western country.

An accurate and extensive knowledge of the numerous tribes and nations of Indians living within the United States' territory can only be attained by a long residence with them. They are seldom communicative, except upon subjects intimately connected with their personal experience or present interests and welfare. In regard to matters of an abstract or metaphysical nature their ideas appear to be very limited; at any rate very little is known of their sentiments upon subjects of this kind, owing, in a great measure, to the inability of the persons usually employed as interpreters to converse intelligently concerning them. The delicate trains of thought and reflection attributed to them by writers who have attempted to enlarge our acquaintance with the Indian character, usually have their origin in the ingenuity of the writers themselves. The exploits of their war-parties, and particularly those of individuals, are often recounted, but are seldom transmitted to succeeding generations, unless they are characterized by some signal advantage to the tribe or nation to which the party or individual belongs. Hence their history is very defective, affording but few incidents, and characterized by no regular series of events. In regard to the number of persons, and strength of the several tribes and nations, also the ages of individuals, no precise statements can be made; all the information given under these heads is almost without exception conjectural. In relation to subjects of this kind the Indians are either ignorant or wilfully silent; and deem it an impertinent curiosity that prompts a stranger to the investigation of them.

Notwithstanding these obstacles in the way of acquiring authentic and credible information concerning the savages, yet there are certain traits in their general character that are observable on a partial acquaintance with a variety of tribes and nations, and upon these the following remarks are grounded.

They are, almost without exception, addicted to habits of extreme indolence; self-preservation, self-defence, and recreation being their usual incitements to action. The laborious occupations of the men consist almost exclusively in hunting, warfare, and tending their horses. Their amusements are principally horse-racing, gambling, and sports of various kinds. The cultivation of corn and other vegetables, the gathering of fuel, cooking, and all other kinds of domestic drudgery, is the business of the women, the men deeming it degrading to their dignity to be occupied in employments of this kind. Their religion consists in the observance of a variety of rites and ceremonies, which they practise with much zeal and ardour. Their devotional exercises consist in singing, dancing, and the performance of various mystical ceremonies, which they believe efficacious in healing the sick, frustrating the designs of their enemies, and in giving success to any enterprize in which they may be embarked.

Amongst all these tribes and nations secret associations or councils are common, the proceedings of which are held sacred, and not to be divulged, except when the interests of the people are thought to require a disclosure. To these councils, which they denominate medicine, or rather magic feasts, none are admitted but the principal men of the nation, or such as have signalized themselves by their exploits in battle, hunting, stealing horses, or in any of the pursuits accounted laudable by the Indians.

In these assemblies the policy of making war or peace, and the manner in which it is to be effected, also all matters involving the interests of the nation, are first discussed. Having thus been the subject of deliberation in solemn council (for the proceedings at these feasts are conducted with the greatest solemnity,) the decision, of whatever nature it may be, is published to the people at large by certain members of the council performing the office of criers. On such occasions, the criers not only proclaim the measures that have been recommended, but explain the reasons of them, and urge the people zealously to support them. It is also the business of the criers, who are generally men of known valour and approved habits, and are able to enforce their precepts by the examples they have set, to harangue the people of their village daily, and exhort them to such a course of life as is deemed praiseworthy. On such occasions, which are usually selected in the stillness of the morning or evening, the crier marches through the village, uttering his exhortation in a loud voice, and endeavouring to inculcate correct principles and sentiments. The young men and children of the village are directed how to demean themselves, in order to become useful and enjoy the esteem of good men, and the favour of the good spirit. In this way they are incited to wage war or sue for peace; and to practise according to their ideas of morality and virtue; and may be swayed to almost any purpose that their elders, for such are their men of *medicine* (or as the term imports, magic wisdom), think proper to execute. They appear to have no laws, except such as grow out of habitual usages, or such as are sanctioned by common consent. The executive of their government seems to be vested in the chiefs and warriors; while the grand council of the nation is composed of the medicine council above mentioned, at which the principal chief presides. In all their acts of devotion, as also on all occasions where their confidence is to be won, or their friendship to be plighted, the smoking of tobacco seems to be invariably regarded as an inviolable token of sincerity. They believe in the existence of a Supreme Being, whom they denominate " Master of Life" or " Good Spirit," but of his attributes their ideas are vague and confused. They are generally in the habit of offering in sacrifice a portion of the game first taken on a hunting expedition, a part of the first products of the field, and often a small portion of the food provided for their refreshment. In smoking, they generally direct the first puff upward, and the second downward to the earth, or the first to the rising and the second to the setting sun; after which they inhale the smoke into their lungs, and puff it out through the nostrils for their own refreshment.

They have some indistinct notions of the immortality of the soul, but appear to know no distinction of Heaven or Hell, Elysium or Tartarus, as the abode of departed spirits.

The arts of civilized life, instead of exciting their emulation, are generally viewed by the Indians as objects unworthy of their attention. This results, as a natural consequence, from their habits of indolence. They are aware that much labour is requisite in the prosecution of them, and being accustomed from their infancy to look upon manual labour of every description as a drudgery that pertains exclusively to the female part of their community, they think it degrading to the character of men to be employed in them. Hunting, horsemanship, and warfare are the only avocations in which their ambition or sense of honour prompts them to engage.

Their reluctance to forgive an injury is proverbial. "Injuries are revenged by the injured; and blood for blood is always demanded, if the deceased has friends who dare to retaliate upon the destroyer." Instances have occurred where their revenge has become hereditary, and quarrels have been settled long after the parties immediately concerned have become extinct.

Much has been published in relation to the high antiquity of Indian tradition, of those particularly which relate to their origin and their religion. But from the examples afforded by the several nations of Indians resident upon the Mississippi and its waters, but little proof is to be had in favour of the position. It is not doubted that the immediate objects of their worship have been held in reverence by their predecessors for a long succession of ages; but in respect to any miraculous dispensations of providence, of which they have a traditional knowledge, their ideas are at best exceedingly vague and confused; and of occurrences recorded in sacred history they appear to be entirely ignorant. The knowledge they have of their ancestry is also very limited; so much so, that they can seldom trace back their pedigree more than a few generations; and then know so little of the place whence their fathers came, that they can only express their ideas upon the subject, in general terms, stating, that they came "from beyond the lakes,"—"from the rising or setting sun"— "from the north or south," &c. In some instances, where their term of residence in a place has evidently been of limited duration, they have either lost or conceal their knowledge of the country whence their ancestors came, and assert that the Master of Life created and planted their fathers on the spot where they, their posterity, now live. They have no division of time, except by years, seasons, moons, and days. Particular periods are distinguished by the growth and changes of vegetables, the migrations, incubations, &c. of birds and other animals.

Their language is of two kinds, viz. verbal and signal, or the language of signs. The former presents a few varieties, marked by radical differences, and a multiplicity of dialects peculiar to individual tribes or nations descended from the same original. The latter is a language common to most, if not all, of the western Indians, the motions or signs used to express ideas being, with some slight variations, the same amongst all of them. Nearly allied to the language of signs is a species of written language which they make use of, consisting of a few symbolical representations, and of course very limited and defective. The figures they make use of have but a faint resemblance to the object described, and are rudely imprinted upon trees, cliffs, &c. by means of paints, charcoal, and sometimes by carving with a knife or other edged tool, and are significant of some movement, achievements, or design of the Indians. A variety of figures of this description are to be seen upon the cliffs, rocks, and trees in places held sacred and frequently resorted to by the Indians, but of their import little is known. Many of these symbols are made by the magicians, or men of medicine, and are probably of sacred or devotional import.

Much intrigue, cunning, and artifice are blended with the policy of the Indians, and judging from their usual practice, it is a favourite and well approved maxim with them, that "the end sanctifies the means." In an interview with strangers it appears to be their first object to ascertain their motives and the objects of their visits; and after regarding them for some time without a show of curiosity, a variety of interrogatories are proposed, in order to satisfy themselves upon these points. This they appear to do with the view also of scrutinizing into the character and disposition of their guests. In the course of the conversation they become more and more familiar and impertinent, till at length their familiarity is succeeded by contempt and insult. Thus, from the coldest reserve, they are in a short time impelled by curiosity and a propensity to abuse, where they are not in some measure compelled to respect, to the commission of outrages, even without the slightest provocation. This kind of treatment, however, is easily obviated at the commencement of an interview, by resisting every advance made by the Indians towards familiarity, and by uniformly opposing firmness and reserve to the liberties they are disposed to take.

These attributes of the Indian character manifest themselves not only in the well-known stratagems they adopt in warfare, but in the management of their domestic concerns, in which rivalships of one kind or other are created; parties are formed and pretenders arise, claiming privileges that have been withheld from them, and placing themselves at the head of factions, occasionally withdraw from the mother tribe. Thus new tribes are formed and distributed in various directions over the country, with nothing to mark their genealogy, but the resemblance of their language to that of the parent stock, or of other Indians that sprung from the same origin.

The chiefs, or governors of tribes, have their rank and title by inheritance; yet in order to maintain them, and secure themselves in their pre-eminence, they are under the necessity of winning over to their interests the principal warriors and most influential men of their tribe, whose countenance and support are often essential to their continuance in authority. In conciliating the friendship of these, the chief is often compelled to admit them to participate in the authority with which he is invested, and to bestow upon them any effects of which he may be possessed. Thus it often happens that the chiefs are amongst the poorest of the Indians, having parted with their horses, clothes, trinkets, &c. to ensure the farther patronage of their adherents, or to purchase the friendship of those that are disaffected.

The situation of principal chief is very frequently usurped during the minority of the rightful successor, or wrested from an imbecile incumbent by some ambitious chief or warrior. In this case the ascendancy obtained over the nation by the usurper is gradual, and depends upon the resources of his own mind, aided by his reputation for generosity and valour.

The condition of the savages is a state of constant alarm and apprehension. Their security from their enemies, and their means of subsistence, are precarious and uncertain, the former requiring the utmost vigilance to prevent its infraction, and the latter being attended with no regular supplies of the necessaries of life. In times of the most profound peace, whether at their villages or on a hunting expedition, they are continually on the alert lest they should be surprised by their enemies. By day scouts are constantly kept patrolling for a considerable distance around them, and by night sentinels are posted to give notice of the approach of strangers.

When they engage in a hunt, they generally abandon their villages, old men, women, and children joining in the enterprize, through fear of being left at home without the strength of their nation to protect them. On their march they endeavour to make as great a display of force as practicable, in order to intimidate any of their enemies that may be lurking to spy out their condition. With this view they are careful to pitch their lodges or tents at the places of their encampment in such a manner, and in such numbers, as to give the impression, at a distance, that they are numerous and formidable. We have witnessed a hunting party on their march, consisting of not more than one hundred persons, including men, women, and children, yet at their encampment more than thirty lodges were pitched, each of which would accommodate at least twelve adult persons.

It is an opinion generally credited, that the Indians are possessed of strong natural appetites for ardent spirits, but there is at least room to doubt of its being well-founded. That the appetites for them are often strong and ungovernable is very certain; but they may be considered as factitious rather than natural, having been created by occasional indulgencies in the use of intoxicating liquors. Instances are not rare in which Indians have refused to accept liquor when offered them. After a long abstinence from food, any thing calculated to allay the cravings of the appetite is eagerly swallowed, and on such occasions nothing perhaps produces such an effect more speedily than spirituous liquors. Indians, while lounging about a trading establishment, are often destitute of food for a considerable time, and can obtain no other kind of refreshment from the trader but liquor, which is bestowed partly in exchange for commodities they may have to dispose of, and partly by way of encouraging them to return to him with the products of their next hunt. A small draught, on such occasions, produces intoxication, and the sudden transition from a state of gnawing hunger to that of unconcerned inebriety cannot fail to make them passionately fond of a beverage that can thus change their condition so much to their immediate satisfaction. In their use of ardent spirits, the Indians appear to be less captivated with their taste than with their exhilarating effects. The quality of liquor is not a subject of discrimination with them; provided it has sufficient strength to inebriate they are satisfied, let its character in other respects be what it may. Having contracted the habit of intoxication, they seldom appear thankful for liquor, unless it has been bestowed in such quantities as are sufficient to produce that effect.

In the indulgence of their appetites they display but few or no traits of epicurism, choosing those kinds of food that are most nutritive, without regarding their taste or flavour. In the preservation of their food, no pains are taken to render it savoury or palatable; their object is solely to reduce it to a state of security against putrefaction. They make no use of spices or other aromatics, either in preserving or cooking their food. Even salt is not considered as an essential, and is seldom used as an appendage in their cookery. This article is only prized by them on account of its usefulness for their horses. In regard to their choice of food, however, and manner of cooking it, the small variety within their reach, and the impracticability of obtaining condiments of different kinds, perhaps renders them less particular in these respects, than they would be under different circumstances. It cannot be supposed that they are entirely insensible to dainties of every description; on the contrary, they appear remarkably fond of sugar and saccharine fruits.

They appear to have a natural propensity for the fumes of tobacco, which they invariably inhale into the lungs, and eject through the nostrils. They make no use of this article except in smoking, which is an indulgence of which they are exceedingly reluctant to be deprived. When they cannot obtain tobacco, they use as a substitute the dried leaves of the sumac, the inner bark of the red willow dried, and the leaves and bark of a few other shrubs, the fumes of which are less stimulating, but equally as palatable as those of tobacco.

The Indians under consideration know not the use or value of the precious metals, except as trinkets or ornaments for their dress. They use wampum, and in some few instances shells of a small size and of a particular character, as a substitute for money. But in general furs, peltries, horses, and various articles of dress at standing or fixed rates of barter, are the immediate objects, both of internal and external trade. They do not hold their property in common, but each individual enjoys the fruit of his own toil and industry. They are accounted more or less wealthy according to the number of horses they are possessed of, and the style in which they are able to dress.

Polygamy is common amongst them, every man being allowed to have as many wives as he can maintain. Marriages are binding upon the parties only as long as they think proper to live together, and are often contracted for a limited term particularly specified. Females, during the periods of their catamenia, are excluded from society, and compelled even to sleep apart from their families, in small tents or lodges constructed for their use.

Dancing is common amongst them, both as a devotional exercise and an amusement. Their gestures on both occasions are similar, except that on the former they are accompanied by solemnity, and on the latter by cheerfulness; and are characterized by extraordinary uncouthness, rather than by gracefulness. No ribaldry, however, or tricks of buffoonery are practised on these occasions; on the contrary, their deportment is uniformly accordant with their ideas of decorum. This exercise is invariably accompanied by singing, or a kind of chanting, in which the women, who are usually excluded from a participation in the former, perform their part. Their music consists in a succession of tones of equal intervals, accompanied by occasional elevations and depressions of the voice. The modulations with which it is variegated are by no means melodious; the voices of all the chanters move in unison, and all appear to utter the same aspirations. The same series of sounds appears to be common to the chanting of all the tribes.

The foregoing are among the most common features in the general character of the western Indians. Although in a region so extensive as that inhabited by them, and amongst so great a variety of tribes and nations, a considerable diversity of character is to be expected and admitted, yet it is believed that the traits above considered are common to the whole, as a race of barbarians. And although the shades of barbarism in which they are enveloped uniformly exclude the light of civilization, yet it is not to be presumed that they are equally dark and malignant in all cases.

OF THE MISSISSIPPI, MISSOURI, AND OHIO RIVERS.

I trust it will not be deemed improper on this occasion, to offer a few remarks upon the character of these rivers, embracing more particularly the condition of their navigation.

The causes heretofore alleged as giving occasion to a diversity of soil within the valleys of the western rivers, have an effect also in giving character to their channels or beds. For example: the banks near the mouths of the rivers, being composed of a fine unctuous and adhesive alluvion, are less liable to crumble and wash away, and constitute a more permanent barrier to resist the force of the current, than those higher up, that are composed of coarser materials. In consequence, the beds of the rivers are rendered narrower and deeper towards their mouths than at greater distances above them. This is more particularly the case with the Mississippi, Red, Arkansa, and some others, whose beds or channels gradually dilate, and become more shoal on ascending from their mouths. Thus it happens also, that the navigation of the Mississippi has fewer obstructions between Natches and its mouth than above this part of the river, having so great a depth of water, that snags, bars, &c. are sunk below the reach of any kind of water-craft employed in its navigation. From Natches upward to its confluence with the Missouri, the river presents impediments that become more and more numerous and difficult to pass. Still, however, the main channel, though intricate in many places, affords a sufficient depth of water in all stages for boats of five or six feet draft to ascend to the mouth of the Ohio. From this point to the Missouri, a distance of more than two hundred and twenty miles, the navigation is partially obstructed, during a very low stage of the water, by shoals, so that it is navigable only for boats of moderate burthen, requiring but about three feet of water. At the distance of about thirty miles above the mouth of the Ohio there are two rocky bars extending across the Mississippi, called the Big and Little Chains, which in the deepest channel across them afford no more than five or six feet of water in a low stage, and occasion a great rapidity of current. The Mississippi is usually at its lowest stage about the middle of August, the summer freshet of the Missouri having subsided previously to that time. It usually continues in this stage till it is swollen by the fall freshet of the Ohio, after which it subsides again, and remains low during the winter. The distance from New Orleans to the mouth of the Missouri is estimated at about twelve hundred miles; its current in the main channel of the river is supposed to have an average velocity of three miles and three quarters per hour, in a moderate stage of the water; but when the river is high its velocity is considerably accelerated. Its water is turbid, being charged with a fine argillaceous mud, of a light colour, derived exclusively from the Missouri.

The Missouri is a very wild and turbulent river, possessing the ruder features of the Mississippi, but destitute of the gentleness characteristic of the latter in many places. The obstructions to the navigation of the Missouri, although they are of the same character with those of the Mississippi, are far more numerous and formidable than those of the latter. The channel is rendered exceedingly intricate by means of sand-bars and islands, and the navigation in many places is very hazardous, on account of the multiplicity of rafts, snags, sand-bars, &c. with which the channel is beset. No part of the river is exempt from these obstructions for any considerable distance, particularly when the water is low.

As this river in connexion with some of its principal tributaries traverses a considerable variety of climates, embracing more than ten degrees of latitude, a succession of spring freshets invariably takes place, and maintains an elevated stage of water from the breaking up of winter early in March, to the middle, and sometimes the last of July, when the summer freshet, yielded by the most northerly of its tributaries, takes place. During this period there is a sufficient depth to admit boats of almost any burthen; but during the residue of the year it can hardly be called navigable, except for boats drawing no more than twenty-five or thirty inches. The river is usually blocked up with ice during the winter season. The average velocity of its current, in a middling stage of water, may be estimated at four miles and one third. In time of a high freshet it moves with an accelerated velocity, equal to five or five and half miles per hour.

The Ohio river, as before hinted, differs from those just described, in the rapidity of its current, the width of its bed, the character of its channel, and in several other respects ; but as its general character is well known, a few remarks in relation to it will here suffice. The obstructions to its navigation are sand-bars, some few rafts and mags, and rapids, to which the intricacy of its channel in several places may be added. During a middle and high stage of water, the obstructions entirely disappear, and an accelerated current is the only difficulty to be encountered. The average velocity of the current, in a moderate stage of water, may be estimated at two miles and a half, and in a high stage, at three miles per hour. The season in which the navigation of the Ohio can be relied on, commences between the middle of February and first of March, and continues to the latter part of June. A fall freshet usually takes place in October or November, and the river is again navigable for a few weeks. During the rest of the year, boats of inconsiderable burthen meet with numerous obstructions in their progress from the lowness of the water, and in many places no channel can be found of sufficient depth to admit their passage. At the distance of about seventeen miles from its mouth is the first serious obstruction to its navigation, consisting of a lime-stone bar extending across the river, denominated the Big Chain. Three miles above is another of a similar description. The range of rocks, of which these appear to be a portion, seems to extend across the point of land situated between the Ohio and Mississippi, presenting itself again on the latter, at the Big and Little Chains before mentioned. The falls of the Ohio at Louisville are impassable for boats of burthen, except in the higher stages of the water. Le Turt's Falls, and numerous other rapids, denominated ripples, are also impassable for boats of heavy burthen when the river is at its lowest stages. In this state the river is fordable in numberless places.

OF THE GREAT VALLEY OR BASIN OF THE MISSISSIPPI.

This vast region, embracing more than twenty degrees of latitude and about thirty of longitude, although it has been explored in various directions by men of intelligence, is yet but imperfectly known; and probably no country in the world affords a more ample or interesting field for philosophic investigation. A thorough acquaintance with its geological character would in all probability lead to the most important conclusions in forming a correct theory of the earth, while a knowledge of its vegetable and mineral productions may be conducive to the comforts and enjoyments of a large portion of the human family. All we shall presume to offer under this copious head, will be a few general remarks relative to the position and conformation of the valley, grounded almost exclusively upon the hydrography of the country, so far as it has come under our observation.

The valley is bounded on the west by the Rocky Mountains, on the east and south-east by the Alleghanies, and on the south by the Gulf of Mexico. To the northward, no precise limits can be assigned as its boundary. Although many have supposed that the waters of the Mississippi are separated from those running north-westwardly into the Pacific Ocean, and north-eastwardly into the Atlantic, by a mountainous range of country, yet, from the best information that can be had on the subject, the fact is quite otherwise. The old and almost forgotten statement of savage origin, viz. that " four of the largest rivers on the continent have their sources in the same plain," is entitled to far more credit. The rivers alluded to are the Mississippi, the St. Lawrence, the Saskashawin, and the Oregon or M'Kenzie's river. Agreeably to the accounts of Colonel Dixon and others who have traversed the country situated between the Missouri and the Assinaboin, a branch of Red river of Hudson's Bay, no elevated ridge is to be met with; but, on the contrary, tributaries to both these streams take their rise in the same champaign, and wind their way in various directions to their far distant estuaries. Judging from the maps that have been given of the country near the sources of the Mississippi, and of the region generally situated northwardly of the great lakes, as also from the accounts of various travellers who have penetrated many parts of those countries, the same remarks appear equally applicable to a large portion of the whole. The watercourses are represented as chains of lakes of various magnitudes, while lakes and stagnant pools are scattered in almost every direction, without ridges or perceptible declivities to show the direction in which they are drained. But we forbear to enlarge on this subject, and beg leave that reference may be had to Bouchette's map of the region of which we have just been treating, as a document containing ample illustrations of our opinion. Hence it will be inferred that the valley of the Mississippi is merely a portion of an immense region of valley or flat country, extending from the Gulf of Mexico north-eastwardly to the Atlantic, and north-westwardly to the Pacific Ocean.

Within the valley or region drained by the Mississippi, are situated no less than three distinct ranges of mountainous country, the localities of which we will attempt to point out. The first and most considerable is a range of mountains commencing within the Spanish province of Texas, and stretching in a north-eastward direction, till it is terminated by the high lands on the lower part of the Missouri river. To this range we have given the name of the Ozark

Mountains, an appellation by which the Arkansa river was formerly distinguished, as also the tribe of Indians, since denominated the Quawpaws, inhabiting near that river. Its direction is nearly parallel to that of the Alleghanies. Its peaks and ridges are less elevated than those of the latter, and do not present the same regularity in their arrangement. The second is denominated the Black Hills, commencing on the South or Padouca fork of the river Platte, at the distance of about one hundred miles eastward of the Rocky Mountains, and stretching north-eastwardly towards the great northerly bend of the Missouri. Of this range very little is yet known; and the fact that there is such a range is partially substantiated by the concurrent testimony of the traders and hunters of the Missouri, with whom it is a noted landmark, but it is more fully corroborated by the hydrography of the country, as may be shown by the map.

The third is a range of hilly and broken country, commencing on the Wisconsan near the Portage, and extending northwardly to Lake Superior. To this range we have taken the liberty to give the name of the Wisconsan Hills. The Ocooch and Smokey Mountains before mentioned, are connected with this range. In its geological character, and more especially in its metallic productions, so far as our inquiry will enable us to decide, it appears nearly allied to the Ozark Mountains, and circumstances are not wanting to induce the opinion, that they were once the same continuous range. Dr. James is decidedly of opinion, that the metalliferous region of the Mississippi, which extends from Red river to Lake Superior in the direction of these two ranges, strongly indicates that a continuous range, as just hinted, once had an existence.

The Mississippi river may be regarded as occupying the lowest part of the valley, from its great estuary, the Gulf of Mexico, to its confluence with the Missouri and Illinois. Thence to Lake Michigan, the immediate valley of the Illinois is to be viewed as the lowest part of the great valley under consideration. This conclusion necessarily results from an attentive consideration of the characters of the three rivers just mentioned. If the inclinations of the plains down which these rivers respectively flow, be in any degree proportionate to the velocities of their currents, the plain of the Illinois will be found to have far the least inclination, inasmuch as the velocity of its current is not more than one-fourth of that of either of the others. But in order to have a more distinct view of the matter, let us assume the parallel of latitude intersecting the Illinois at its head, or point of confluence of the Kankakee and Des Plaines rivers, and suppose a vertical section cut in the direction of the parallel. Such a section would intersect the Missouri at the distance of nearly seven hundred miles from its mouth, the Mississippi at about two hundred and sixty, and the Illinois at two hundred and fifty from the same point. Hence, allowing that the plains of each have the same inclination, the point of intersection on the Missouri would be at a greater elevation than that on the Mississippi, and that on the Illinois would be less elevated than either. But the difference of inclination in these plains is manifest, not only from the comparative velocities of the several streams alluded to, but from the circumstance, that the Illinois is destitute of any considerable rapids throughout its whole course, whereas the Mississippi, in addition to a current uniformly more rapid, is hurried down the De Moyen rapids, eleven miles in length; and the Missouri, without a perversion of terms, may be denominated a rapid throughout the distance above specified. By a similar course of reasoning it may also be made to appear, that the assumed point of intersection on the Illinois is less elevated than any other point in the same parallel of latitude between that river and Lake Erie, and even that it is somewhat lower than the surface of the lake itself; for the aggregate descent, from the surface of Lake Michigan to the point under consideration, is evidently greater than from the surface of the same lake to that of Lake Erie; or, in other words, the descent of the Des Plaines, from Chicago to its confluence with the Kankakee, is greater by a few feet than that of the stream uniting Lakes Huron and Erie.

This view of the subject affords us a clue whereby to ascertain, with some degree of precision, the aggregate fall of the water, from the head of the Illinois, to the Gulf of Mexico. Agreeably to the surveys of the Great Canal of New York, the elevation of Lake Erie above tide-water is found to be 564 feet. Hence we may assume, in round numbers, 450 feet as the altitude of the head of the Illinois above the ocean.

Of the conformation of the valley in other respects, no other ideas can be advanced but such as are suggested by a general view of the topography of the country, and especially of the courses of the principal rivers, as exhibited in the map of the country drained by the Mississippi. We will only add, that the inclined plain constituting the western side of the valley, or, in other words, the great slope down which the Red, Canadian, Arkansa, Konzas, Platte, and other large rivers have their courses, has probably a greater general inclination than any other side of the valley. In forming an estimate of the aggregate descent of this slope, commencing at tide-water, and extending to the base of the Rocky Mountains, Pike allows 8000 feet, which probably exceeds the truth by more than one-half. We would substitute 3000 feet as the aggregate elevation of the base of the mountains above the ocean, and are of opinion, that this amount rather exceeds the truth. This altitude, added to that of James's Peak as before stated, would give for the height of that Peak above the ocean, 11,500 feet; comparing this altitude with that of the " inferior limit of perpetual snow," as estimated by M. De Humboldt for the latitude of 40 degrees, viz. 9846 feet above the ocean, we find the summit of the Peak 1654 feet higher than that elevation; and judging from appearances, this difference of altitude seemed sufficiently well marked by the distance to which the snow extended from the summit downward, upon the sides of the Peak, to authenticate in a good degree the calculation above stated.

The foregoing report is intended as a civil rather than a military description of the country. For a partial description of its military features, I beg leave to refer to my report of the 12th May, 1818, to Brigadier General T. A. Smith, on file in the War Department.

In the performance of topographical duties I have been aided by Lieutenants Graham and Swift, who have rendered essential service in these and other operations. The former of these gentlemen is at present occupied in completing the calculations upon the various astronomical and other observations we took in connexion with our duties; the latter is engaged in delineating the surveys made in behalf of the expedition.

The services of Captain Bell are to be recognized as highly important and useful to the expedition, in keeping a journal of our proceedings, and conducting detached parties whenever an occasion required. He is now busily engaged in revising his journal, a copy of which will soon be in readiness to be disposed of agreeably to your instructions.

The duties in the various departments of natural science were discharged with zeal and ability by Mr. Say and Dr. James, assisted by Mr. Peale, who was active and industrious in the collection and preservation of such rare specimens of animals, &c. as came under our observation. The vessel on board of which most of these specimens were shipped from New Orleans, has very lately arrived in this port, and discharged our packages in good order. I take this opportunity to express my acknowledgements of the politeness of her owners, Messrs. Price and Morgan, who have kindly franked the transportation of the collections. A catalogue, embracing the zoology of the country explored by us, is shortly expected from Mr. Say, and shall be forwarded by the earliest opportunity. Dr. James has been instructed also to furnish a mineralogical and botanical catalogue, which is daily expected. Both of these are intended as accompaniments to this report.

Mr. Seymour has taken numerous landscape views, exhibiting the characteristic features of various parts of the country, besides many others of detached scenery.

A map of the country situated between the meridian of Washington City and the Rocky Mountains, shall be reported as soon as the necessary elements and data can be compiled and the drawings executed.

I have the honour to be, Sir,
most respectfully,
Your obedient and humble Servant,
S. H. LONG,
Major U.S. Engineers.

Honourable J. C. Calhoun,
Secretary of War.

OBSERVATIONS

ON

THE MINERALOGY AND GEOLOGY

OF

A PART OF THE UNITED STATES

WEST OF THE MISSISSIPPI.

Extracted from a Report to Major Long.

OBSERVATIONS, &c.*

The following remarks are designed to give a summary and connected view of the facts and observations collected during the progress of the exploring expedition, relative to the geology and mineralogy of the several regions traversed by the party, more particularly of the Rocky Mountains, and the western portions of the great valley of the Mississippi. In an attempt of this kind, some difficulty arises from the unsettled and progressive condition of geognostic science. A nomenclature, constructed upon principles applicable to the other branches of natural history, has been extended to this. Attempts have been made to define classes, orders, genera, and species of rocks; while it must be acknowledged, that the inventors of systems have hitherto failed to point out such infallible foundations for distinction of character as exist in the animal and vegetable kingdoms. Among minerals, from one extreme of the series to the other, there is a constant transition of approximating aggregates into each other. The particles of unorganized matter, being exempt from the influence of those peculiar laws which regulate the forms and characters of living

---

* The Report from which these observations are extracted was drawn up at Smithland, Kentucky, in January, 1820, soon after the return of the exploring party from the Rocky Mountains. Since that time, opportunities have been wanting to supply the deficiency of study and comparison, for which that place, remote from all collections of books and minerals, did not afford the means. We may be allowed to mention these circumstances in extenuation of our apparent neglect of many recent innovations in geology, and of some late works, with which we had not the opportunity to be acquainted.

beings, and moving in obedience only to the impulses of attraction and affinity, arrange themselves together not always in an invariable order, and after a permanent and unalterable type, but are variously intermixed and confounded, as circumstances may have variously influenced their aggregation. Definitions, it must be acknowledged, have been constructed, strictly applicable to particular portions of matter, which may occur under similar circumstances in remote quarters of the globe. Fragments of granite may be found in the Rocky Mountains of America which could not be distinguished from the granite of Egypt, such as is seen in our collections. These definitions, then, may be sufficient for the purposes of the naturalist who confines his inquiries to his cabinet; but when examinations are extended, when we approach the imaginary limits of these artificial divisions, we not uncommonly find ourselves deserted by our boasted distinctions and definitions. It must be evident to any person in the slightest degree familiarized to the examination of the rocky materials composing the earth's surface, that between any two of the contiguous artificial divisions there is oftentimes no definite and discoverable boundary. Granite must consist essentially of felspar, quartz, and mica; so must gneiss and mica-slate; and between the two former, it is often extremely difficult to point out the line which shall be considered as marking the termination of the one and the commencement of the other. It will, we think, be acknowledged, that not one of the names applied to rocks, as constituting extensive strata, conveys of itself a definite and satisfactory idea. Hence the necessity which is felt, in attempting to give a detailed account of the rock formations of any particular district, to define the names in almost every instance of their application. If the following remarks should on this account seem faulty, by a certain monotony and appearance of repetition, we hope there are a few, who, for the sake of the facts detailed, will excuse any want of precision in the language which may have necessarily resulted from the unsettled condition of the nomenclature.

No part of the earth, it is probable, presents a greater degree of simplicity and uniformity in the structure and conformation of its surface than North America. The mountain ranges are here distinct, forming each its own particular system, and preserving severally, through their whole extent, a similarity in external appearance, as well as in the structure and aggregation of the various rocks of which they are composed.

The outlines of a physical delineation of the continent of North America would present, first, the great chain of the Rocky Mountains, evidently a continuation of the Andes of the southern hemisphere, stretching parallel to the direction of the western coast from the isthmus of Panama to the northern ocean. Their summits penetrating far into the regions of perpetual winter, look down upon the vast plains of the Mississippi and its tributaries; in which we distinguish a comparatively inconsiderable range of rocky hills, commencing near the confluence of the Missouri and Mississippi, and running south-west of the Gulf of Mexico, near the estuary of the Rio del Norte. Beyond these, the surface subsides to a plain, stretching eastward to the commencement of the great chain of the Alleghanies. The range of the Alleghanies, far less elevated and alpine than that of the Rocky Mountains, traverses the continent in a direction nearly parallel to the Atlantic ocean, from the Gulf of St. Lawrence, on the north-east, to the confluence of the Alabama and Tombigbee rivers, in the south-west. Compared to the Rocky Mountains, this range is without summits, presenting, instead of conic peaks, long and level ridges, rising in no point to the inferior limit of perpetual frost, and scarce in any instance reaching that degree of elevation which is incompatible with the growth of forests.

In many particulars there is a manifest resemblance between the Alleghanies, and the comparatively inconsiderable group known by the name of the Ozark mountains. They are parallel in direction, making an angle of about forty degrees with the great range of the Andes. They agree in having their most elevated portions made up of rocks of recent formation. It is well known, that, from the highly primitive gneiss rock at Philadelphia, there is a gradual ascent, across strata more and more recent, to the rocks of the coal formation, about the summit of the Alleghanies. Whether the same thing happens in every part of the range, our examinations have not yet been extensive enough to decide. We know that some of the granitic mountains of New England are far surpassed in elevation by the neighbouring hills and ridges of mica slate, talcose rocks, or even more recent aggregates.

In the Ozark mountains, as far as they have been hitherto explored, the granites and more ancient rocks are found at the lowest parts, being surmounted by those of a more recent date, the newest horizontal sandstone, and strata of compact limestone, forming the highest summits. What we wish to remark is, that the reverse of this being the case with the Rocky Mountains, the granite there far surpassing, both in extent and elevation, all the other aggregates forming the central and higher portions of all the ridges, that range has a character very distinct from the Ozark or Alleghany mountains.

It has been suggested by Major Long, that the hydrography of the upper portion of the Missouri seems to indicate the existence of a mountain range, approaching that river from the south-west, near the great northern bend, in the country of the Mandans. From Lewis and Clarke we have also some accounts tending to the confirmation of this opinion. Further examination may perhaps prove this third range, called the Black hills, to resemble in direction and general character the Alleghany and Ozark mountains. The Rocky Mountains have not inaptly been called the backbone of the continent: these three lateral ranges, going off at an angle of about forty degrees, may with equal propriety be called the ribs. In latitude 38° north, the eastern base of the Rocky Mountains is found to be in about 106° west longitude: following the same parallel of latitude eastward, you arrive at the base of the Ozark mountains, nearly in longitude 94°. The intervening space, occupying the extent of near twelve degrees of longitude, is a wide and desolate plain, destitute of timber; scorched in summer by the reverberation of the rays of the sun, howled over in winter by the frozen west winds from the Rocky Mountains.

Though we have assumed twelve degrees of longitude as the medium width of this great plain, it is to be remarked, that to many parts of it our examinations have not been extended. In the latitude of 41°, no mountain, and scarce an elevation deserving the name of a hill, occurs between the western range of the Alleghanies and the Rocky Mountains. But at no great distance north of this parallel, low ranges of hills begin to appear in the region south-west of Lake Michigan; and though too inconsiderable in point of elevation to deserve particular notice, still they exhibit peculiar characters, which seem to designate an intimate connection with the Ozark mountains, south of the Missouri. The same succession of strata, the same alternation of crystalline beds, with those of mechanical deposition, and similar depositories of metallic ores, are observed here, as in the regions about the Merameg and St. Francis. A marked difference is also, as we think, to be discovered between the rocks and soils on the different sides of this range. Of this we shall speak more particularly in another place. For our present purpose, it is sufficient to assume as a boundary of the region we propose first to consider, a line running from the confluence of the Arkansa and Canadian rivers on the south-west, to the junction of the Mississippi and Wisconsan, on the north-east. Assuming this as the direction of the range of the Ozark mountains, it will be perceived, by examining the map, that to the north-west of this line spreads an extensive plain, reaching to the base of the Rocky Mountains. This plain has been crossed in three different places by the exploring party, as already detailed in our narrative; once in ascending by the River Platte, between latitude 40° and 41° 30'; again, in descending the Arkansa, in 38°; and, thirdly, by the route of the Canadian, in 34°. To the information collected in these journeys, we have added a little from other sources; but the greater part of this extensive region yet remains unknown.

Of the Great Desert at the base of the Rocky Mountains.

The portion of country which we design to consider under this division has an average width of five or six hundred miles, extending along the base of the Rocky Mountains from north to south: as far as we have any acquaintance with that range, consisting entirely of granitic sands, or of secondary aggregates made up of the *detritus* of that great chain of primitive mountains, there seems to be a degree of propriety in designating it by some name recognising relation to those mountains. It has been mentioned as the " Mexican desert ;" a name sufficiently applicable, perhaps, to some portions of it, but one by no means to be extended to every part alike, as there can be little doubt of its occupying an extensive portion of the interior of North America. That a similar desert region exists on the western side of the mountains, we have sufficient evidence; but whether as uninterrupted and as extensive, we have not the means of determining.

The Jesuit Venegas, speaking of the early history of California, says " Father Kino and his companions, after travelling thirty leagues from San. Marcelo, came to a small rancheria (Indian village); and leaving on the north the great mountain of Santa Clara, whose sides, for the length of a league, are covered with pumice-stone, they arrived at the *Sandy Waste*, on the 19th of March." Our information is, however, too limited to justify an attempt to fix the boundaries of this desert; we will, therefore, content ourselves with communicating the observations our opportunities have enabled us to make.

The channel of the Missouri, near the mouth of the Platte, discloses here and there rocks of horizontal limestone; which, from their peculiar character, we are disposed to consider as belonging rather to the Ozarks, than having any connection with the Rocky Mountains. These rocks appear at the lowest parts of the valleys, and are usually surmounted by extensive beds of soil, consisting principally of flinty sand in the most minute state of division, but variously intermixed with the remains of organized beings, and sometimes with calcareous and aluminous earth. Proceeding westward, the sand becomes deeper and more unmixed; not a rock or a stone, in place or out of place, is to be met with for some hundreds of miles. It is believed that no rocky bluffs appear along the valley of the Platte, within three hundred miles of its mouth, though a small part of this distance, on the lower portion of the river, has not hitherto been explored. The surface is not an absolute plain, but is varied with gentle undulations, such as the draining of water, from an immense table of a light arenaceous earth, for a succession of centuries, may be supposed to have occasioned. The gradual intermixture of the exuviæ of animals and vegetables, with what was formerly a pure siliceous sand, has at length produced a soil capable of supporting a scanty growth of grasses ; now almost the only covering of these desolate regions. Scales of mica, little particles of brownish felspar, and minute fragments of hornblende, may here be detected in the soil.

About four hundred miles west of the mouth of the Platte, a low range of sandstone hills crosses the country from south-west to north-east. The strata composing these hills have no perceptible inclination, and present appearances which indicate their deposition to have been nearly contemporaneous to that of many of our coal formations. It has already been suggested that this range may probably be a continuation of the Cotes Noir, or Black hills, said to contain the sources of the Shienne, the Little Missouri, and some branches of the Yellow Stone. *

These inconsiderable hills being passed, the surface again subsides nearly to a plain. The fine and comparatively fertile sand which prevailed to the east of the ranges, is exchanged for a gravel made up of rounded granitic fragments, varying in dimensions from the size of a six-pound shot to finish sand. This great mass of granitic fragments, evidently brought down by the agency of water from the sides and summits of the Andes, slopes gradually from their base, appearing, as far as examinations have extended, to correspond in some measure, in magnitude, to the elevation and extent of that part of the mountains opposite which it is placed. The minute particles derived from the quartzy portions of the primitive aggregates, being least liable to decomposition, have been carried to the greatest dis-

* Lewis and Clarke's History, vol. i. p. 83. Philadelphia, 1814.

tance, and now form the almost unmixed soil of the eastern margin of the great sandy desert. The central portions are of a coarser sand, with which some particles of felspar and mica are intermixed: nearer the mountains, pebbles and boulders become frequent, and at length almost cover the surface of the country.

The opinion above advanced, that the great sandy desert has resulted from the wearing down of the mountains, both before and since the retiring of the ocean, should, perhaps, be received with some caution. We have no foundation for the belief, but in the examinations which enabled us to discover that the materials composing both regions are similar in kind; that the granitic soils of the plain are precisely such as would result from the disintegration of the rocks now existing in the mountains; and that the numerous deep ravines and water-worn valleys traversing the mountains in various directions, indicate the change here supposed to have happened.

It is probable many parts of this extensive desert may differ from that traversed by the Platte, in having the surface more or less covered with horizontal strata of sandstone and conglomerate, instead of loose sand and pebbles. Indeed, there are many appearances indicating that a formation of this kind formerly extended down the Platte much farther than at present. From the minute account given in the narrative of the expedition, of the particular features of this region, it will be perceived that its eastern portions bear a manifest resemblance to the deserts of Siberia. The soils, and I believe the rocks, wherever any occur, are saline: plants allied to chenopodium and salsola are peculiarly abundant, as are the astragali and other herbaceous leguminæ; while trees and forests are almost unknown.

The surface of the sandy plain rises perceptibly towards the base of the mountains; and becoming constantly more and more undulating, is at length broken, disclosing some cliffs and ledges of micaceous sandstone. Near the Platte this sandstone occurs in horizontal strata, sometimes divided by the beds of the streams, and forming low ridges parallel to the Rocky Mountains. Whether they continue in an uninterrupted line along the base of the mountains, we have not been able to ascertain. They are separated from the first range of primitive, by more elevated cliffs of a similar sandstone, having its strata in a highly inclined position. Behind these, occur lofty but uninterrupted ranges of naked rocks, destitute of any covering of earthy or vegetable matter, and standing nearly perpendicular. At a distant view, they present to the eye the forms of walls, towers, pyramids, and columns, seeming rather the effects of the most laborious efforts of art, than the productions of nature. When surveyed from the more elevated summits of the first granitic range, these immense strata of sandstone standing on edge, and sometimes inclining at various angles towards the primitive, resemble the plates of ice often seen thrown into a vertical position in the eddies and along the banks of rivers.

Climbing to the summits of such of these elevations as are accessible, and crossing their stratifications towards the primitive, we observe appearances similar to those found in the valleys, when circumstances enable us to push our inquiries to a corresponding extent below the surface. Having crossed the upturned margin of the whole secondary formation which occupies the plain, and arriving at the primitive, we find these highly inclined strata of sandstone reposing immediately against the granite. We search in vain for any traces of those rocks distinguished by the Wernerians as rocks of the transition period. We also observe an entire deficiency of all those primitive strata which the doctrine of universal formations may have taught us to look for in approaching the granite.

The sandstone along the base of the mountains,

though apparently not very recent, contains the remains of marine animals and plants, and embraces some extensive beds of puddingstone. It may be remarked that the sand and gravel composing these aggregates have in general the same close resemblance to the materials of the granitic mountains, as we have already observed in the uncemented materials of the plain. Indeed, it does not seem easy to determine whether the sands, gravel-stones, and pebbles, now loosely strewed over the extensive plains of the desert, have been brought down immediately from the granitic mountains whence they were originally derived, or have resulted from the disintegration of the stratified sandstone and conglomerates deposited during a long series of ages, while the waters of the ocean rested upon the great plain, and washed the bases of the Rocky Mountains. The very wide and equal distribution of these sands, in other words, the very gradual slope of the *débris* of the mountain, would seem to countenance the latter supposition.

The position of the strata of sandstone varies in the distance of a few miles from nearly horizontal to an inclination of more than sixty degrees, and that without any very manifest change of character, or the interposition of any other stratum. The laminæ most distant from the primitive, occupying the eastern sides of the first elevations, though lowest in actual elevation, may with propriety be considered the uppermost, as resting on those beyond. At the level of the surface of the great plain, they sink beneath the alluvial; and in the neighbourhood of the river Platte, they are no more seen. The uppermost are of a yellowish-gray colour; moderately fine; compact and hard; constantly varying, however, at different points, in colour as well as most other characters. The light-coloured varieties usually contain small round masses about the size of a musket-ball, which are more friable than the rock itself, from which they are easily detached, leaving cavities corresponding to their own shape and dimensions. They are commonly of a dark-brown colour, and of a coarser sand than that which constitutes the rock itself. Where these are found, I could never discover any of those remains of shellfish so distinctly seen in many of the secondary rocks in this neighbourhood.

Passing downwards, or in other words, proceeding towards the primitive, crossing the edge of the secondary, the sandstone becomes more coarse and friable, its colour inclining more to several shades of brown and red. This variety contains numerous masses of iron ore, and does not appear to abound in the remains or impressions of organized beings. It is also less distinctly stratified than that just mentioned; and it often becomes exceedingly coarse, with angular fragments intermixed, being in no respect different from the rock denominated breccia, and by some geologists considered a distinct stratum.

This tract of sandstone, which skirts the eastern boundary of the Rocky Mountains, and appears to belong to that immense secondary formation which occupies the valley of the Mississippi, abounds in scenery of a grand and interesting character. The angle of inclination of the strata often approaches $90°$, and is very rarely less than $45°$. That side of the ridges next the primitive appears to have been broken off from a part of the stratum beyond; and is usually an abrupt and perpendicular precipice, sometimes even overhanging and sheltering a considerable extent of surface. The face of the stratum is usually smooth and hard, and both sides are alike destitute of soil and verdure. Elevations of this description are met with, varying from twenty to several thousand feet in thickness; neither are they by any means uniform in height. Some of them rise, probably, three hundred or four hundred feet; and considering their singular character, would appear high, were they not subjected to an immediate and disadvantageous comparison with the stupendous Andes, at whose feet they are placed. Their summits in some instances are regular and horizontal, and are crowned with a scanty growth of cedar and pine. Where the cement and most of the materials of the sandstone are siliceous, the rock evinces a tendency to break into fragments of a rhombic form; and in this case the elevated edge presents an irregularly notched or serrated surface.

Sandstones consisting of silex, with the least intermixture of foreign ingredients, are the most durable. But in the region of which we speak, the variations in the composition, cement, and characters of the sandstone, are innumerable. Clay and oxide of iron entering into its composition in certain proportions, seem to render it unfit to withstand the attacks of the various agents, whose effect is to hasten dissolution and decay. Highly elevated rocks of this description may well be supposed in a state of rapid and perceptible change. The sharp angles and asperities of surface which they may have originally presented, are soon worn away; the matter constantly removed by the agency of water from their sides and summits is deposited at their feet; their elevation gradually diminishes, and even the inclination of their strata becomes at length obscure or wholly undiscoverable. This appears to have been a part of the process by which numerous conic hills and mounds have been interspersed among the highly inclined naked rocks above mentioned. These hills, often clothed with considerable verdure to their summits, add greatly to the beauty of the surrounding scenery. The contrast of colours in this rude but majestic region, is often seen to produce the most brilliant and grateful effects. The deep green of the small and almost procumbent cedars and junipers, with the less intense colours of various species of deciduous foliage, acquires new beauty from being placed as a margin to the glowing red and yellow seen in the surfaces of many of the rocks.

Of the Sandstones of the Rocky Mountains.

Having commenced our account of the Rocky Mountains with the consideration of that vast accumulation of rounded fragments constituting the Great Desert, which may be reckoned the most recent formation connected with that great range of mountains, we proceed to speak of the sandstones, the next member in the inverted order we have adopted; and here we take occasion to remark the peculiar grandeur and simplicity of features which distinguish the mineral geography of this part of our continent. We have here a stupendous chain of granitic mountains, many hundred miles in extent, and with no stratified rocks resting about their sides, except a few sandstones, equally granitic, and almost equally primitive. We discover here comparatively few traces of that magnificent profusion of animal and vegetable life, which in other parts of the globe has reared mountains of limestone, clay-slate, and those other aggregates, which if not entirely, are often in a great measure, made up of the exuviæ of living beings. We shall not here be understood to contradict the assertion we have before made, that the sandstones along the base of the Rocky Mountains contain organized remains, and bear abundant evidence of having been at a comparatively recent period deposited gradually from the waters of the ocean. The particular we wish to remark as distinguishing these mountains most strikingly from the Alleghanies, and many other ranges, is the entire want of the aggregates referred by the Wernerians to the transition period, as well as nearly all the stratified primitive rocks, and the limestones of the secondary formations. [19] This great range, as far as hitherto known to us, lies nearly from north to south. Considered topographically, the sandstone formation belongs both to the mountains and the plains, sloping down from the sides of the granite, and disappearing under the sands of the Great Desert.

The western boundary of this formation of sandstone, as far as our examinations have searched, appears to be defined, and corresponds to the side of the easternmost granitic ranges. From the Platte towards the south, the sandstone increases in width, and on the Canadian it extends more than half the distance from the sources of that river to its confluence with the Arkansa. This sandstone formation we consider as consisting essentially of two members.

1st. *Red sandstone.* — This rock, which is the lowest of the horizontal or fletz rocks met with in this part of the country, is very abundant in all the region immediately subjacent to the Rocky Mountains. We have never met with a similar rock in the eastern part of the valley of the Mississippi. It occurs at intervals along the base of the mountain, reposing against the primitive rocks, in an erect or highly inclined position. It varies in colour from bright brick red, to dark brown; and is sometimes found exhibiting various shades of yellow and gray. It is, however, almost invariably ferruginous; and the predominance of red in the colouring certainly entitles it to the distinctive appellation of red sandstone. The lowest part of the stratum has frequently least colour, and is also the most compact and hard. This is not, however, invariably the case; for in the neighbourhood of the Platte, that part of it which lies immediately upon the granite is white, and contains beds of coarse conglomerate or puddingstone. At the lowest points we have been able to examine, are found embodied large oval or irregular masses of hornstone, usually of a yellowish-white, or bluish colour; and near the surface of these masses are found the few well-marked organic relics the stratum can be said to contain. Higher up the rock becomes much softer, and usually of a browner colour. It is disposed in immense horizontal laminæ or strata, which, when broken transversely, exhibit some tendency to separate into fragments of a rhombic form. Near the upper part of the stratum are frequently seen broad belts of a lighter colour, conspicuously marked with reticulating yellowish veins. The cross fracture of the stone is even and earthy, except in the conservatories. When divided in a direction parallel to that of the strata, small scales of mica are seen; but this is usual only in those parts of the stone where natural seams or fissures existed. Small specimens from many parts of this stratum could not be distinguished from the red sandstone quarried at Nyae in New Jersey, and used in great quantities in the cities of New York, Albany, &c. for building. The character which most particularly distinguishes this rock from " the old red sandstone of Werner," pointed out by Maclure in New York and New Jersey, appears to be the constant accompaniment of gypsum, and muriate of soda; the colour of the stratum is also in general of a brighter red, approaching vermilion, and is more copiously imparted to such streams of water as traverse it.

2d. *Argillaceous or gray sandstone.* — Immediately above the red sandstone, we have invariably found, where any rock rests upon it, a grayish or yellowish-white sandstone, which we distinguish as the second variety. It most frequently contains a large proportion of argillaceous earth in the cement, and has a more or less slaty structure. Hence it may with propriety be denominated argillaceous sandstone, though it may in some respects differ from the rock known to many by that name. This variety being uppermost in actual position, is perhaps more frequently seen than the other, while at the same time it is probably less abundant. The line of separation betwixt the two is often manifest and well defined; and in other instances, they pass by imperceptible gradations into each other.

The upper, or gray sandstone, is usually more compact and homogenous than the red; it breaks like the other, though more rarely, into large cubic or rhombic masses, which, on account of the more compact texture of the stone, retain their form longer than those of the other variety. The precipices formed by both are often lofty and perpendicular; but the projections and angles of the red are more worn and rounded than those of the gray. The narrow defiles and ravines which the streams of water have excavated, are less tortuous when they are made entirely in the gray sandstone, than in other instances. The springs of water flowing from it are more free of mineral impregnations, than such as are found in the other variety. It sometimes consists of glittering crystalline particles, but does not in this case appear to be a chymical deposit. In fine, it appears under an endless variety of characters, of which it would be in vain to attempt the enumeration. Although the gray sandstone is not invariably distinguished by the presence of an argillaceous ingredient, yet it is constantly found accompanying soft clay-slate, or bituminous shale and coal, wherever these last are met with.

If this formation of sandstone, consisting of the two varieties just mentioned, ever extended across the valley of the Mississippi to the Alleghany mountains, as some might be disposed to believe, we cannot pretend to determine what was its position relative to the immense masses of fletz, limestone, and other rocks now found in that valley. But as the red variety is still extensively disseminated, and usually accompanied by those valuable substances, salt and plaister, it may not be amiss to trace, as far as our examinations have enabled us to do it, the outline of the region which it occupies. As we have before mentioned, it is found in the vicinity of the river Platte, in a highly inclined position, covering a narrow margin immediately at the foot of the Rocky Mountains.

From the accounts of Lewis and Clarke, we are induced to believe that it exists under similar circumstances, near the falls of the Missouri. On the Canadian it is constantly met with, from the sources of that river on the borders of New Mexico, near Santa Fé, 106° west, until you arrive within a short distance of its confluence with the Arkansa, in long. 97° west. The waters of the Canadian, from flowing over the sandstone in question, acquire an intense red colour, and are so impregnated with muriate of soda and other soluble salts as to be unfit for use. This, we are credibly informed, is also the case with the waters of three small rivers tributary to the Arkansa, above the Canadian, on the same side; also with the waters of Red river. Hence the conclusion appears to be justified, that this rock extends from near the Arkansa on the north, to a point beyond Red river on the south; and from near the mouth of the Canadian, an unknown distance to the west. It is not unlikely it may exist about the sources and upper branches of the Rio Colorado of California, the Red river of Santa Fé, and the other Red rivers of New Mexico. Near the mountains, and for a great distance to the south and east of the High Peak, it is covered by the gray sandstone already mentioned. This gray sandstone is the uppermost of those horizontally stratified rocks which are seen in this region, possessing convincing evidence of their being the deposition of an ocean or lake of salt water.

Perhaps the most striking feature of this formation of sandstone, is the great and abrupt change in the inclination of the strata in the parts near the granite. We have already described this in a manner sufficiently explicit, as we suppose, to convince most of our readers that since the deposition of the sandstones, a signal change must have happened in the elevation of the secondary aggregates as compared with the granite. The appearances are precisely such as we must suppose would have ensued, had the sudden emerging of the granite broken off, and thrown into an inclined or vertical position the margin of the horizontally stratified rocks of the plains. We are conscious that inclined strata of sandstone are by no means infrequent about the declivities of lofty mountains, but we are not well assured that the same strata being traced to a little distance, are often found in a horizontal position in the plains, as is the case in the instance under consideration.

It may perhaps be thought possible that the gradual wearing away, by the agency of rivers, of some portions of the sandstone, may have been sufficiently extensive to have occasioned that change of elevation of which we speak; and that those rocks now found in an inclined position, are insulated portions of what was formerly the upper part of the stratum, which having been undermined on their eastern side, and supported by the granite on their western, have fallen into their present situation.

This supposition, however, seems incompatible with the vast magnitude and extent of these rocks, and entirely irreconcilable to the fact that they dip to a great and indefinite extent below the present level of any of the beds of the river.

The position of this formation in relation to the granite is similar to that of the sandstone of Guachaco, in South America, observed by Humboldt; also to that spoken of by Mr. Burkhardt, at the entrance of Nubia, superimposed upon the granite of Syene, and to that mentioned by Mr. Schoolcraft, as found near Lake Superior, but it does not appear that those formations have the same peculiarities in in regard to inclination.

FLETZ TRAP ROCKS.

Another family of rocks, of recent formation, and connected with the sandstone last mentioned, remains to be noticed.

These are rocks of basaltic conformation, belonging to the class, by some mineralogists denominated superincumbent rocks, and by many considered of volcanic origin. They present a striking contrast, by their dark colour, by the vastness and irregularity of their masses, to the smooth, light, and fissile sandstone on which they rest. Sometimes they are observed compact and apparently homogeneous in their composition, and in many particulars of structure, form, hardness, &c. seeming more analogous to the primitive rocks than to those recent secondary aggregates with which they are associated. In other instances, black and formless masses of porous and amygdaloidal substances are seen scattered about the plains or heaped in conic masses, but having no immediate connection with the strata on which they rest. Most of the rocks belonging to this class were observed in the neighbourhood of the sources of the Canadian. Among them we distinguish two kinds, referable to the two divisons called greenstone and amygdaloid.

1. *Greenstone,* JAMESON.—It appears in the limited district we examined under almost every variety of form and character noticed by mineralogists. Sometimes it is nearly or quite free from any intermixture of hornblende, is of a fine dark green colour, and closely resembles some varieties of serpentine. Sometimes its colour is a dull gray, graduating into brown and black of various shades and intensities. It forms numerous conic hills of considerable elevation, scattered without order, or grouped in various directions. These hills are usually of a regular and beautiful form. The great plain on which they are based is elevated and destitute of timber or water, but ornamented with a carpet of thick and verdant grasses. The hills, though steep and high, are sometimes smooth and green to the summit, the surface on all sides being unbroken by trees or rocks, and covered with thick turf. The whole forms a scene of sin-

gular beauty. During our journey across the district, based upon the rocks now under consideration, we had constantly occasion to admire the freshness and abundance of the grasses and other herbaceous plants. The plains of the Platte and Arkansa we had seen brown and desolate, as if recently ravaged by fire; but here we passed elevated tracts, where, for many miles, we could find no water for our own necessities, yet the vegetation possessed the freshness of spring in the most fertile regions. But the conic hills just mentioned, are not invariably the form under which the greenstone appears. It sometimes rises in low irregular ridges, extending a considerable distance, and sloping on both sides into the level of the plain.

In the narrow channels which the streams of water have sunk in it, may be seen perpendicular precipices of great elevation, but the valley between them is usually almost filled with large broken masses of the rock, which frequently exhibit a prismatic form. It falls readily into large masses, but seems strongly to resist that progress of disintegration which it must undergo before it can be removed by the water. The face of the perpendicular precipices are almost invariably marked by distinct and large seams running nearly parallel to each other, and at right angles with the horizon. Following the water-courses, which are sunk considerable distance below the surface, the line of separation from the sandstone on which the greenstone rests, at length becomes visible on account of the descent of the surface.

2. *Amygdaloid*, Kirwan, Jameson. — We apply this name to a porous or vesicular rock, of a very dark gray, greenish or black colour, usually found near the greenstone, but sometimes in connection with the sandstone. In its ultimate composition it resembles greenstone, but we have never seen in it such large fragments of felspar and scales of mica, as are observed in that rock. The amygdaloidal

cavities which every where penetrate this rock, are of various sizes, some of them appearing like bubbles which have been formed in a semifluid mass, and afterwards lengthened and variously distorted by the motions of the contiguous matter. Near the surface they contain a soft white, or yellowish white substance, very different from the rock itself, usually a soft chalk-like carbonate of lime. This gives the recent surface a mottled appearance. In surfaces which have been for some time exposed to the air, this soft substance has been removed, and the pores and vesicles are found empty.

Amygdaloid does not appear to occupy any very great extent of the country near the Rocky Mountains. We have not met with it imbedded in, or surmounted by any other rock. Like the greenstone, it forms conic hills which sometimes occur in deep water-worn vallies, bounded on both sides by perpendicular walls of sandstone. It is likewise seen in the high plains, sometimes in the form of narrow and crooked ridges, apparently following what were anciently the beds of small brooks. Some very high and sharp conic hills were visible to the westward, but at a great distance. Two of this kind which stand near each other, and seem to be detached from the primitive mountains, are called the Spanish peaks, and at the end of July, snow was still to be seen on them.

When either of the two rocks last mentioned occur, it is not uncommon to find detached masses of a stone somewhat resembling the pumice-stone of commerce. It is usually of a faint red, or yellowish white colour, but sometimes it is brown, or nearly black. It feels less harsh than the pumice-stone which is used in the arts, and seems to consist in a great degree of clay. It appears to be entirely similar to the substance brought down the Missouri by the annual floods, and by many considered as a product of pseudo-volcanic fires, said to exist on that river.

With regard to the soils resting upon the rocks of this trap formation, it may be worthy of remark, that gravel and water-worn pebbles rarely occur, except in situations where it is easy to see they may have been derived from the subtratum of sandstone. We are not disposed to enter into any discussion concerning the origin of the trap rocks. The volcanists, and those who believe the trap formations to have been thrown up in a state of fusion from beneath the crust of the earth, will have an easy method of accounting for a fact mentioned in our journal, namely, that pieces of charred wood were found enclosed in the sandstone underlaying the formation in question. Though we sought in vain for some evidence that the rocks of this formation traversed the strata of sandstone in the manner of the whin dikes of England, we are conscious our examinations were far too limited to justify us in asserting that this is not the case; nor can we adduce a single fact from which it could be inferred that these basaltiform rocks have been deposited, like the accompanying strata of sandstone, from suspension in water. The country occupied by this formation, exhibits scenery of a very peculiar and interesting character. It is remarked by Humboldt*, that " in the Canary islands, in the mountains of Auvergne, in the Mittelgebirge in Bohemia, in Mexico, and on the banks of the Ganges," and we may add, in the United States, the formation of trap is indicated by a symmetrical disposition of the mountains by truncated cones, sometimes insulated, sometimes grouped, and by elevated plains, both extremities of which are crowned by a conical rising. In some of the unpublished drawings by Mr. Seymour, these peculiar

* Personal Narrative, vol. i. p. 87. American edition.

features of the scenery of the fletz trap formation, have been preserved.

RECAPITULATION.

The secondary formations along the eastern base of the Rocky Mountains, are:

1st. *Red Sandstone* — Rests immediately upon the granite, is rather indistinctly stratified; strata sometimes inclined and sometimes horizontal; abounds in gypsum, salt, and iron, but exhibits no indications of coal.

2d. *Argillaceous,* or *Gray Sandstone* — Overlays the red, conforming to it in the inclination of the strata, occurs principally near the primitive; contains coal and iron.

3d. *Greenstone* and *Graystone** — Of an imperfectly columnar structure, resting on the argillaceous sandstone.

4th. *Amygdaloid* — Sometimes containing argil, and sometimes hornblende, occurs with the greenstone about the sources of the Canadian river, constituting with te former the newest fletz trap formation.

5th. *Sand* and *Gravel* — Accompanying the sandstones and extending over the great desert, but rarely found resting on the trap rocks.

The sandstones being entirely mechanical aggregates, consisting of rounded fragments of rocks formerly constituting a part of the primitive mountains, would seem to have been deposited at a very remote period, when the waters of the primeval ocean covered the level of the great plain and the lower regions of the granitic mountains.

Subsequent to the deposition of the horizontally stratified rocks, the position of these in relation to the primitive, has been somewhat changed either by the action of some force beneath the primitive rocks,

* Pinkerton.

forcing them up to a greater elevation than they formerly possessed, or by the sinking down of the secondary, produced by the operation of some cause equally unknown. Without supposing some change of this kind, how can we account for the great inclination of the margin of the sandstone rocks which is found resting against the granite almost perpendicularly? Nearly contemporaneous to this change, was the retiring of the sea, and the formation of the trap rocks. The beds of loose sand and gravel which are still constantly accumulating, have been formed in part from the disintegration of the sandstones and puddings, and partly by the action of those currents of water which are constantly bringing down small fragments from the primitive rocks, and depositing them in the plains.

The absence of any formation of limestone is a distinguishing characteristic of the country under consideration. A traveller to the upper part of the Missouri mentions " calcareous and petrosiliceous hills," as existing in the coal districts on that river. But in ascending the Platte from its confluence with the Missouri to the mountains, we saw not a single fragment of limestone. Small veins of carbonate of lime crystallized in the usual form, are met with in the argillaceous sandstone of the Arkansa, also the sulphate in small quantities. Gypsum is very abundant on the Canadian river, at a distance of three or four hundred miles from the mountains. It is disseminated in veins and thick horizontal beds in the red sandstone. The extent and thickness of these horizontal beds are, perhaps, such as would justify the appellation of stratum, but as it is not met with in great quantities, except in connection with the sandstone, with which it often alternates, it may with propriety be considered a subordinate rock.

Rock Salt. — This substance has often been said to exist in some part of upper Louisiana, in the form of an extensive stratum : we have met with salt among the natives in masses of twenty or thirty pounds weight. The interior of these masses when broken, presented a crystalline structure, being made up of incomplete cubic crystals variously grouped together. On one of the surfaces, which had probably been the one in contact with the ground or rock on which the salt had rested, a considerable mixture of red sand was discoverable. These masses had apparently been produced by the evaporation, during the dry season, of the waters of some small lake. The whole country near the mountains abounds in licks, brine springs, and saline efflorescences, but it is in the neighbourhood of the red sand-rock before mentioned, that salt is met with in the greatest abundance and purity. The immediate valley of the Canadian river in the upper part of its course, varies in width from a few rods to three or four miles, but it is almost invariably bounded by precipices of red sand-rock, forming " the river bluffs." In the valley between these, incrustations of nearly pure salt are often found, covering the surface to a great extent, in the manner of thin ice, and causing it to appear when seen from a distance, as if covered with snow.

Most of the remarkable formations of rock-salt hitherto known, have been found in the stratum denominated " the lowest red sand rock, which appears to correspond in character, position, &c. with the sandstone above mentioned. Rock salt is found in connection with this sandstone in Cheshire, and at Northwich and Droitwich, in England, at Cardona in the province of Catalonia in Spain, and at the base of the Carpathian mountains in Moldavia and Poland. In Peru it is accompanied by sandstone and gypsum.

Accident, or further examination, it is probable, may hereafter bring to light those extensive beds of this substance, which there is reason to believe exist in the neighbourhood of the Rocky Mountains. The briny character of those great streams, the Arkansa and Red rivers, flowing over the red sandstone formation, and receiving from it the peculiar character and colour of their waters, affords sufficient evidence of the existence of such beds, and the greatness of the quantity washed away in any given time, would lead to the conclusion, that they must be of vast extent. By the analogy of other rock salt formations apparently similar in character, we should be instructed to search for these beds in depressed situations and basin-shaped cavities, whose contents had not been worn down and removed by the currents of water.

Other secondary rocks found in different parts of the great valley of the Mississippi will be noticed hereafter. Those above enumerated seem to have a peculiar dependence upon the Rocky Mountains, and for this reason, we thought proper to consider them in connection with that range; they also appear to be, in some measure, independent of the other members of that great secondary formation on the borders of which they occur. The peculiar features of the region occupied by these rocks have been minutely described in the narrative of our journey. It is a region unfitted by the barrenness of its soil, the inhospitable character of its climate and other physical disadvantages, to become the residence of a permanent and numerous population. The immense grassy plain of the southern and eastern portions are adapted to the feeding of cattle and horses; and it is not improbable the countless herds of bisons and wild horses will soon give place to domesticated animals. The coal, salt, plaster, and iron, which constitute the mineral wealth of this portion of the United States' territory, lose much of their value on account of their remoteness from navigable streams. Beautiful carnelions and agates occur in the alluvial regions of the Platte and the Missouri; but these will never become objects of any importance.

Of the Ozark Mountains.

Leaving the newest fletz trap rocks, about the sources of the Canadian, and returning eastward along the great woodless plain between the Arkansa and Red rivers, we find an extensive tract occupied exclusively by the red sandstone of the salt formation. This rock, as we have already remarked, is constantly accompanied by gypsum and muriate of soda. The red and somewhat argillaceous soil which results from its disintegration is far more fertile than that of the gravelly plains of the Platte, being often covered with a luxuriant growth of grasses, and affording pasturage to great numbers of herbivorous animals.
About one hundred and fifty miles west from the confluence of the Arkansa and Canadian, this red sandstone is discontinued, being succeeded, or perhaps overlaid by an extensive coal formation. The argillaceous sandstone of this formation assumes various characters at different points. The Falls of the Canadian, particularly described in our narrative, are occasioned by a small ridge of fine argillaceous sandstone of a deep green colour, crossing the bed of the river obliquely. The coal beds in this region are of great thickness, and are apparently extensive and numerous. This formation appears, in a great measure, unconnected with the coal strata along the base of the Rocky Mountains, and the sandstone of the two districts are often remarkably dissimilar. Though the strata in both instances are nearly horizontal, the formation at the base of the Rocky Mountains must have an actual elevation greatly surpassing that of the district now under consideration. For these reasons, we have been induced to consider

this as belonging to the small group of mountains we have already had frequent occasion to mention, and which have received from Major Long, the name of Ozark mountains. These we shall now proceed to describe, according to their formation in our possession.

From an inspection of the map annexed to this volume, it will be perceived that the course of the Missouri, below the mouth of the Konzas, is considerably inflected to the east, in order to pass round the end of a range of hills, rising in the angle between this river and the Mississippi. This range increases in elevation for some distance to the south-west, its highest point being somewhere near the sources of the White and Osage rivers, the two most considerable streams originating in these mountains. Farther to the south-west, losing a part of its elevation, it is traversed in succession by the Arkansa and Red rivers from the west, and gives origin to the Washita, the Sabine, and some other rivers of inconsiderable magnitude. Our acquaintance with the country between Red river and the Rio del Norte is too imperfect to enable us to trace particularly the continuation of the Ozark mountains, which is believed to extend to that river, and to have some connection with its great southern bend, below the confluence of the Rio Conchos. We will, therefore, at present, confine our attention to that portion north-east of Red river.

Though there is no point of great elevation in any part of the range, the whole is truly a mountainous region, and well entitled to a distinctive appellation. Its parallelism in general direction to the Atlantic coast, and the great chain of the Alleghanies, as well as the character and inclination of its component strata, afford unequivocal indication that it belongs to a different system from the great chain of the Rocky Mountains. In several particulars, there is a striking resemblance between this range and the Alleghanies, and in some, as we shall notice hereafter, as manifest a dissimilarity.

Near the western limits of the coal formation, which are also the limits of the mountainous countries on the Canadian and Arkansa, compact limestone occurs for the first time (as far as our acquaintance extends) on this side the Rocky Mountains. This formation of limestone, and the accompanying strata of argillaceous sandstone, though they do not, perhaps, always strictly coincide in position, may be traced far to the north; and these we consider as marking the western limits of the Ozark mountains. It is to be remarked, however, that in these observations, we do not intend to apply this name with strict geographical precision to those portions only which are sufficiently elevated to be called mountains; but so far to extend its signification as to include not only the high and broken ridges, but several less elevated tracts possessing the same peculiar mineralogical features.

The few facts and observations we have it in our power to contribute towards an account of this interesting range, were collected during a pedestrian excursion from Bainbridge on the Mississippi, through the country of the lead-mines, at the sources of the Merameg and St. Francis, and a journey from Belle Point, by the way of the hot springs of the Washita, and the upper settlements of White river, to Cape Girardeau. For many important facts we are indebted to Major Long's unpublished journals of tours in various parts of the region in question, and to Mr. Nuttall's "Travels into the Arkansa Territory."

Compact Limestone. — We commence with the consideration of this stratum, as it is one of frequent occurrence, and perhaps occupies a greater extent of surface than any other. It so frequently alternates with the micaceous sandstones, and with the peculiar flint-rock of this district, that we have never been able to devise any theory of arrangement which appeared applicable to more than an inconsiderable extent of territory.

A few miles west of the Rapids of the Canadian, a thin stratum of compact limestone, of the common blue variety, and abounding in organized remains, overlays the argillaceous sandstone of the coal formation. This limestone becomes more abundant towards the south, and is the prevailing rock on that part of Red river, near the confluence of the Kiamesha. [20] At Cape Girardeau, in the country a few miles in the rear of Herculaneum and St. Genevieve, and in many places throughout the district of the lead-mines, there is a coarse crystalline limestone, of a light gray colour, which is usually the lowest rock exposed in those places. It is very indistinctly stratified, and has in many respects a considerable resemblance to the more crystalline varieties of primitive limestone: for such it appears to have been mistaken by Mr. Schoolcraft, who, in his work on the lead-mines, asserts that the " mineral soil at Mine a Burton, and the numerous mines in its vicinity, reposes on primitive limestone," page 108. Afterwards, at page 119., speaking of this same primitive limestone, he says, " On going deeper, the rock again graduated into a compact limestone, very hard, and of a bluish gray colour, in which were frequently found small cavities studded over with minute pyramids of limpid quartz." And again, at the page first referred to, he informs us, " The primitive limestone passes into transition, and secondary, in various places on the banks of the Mississippi, between Cape Girardeau, and Saint Louis. We adduce these statements as confirming our own observations of the alternation of the *crystalline* or *sparry* limestone, with the compact blue variety; but as we have examined with great care several of the places mentioned by Mr. Schoolcraft, and many others apparently similar, we are disposed to think he has mistaken the character of the rock. We have never met with any limestone about the lead-mines which did not contain organized remains; and the white crystalline variety abounds particularly in casts of encrinites, though these are not always manifest without careful examination.

This limestone, though rather indistinctly stratified, is marked by horizontal seams, distant one or two feet, and sometimes more, from each other. Its exposed surface becomes somewhat bleached and rough with small prominences, in which we may often distinctly trace the forms of animal remains. The recent fracture is uneven, distinctly crystalline, and much like that of many moderately fine-grained granites. Careful examination shows that in many instances the most minute particles visible under a lens, have assumed the rhombic form so common to the carbonate of lime. These crystalline particles vary greatly in size, and are sometimes half an inch across. In the interior of the casts of animal remains, they are sometimes less distinct than in parts of the rock where no such remains are discovered.

These vast beds of sparry limestone, made up almost exclusively of deposits from chymical solution, would seem to have been formed during periods when great tranquillity prevailed in the waters of the primeval ocean; and their alternation with limestones of the common earthy variety, and with sandstones made up of fragments rounded by attrition, may be considered as proofs that those periods, whatever may have been their distinguishing peculiarity, alternated with other periods of a different character.

This variety of limestone is perhaps the lowest rock hitherto noticed in the country of the lead-mines, and it may, according to the suggestion of Schoolcraft, be considered as the basis rock in that district; but as it certainly passes through every intermediate variety into the compact blue limestone, there seems to be no propriety in separating it from that rock, which often overlays the newest sandstones. If this view of the subject be admitted, it results that we are to consider the whole of that part of the Ozark mountains which contains the lead-mines as belonging to a coal formation. We have met with nothing north of the Arkansa which appears to us to have any claim to be considered as belonging to the class of primitive rocks.

Mr. Schoolcraft informs us, that granite, gneiss, and mica slate exist in Missouri, but has omitted to point out the particular localities. See Views of the Lead Mines, page 92.

At St. Louis, Cote sans Dessein, Isle a Loutre, and at many points on the Missouri, the limestone partakes of the character of both the varieties above mentioned, but is rarely if ever so exclusively crystalline as in the lead-mine district. Most of the limestones between Franklin on the Missouri, and the Council bluffs, are distinctly crystalline, and are usually of a yellowish or reddish white colour.

The horizontal limestone near the mouth of the Ohio, is of a bluish gray colour, of a compact or fine granular structure, and contains some metallic ores often occurring in veins of beautifully crystallized fluat of lime. Near some of these localities of fluat of lime, we have observed the rock itself to contain small and apparently water-worn masses of hornstone, and some fragments of a perfectly white granular limestone.

Petrosilex. — In the vicinity of Bainbridge, ten miles above Cape Girardeau, is a stratified gray flint rock very similar in aspect, and having nearly a similar fracture to the common gun-flint. This rock is here an extensive stratum, and occurs in connection with compact limestone. In tracing it towards the south-west, we have not been able to detect the slightest interruption to its continuity through an extent of more than two hundred miles along the central portion of the mountainous district. Towards the south-west it is found to acquire gradually a more and more primitive character, and losing, near the Chattahoocke mountain the accompanying stratum of compact limestone, it appears near the hot springs of the Washita, associated with the highly inclined argillite of that district. This rock, as far as our limited observations have extended, exhibits no traces of organized remains. Its colour seems gradually to change according to its age, or at least with the apparent age of the rocks associated with it. South of the Arkansa it is of a yellowish or pearly white colour; about White river, it is a dirty yellow, and at the St. Francis a grayish brown. A corresponding change may also be noticed in the inclination of the strata, and in other particulars. Aside from this apparently intimate connection there is a particular resemblance between the petrosilex of the Washita, and the flint rock of the lead-mine district. The rock in both instances falls readily into small masses of a few ounces weight. The hills it forms have usually a rounded outline, and often bear open forests of pine, while the timber on the sandstone hills is usually oak. Open woods of pine and oak occur in almost all the uplands in the Ozark mountains, and are considered unfailing indications of a meagre and flinty soil.

Argillaceous Sandstone. — The sandstones of this small group of mountains appear under almost every variety of character, but in most of them, as far as hitherto examined, we discover traces of coal or of those minerals and organized remains which usually accompany it. In the inclined sandstone near the hot springs, there are, it is true, no indications of coal; and that rock is in every respect similar to what are called the transition sandstones of the Alleghany and Coatskill mountains, but by following it an inconsiderable distance either east or west, it is found passing imperceptibly into the coal strata of the Poteau, and of the Little Red river of White river. In this instance, as in that of the stratum last mentioned, we find a rock apparently possessing as much unity as can belong to such a subject, passing from recent *secondary* down, through all the intermediate grades, to the oldest *transition*, and thus heaping confusion upon our doctrines of the original continuity and systematic succession of strata.

A conspicuous character in the sandstones about the central and western portions of the region under consideration, is the great proportion of mica, in large scales, which enters into their composition. Fragments of the sand-rock, about the mouth of the Poteau, might be mistaken for mica slate. This mica is rarely if ever of that dark coloured variety which prevails in the Rocky Mountains; and in the other materials of these aggregates, there is a manifest want of resemblance to those mountains. A very slight comparison of the secondary formations at the base of the Rocky Mountains, with the similar aggregates in the Ozark range, will be sufficient to convince any one that they have resulted from the wearing down of primitive mountains, very dissimilar in character to each other.

We might have remarked, when speaking of the Rocky Mountains, the absence of any formation of talcose rocks, and indeed of magnesian fossils of any kind, and a corresponding deficiency of talcose and chloritic sandstones among the secondary rocks. We no sooner arrive at the western margin of the secondary belonging to the Ozark mountains, than we meet with extensive beds of sandstone, in which the prevalence of magnesia forms a conspicuous character. The beautiful argillaceous chlorite sandstone at the rapids of the Canadian, has been already described, and similar beds are not uncommon in many places in the vicinity of extensive depositions of coal.

Another peculiar variety of sandstone occurs, in connection with the sulphuret of lead, at the old mines of St. Michael, and at many places thereabouts. This bears apparently the same relation to the common sandstones, as the crystalline limestone above mentioned does to the earthy varieties, and it alternates with and passes into the common rock in a similar manner. Its particles are crystalline, and appear to remain undisturbed in the position in which they were originally deposited from solution in water. Nevertheless the aggregate is manifestly secondary, and embraces the relics of many organized beings, as is common in the other secondary rocks.

There is also about the lead mines a sandstone composed of small glimmering grains of transparent quartz, and so loosely cemented as to fall rapidly to pieces, forming a light gray sand. In this variety we have sometimes observed the lead ore either dissemminated, or forming horizontal veins between the laminæ of sandstone. An examination of some spots might lead to the conclusion that the soil in which most of the lead has hitherto been found, has resulted from the disintegration of a sandstone of this kind.

Sandstone, though often covered at the surface by compact limestone or some other stratum is probably the rock which occurs in the greatest quantity throughout every part of this range of mountains. It is the prevailing stratum in all the country between the Arkansa and Red rivers, from the confluence of the Mamelle westward; rising to the height of two or three thousand feet, to form the summits of the Cavaniol, Sugar Loaf, and Mt. Cerne, and to a less considerable elevation at the Mamelle, Magasin, Caslete, and Short mountains.

North of the Arkansa it forms the body of the Chattahoocke mountain, and of many nameless elevations, which diversify the surface from the sources of the Little Red river to the Mississippi. Beds of coarse conglomerate or puddingstone, are met with in many places; but these are particularly frequent in connection with the inclined or transition sandstones about the Washita.

Native Argil. — Nine miles west of Bainbridge, on

the road to Jackson, and on the right bank of the Mississippi, near the head of Tiawapeti bottom, also in various other places in this vicinity, there are extensive beds of perfectly white native argil, of about the hardness of common chalk, for which it has often been mistaken. [21] See Schoolcraft's "Catalogue of Western Minerals," art. 1st. Notwithstanding Mr. Schoolcraft's confident assertion, it must yet be considered doubtful whether any chalk has ever been found in the region under consideration.

Specimens of the substance called chalk by the inhabitants, were collected at several places between Cape Girardeau and St. Louis. Also on the north side of the Missouri, on the road from St. Louis to Franklin. Some of these which were brought to New York, have been examined by my brother, Dr. J. James, and others, and were found to consist principally of argil, none of them occasioning the slightest effervescence with acids.

This substance, whatever it is to be considered, is distributed extensively throughout the country lying around the confluence of the Missouri and Mississippi. Some specimens have been sent from Illinois to the Lyceum of Natural History at Troy, where they are spoken of as a "littrographic carbonate of lime;" but whether any experiments have been made to ascertain their real character we have not been able to learn. We have not, from our own observation, found occasion to confirm the statement, that nodules of flint are found imbedded in this substance; but we have commonly found it accompanied by the flint rock already mentioned, which has in many respects a manifest resemblance to the flints occurring in chalk formation. We have sought in vain for the remains of echini and other animals so common in chalk beds.

Argillite.—Of the older secondary rocks, we have observed in the Ozark mountains only the inclined sandstones and conglomerates above mentioned, and a limited formation of argillite, extending a few miles around the hot springs of Washita, and re-appearing on the Arkansa at and above the town of Little Rock, being usually accompanied by vast beds of petrosilex. This latter ought, perhaps, to be considered a distinct stratum, but south of the Arkansa we have not been able to trace it uninterrupted for any great distance.

Mr. Nuttall, in his valuable Journal of Travels into the Arkansa Territory, mentions *grauwacke slate* as occurring along the Arkansa river near Little Rock, p. 105. We have observed none here in any considerable degree similar to the grauwacke slate of the transition mountains of New York, or even to that of the Alleghanies. We are aware, however, that some of the aggregates which we call sandstones, have all the characters attributed to grauwacke slates, "*grauwacke is a complete sandstone*,"* and in a district where both are so intimately blended as in that we are considering, perhaps it is unnecessary to attempt any distinction between them; or we may persevere in the use of the two names at the same time, acknowledging they are both applied to the same stratum.

The hot springs of the Washita issue from clay-slate, and if we may judge from the inclination of the strata, and the distance at the surface from the granite of the cove, we may conclude a very large mass of clay-slate is interposed between the surface of the granite and the point at which the springs rise. This however it is not possible to ascertain. The hottest springs on the globe rise from beneath or within the granite†, and it is not improbable this rock may approach near the surface at many points

---

* Jameson in the Edinburgh Encyclopedia, Art. Mineralogy.
† Humboldt's Personal Narrative, vol. iv. p. 171. 195. vol. v. p. 553.

in the Ozark mountains, where it has not yet been uncovered.

The slate rock about the hot springs is highly inclined, often a good deal flinty in its composition, and as far as we have observed, contains no organised remains. It is traversed by large upright veins, filled usually with white quartz, contrasting strongly in colour with the dark blue of the slate-stone. The elevation of the " Hot Springs mountain" is estimated by Hunter and Dunbar at three hundred feet above the surface of the creek at the springs. This point is probably raised twenty or thirty feet above the Washita at Keisler. North of the springs the slate-rocks rise to greater elevation; but it is not probable that at any point where we have seen them, they attain the height of one thousand feet above the Mississippi.

The high lands between Washita and Red river are occupied principally by sandstone, the clay-slate appearing to extend from north-east to south-west, which, as far as we have observed, is the direction of the strata; these, when they are not perpendicular, usually dipping to the north-west.

The country about the sources of the Washita is represented as affording many interesting minerals; among them are enumerated "a martial pyrites, large bodies of crystallised spar, and hexagonal prisms, which are known to contain no small portion of the precious metals."* If the clay-slate in any part of this mountainous region should be found accompanied by its usual attendant, the metalliferous limestone, we should be more ready to credit the accounts of the precious metals being found, as at least some of the valuable mines in America exist in that stratum. But as yet we have no satisfactory accounts of the occurrence of that limestone, or any of the precious metals in that part of the United States.

* Stoddart's Louisiana, p. 391.

Granite.— About fifteen miles south-east from the hot springs, near the Washita, granite is found *in situ*. It forms the basis, and, as far as we could discover, the whole mass of a small hill, but little elevated above the level of the river; we found it emerging from beneath the soil at several parts of an area for two hundred or three hundred acres; but had not an opportunity to trace it to any great distance, nor to observe its connection with any other rock. The extent of surface which it covers, we believe, cannot be very great. This granite is very soft, and disintegrates rapidly when exposed to the air. It is compounded of grayish-white quartz, yellowish-white felspar, and an unusually large proportion of mica, in variously and brilliantly coloured masses. These large laminæ of mica are white, pearl colour, yellow, brown, green, and often black, and in some instances are so large and numerous as to exceed in proportion the other ingredients of the aggregate. Talc also enters in large proportion into the composition of this granite. It is indeed sometimes so abundant as to occasion a doubt whether the whole should not be considered a bed of talc, rather than granite. This talc is in tabular masses, two or three inches in diameter, and about half an inch in thickness. Zeolite is also so abundant as sometimes to seem to take the place of the other materials of the granite. It is of two varieties, radiated and mealy. Stilbite (blaettriger zeolith of Werner) occurs in connexion with zeolite. The bed of one of the small streams which traverses this formation of granite is paved with small crystals of schorl, that of another with native magnet. Sulphuret of iron is disseminated in the granite. Several of the appearances presented by this interesting mass of granite, would seem to countenance the opinion that it is of secondary origin, like that mentioned by Saussure, as existing near the valley of Valorsine, at Semur en Auxois, and at the city of Lyons. In speaking of the granite at these places, he says, " It could not be doubted on seeing these heaps of large crystals, that they are the produce of the rain-waters, which, passing through the granite, have dissolved and carried down these different elements, and have deposited them in these wide crevices, where they have formed new rocks of the same kind. The crystals of these new granites are larger than those of the ancient, on account of the repose which the waters enjoyed in the inside of these reservoirs."

The granite of the Washita, if it is to be considered as of secondary formation, appears to be much more extensive than any of the kind hitherto known. Many more particulars must, however, be ascertained before this question can be settled. We are ignorant of the manner of its connection with any other rock. Nor do we know of any formation of primitive granite from which it could, by the action of water, have been derived. One can have no hesitation, however, in considering the Ozark mountains, as a separate system within themselves, and having no immediate connection with the Alleghanies or Rocky Mountains. The sandstones which lie about these mountains, abound much more in mica than those near the Rocky Mountains, nearly in the same proportion as the granite of the latter has less than what is met with in the little we have seen of the former. The Ozark mountains exhibit evidence of metallic riches far exceeding any thing that appears in the Rocky Mountains. May not an extensive range of granite and other primitive rocks have existed at some distant period where the Ozark mountains now are, containing the vast quantities of the ores of lead, iron, &c. now found in rocks of recent secondary origin, and even in the alluvial? and may not the operations of water during many ages, when an ocean rolled over the summits of these mountains, have worn down those primitive rocks, their detritus having been deposited horizontally upon their submarine sides and summits;

so that the greater part of their surfaces are now covered by secondary aggregates? Our acquaintance with this range is however much too limited to admit of indulgence in such speculations.

Numerous specimens of minerals brought by Lieutenant Graham and Dr. Somerville from the Upper Mississippi and the Illinois rivers and others from that region, now in the possession of Dr. L. C. Beck, of St. Louis, have a peculiar resemblance to similar minerals met with in the Ozark mountains, south of the Missouri. From these resemblances, and the corroborating testimony of all the accounts we have received concerning that country, rich in mines, which lies along the eastern side of the Upper Mississippi, we have been induced to believe that a continuation of the Ozark mountains, or at least, of a region similar in Mineralogical features, extends from the confluence of the Missouri, northward to the sources of the Wisconsan, and the Ontonagon river of Lake Superior, north of the Missouri, the country is very little elevated; but aside from this it appears to possess all the peculiar features of the region we have been considering. The sandstones, the limestones, and other rocks, have a striking resemblance. Both regions abound in the ores of lead, and both afford copper.*

We are aware that the great irregularity in the direction of the ridges accessory to this range, and of the dip and inclination of the older secondary rocks belonging to it, may be considered objections to our idea of the connection and continuity of the different parts and the general direction of the group. But we are by no means anxious to maintain the position we have assumed. Our examinations have been limited, and we shall rejoice in any opportunity of correcting our errors, and enlarging our acquaintance with this interesting range of country.

* Copper has been found in Illinois, near the sources of Cache river.

We subjoin in a note some account of a few of the most interesting minerals hitherto observed in connection with the rocks of this district. [22]

Recapitulation.

The Ozark mountains extend from the sources of the Rio Colorado of Texas on the south-west, to the confluence of the Mississippi and Missouri on the north-east, and are continued in a low range from this point towards Lake Superior. They are widest in the south-west, and in that quarter they mingle with some low tracts of secondary sandstone, extending from near the Gulf of Mexico to the base of the easternmost ridge of the Rocky Mountains. Whether there is any similar expansion at the northern extremity, or whether this range is connected as a spur to the great primitive chain supposed to exist north of the great lakes, and is separated by a wide secondary and alluvial valley from the Rocky Mountains, is yet to be determined. This range consists of low ridges, irregular in direction, rarely rising to an elevation of more than 1500 or 2000 feet, and consisting principally of secondary rocks.

The strata are —

1st. *Granite* — at the cove of the Washita.

2d. *Argillite* — ranging north-east and south-west from Little Rock on the Arkansa to the hot springs, and thence to the sources of the Kiamesha.

3d. *Transition Sandstone* — a narrow margin, following nearly the same direction on the north-west side of the argillite, and usually inclining like it to the south or south-east.

4th. *Flint* (petrosilex) — From the hot springs north-east to the Mississippi, and usually forming the basis of the pine-lands.

5th. *Limestone* — Compact and sparry; distributed in the same direction as the last, but more extensive.

6th. *Argillaceous Sandstone* — with extensive beds of coal, and abounding in mines of lead.

7th. *Alluvial* — There are many extensive tracts of deep argillaceous or calcareous loam; in other instances, a more meagre soil has resulted from the disintegration of the sand-rock.

These are the remarks we have been able, from observation, to make respecting the geology of a part of the United States' territory, west of the Mississippi. Relating to that part of the interior of our country which lies north-west of Lake Superior, and north of the sources of the Missouri, we have little satisfactory information. From the accurate and intelligent Mackenzie, we are however able to collect a few important particulars. This enterprising voyager, it is well known, travelled from Montreal, L.C., in latitude $45° 30'$, longitude $74°$, in a north-west direction, to the mouth of Mackenzie's river, latitude $69°$, longitude $135°$; and again, at a later period, leaving his former route at the Lake of the Hills, about midway between Lake Superior and the mouth of Mackenzie's river, he ascended, in a south-west direction, the Unjegah, or River of Peace, to the Rocky Mountains, and crossing them, fell upon the sources of the northern branch of the Columbia, and from thence arrived at the Pacific, at a point a little north of the inlet of Queen Charlotte's sound. From him we learn that the Rocky Mountains continue in an uninterrupted chain, from the sources of the Missouri in the south, to a point beyond the sixty-fifth parallel of north latitude, near the mouth of Mackenzie's river. The River of Peace which he ascended in his journey to the western ocean, has its source in these mountains in about $55°$ north, nearly opposite to those of the great northern branch of the Columbia. Farther towards the south are the sources of the Saskatchawin, a large river, discharging itself from the north-west into Lake Winnipic. The mountains in this part seem to be less elevated than those more to the south, but in other respects entirely similar. Their northern termination, according to this traveller, is in about north latitude 65°, 130° west longitude. Santa Fé in New Mexico is in latitude 36°, longitude 104° 53′ * west. From this it will be perceived, that the general direction of this great mountain range is nearly from north-north-east to south-south-west. We have no evidence to confirm the conjecture, which, nevertheless, is highly probable, that the principal ridges of this range consist through their whole extent of granite or other primitive rocks. Considering the stupendous character, the great elevation and uniformity of the appearance of that portion of these primitive mountains with which we are acquainted, we should be led to look for similarity of character, and similar uniformity throughout. It is commonly believed, as asserted by Maclure, that " a large mass of primitive occupies all the northern part of this continent ;" and he considers the great Atlantic range of primitive, the mountains of New England, New York, and the Alleghanies, as a spur for this formation. We are not acquainted with the grounds on which this opinion is founded, but we see no reason to consider it an improbable one. Of the northern boundary of that vast formation of secondary which certainly occupies a very large portion of the interior of this continent, we are ignorant. On the south-east, its limit is the irregular border of the transition of the Alleghanies, commencing between the Alabama and Tombigbee rivers, and running north-west to Fort Anne, near Lake Champlain. From this point, a narrow and perhaps interrupted strip of secondary extends through the valley of Lake Champlain to the upper parts of St. John's river. The island and mountain of Montreal are of secondary. The coun-

* Lafora, cited in Humboldt's New Spain.

try also between St. John's and La Prairie is most probably secondary, as is much of that along the St. Lawrence below Montreal. From the termination of the transition near the confluence of the Alabama and Tombigbee, the secondary rocks continue on the south-west, sometimes concealed by the recent alluvial to the Black-lake river, near Natchitoches. Beyond this, the information we have is not satisfactory. From this point, turning north-west, we may for the present consider the Red river of Louisiana as the boundary of the secondary, or rather the limit of our acquaintance with this formation.

Beyond the Ozark mountains, the district between the Red river and the Canadian is occupied by the red sandstone of the salt formation, mentioned when speaking of that region, and is undoubtedly to be considered secondary. How far it extends to the west beyond the sources of Red river and the Canadian, we are unable to determine. At the commencement of the most eastern ridge of the Rocky Mountains, a few south of the high peak, and at no very great distance north from Santa Fé, the boundary again becomes determinate. From this point it runs nearly north one hundred and fifty miles, where it crosses the river Platte. From the narrative of Lewis and Clarke, we are enabled to determine with sufficient accuracy, that it crosses the Missouri not far from the Falls, in longitude 110° west. Beyond this, the little information we have, we owe to Sir Alexander Mackenzie. He informs us, that great quantities of pit coal are found about the sources of the Saskatchawin, which lie near the Rocky Mountains, and between 50° and 55° north latitude. The sources of Saskatchawin are placed by this traveller near the base of the Rocky Mountains; and the coal formation which he mentions, lies on the margin of a plain extending far to the north and east. The Saskatchawin running to the east, traverses 15° of longitude, and discharges its waters into Lake Winnipic in latitude 53° north. Lake Winnipic is connected by the Severn and Port Nelson rivers to Hudson's-bay. There is a water communication, interrupted by one portage, from the Saskatchawin, north-west, to the Mississippi or Churchill's river; and from thence, by the Lake of the Hills, Slave Lake, and Mackenzie's river, to the North Sea. Near the Lake of the Hills, in latitude 59°, Mackenzie found several brine springs. This, though not decisive evidence, perhaps justifies the conclusion, that secondary rocks exist in that neighbourbood. A view of the character and direction of the several large rivers which traverse the region about Hudson's Bay, of their numerous inosculations, and the number and position of the small lakes which abound in every part of it, afford, at least, presumptive evidence, that it is an extensive plain little inclined in any direction.

We may, perhaps, venture to conclude, that the secondary formation extends uninterrupted along the base of the Rocky Mountains, as far as to the Saskatchawin, where coal was observed by Mackenzie. What lies beyond is as yet unknown. From this coal formation, our boundary must for the present run in a direction a little south of east to Lake Superior, whence it may, with a few inconsiderable interruptions, follow the territorial boundary of the United States, until it arrives at 45" parallel of latitude, thence by the St. Lawrence to Montreal. The slight acquaintance we have with the country north of this line, is perhaps insufficient to justify the conjecture, that secondary formations occupy an extensive portion of that country. It is improbable, that formations of secondary extend along the base of the Rocky Mountains through their whole course, and from thence spread themselves to the east, knowing no limits but Atlantic mountains, the shores of the Gulf of St. Lawrence, and the northern ocean. We know that rocks of this formation exist about the

Gulf of St. Lawrence, whence coal, plaster, and sandstone, are brought to our markets.*

This boundary of the great formation of secondary rocks, which occupies so large a portion of the interior of our continent, includes a vast area of surface, extending through 25° of latitude, and 60° of longitude. I intend to consider that portion of it only of which the state of facts at present known enables us to speak with some degree of confidence. This portion may be conceived as occupying the area of a large triangle, the base of which is a line running from Montreal in Lower Canada, south-west to a point, near the outlet of the river Sabine, the western boundary of the state of Louisiana. The summit would be at the sources of the Saskatchawin, which are west of north from the mouth of the Sabine, and north of west from Montreal. The Rocky Mountains on the west, and the Alleghanies on the south-east mark the limits of the secondary in those directions. Its extent towards the north and north-east is as yet unknown.

In the wide space included within the lines above mentioned, we know of but one exception to the remark, that all the rocks found in place are secondary. This is the instance of the Ozark hills traversing the horizontal strata from south-west to north-east, somewhat in the manner of a whindyke. The most striking peculiarity of this range, is the prevalence among the secondary strata of crystalline substances, and what are called rocks of chymical deposition, and the alternation of these with beds and strata whose integrant particles bear evident marks of having been worn and rounded by mechanical attri-

* The banks of the river Montmorenci, from the natural steps downward to the St. Lawrence, are composed of a lime slate placed in horizontal strata from the depth of five to twenty-four inches, each connected by fibrous gypsum of a whitish colour. Heriot's Travels, p. 88. The island of Cape Breton abounds in sandstone, coal, and plaster. *Ibid.* 431.

tion. Appearances of this kind are observed in all formations of secondary rocks, but it is believed, are, in few instances, as extensive or as numerous as in this. It is well known, that the ores of lead, so abundant in many parts of this range, occur in the uppermost strata of horizontal sandstone, or in primary soils superimposed upon those sandstones. It has been suggested, that these ores of lead may have been brought down in the alluvion of rivers from some more ancient and elevated region, but any one who shall examine them in connection with the substances with which they are now found associated, will, we think, be convinced of their having been of contemporaneous origin with the sandstone. That the sparry limestones, the crystalline sandstones, and perhaps the ores of lead, (almost invariably found in the form of crystals,) have been deposited from solution in water, is highly probable; and that these depositions must have taken place in connection with circumstances not unfavourable to animal life is evident, as all these crystalline rocks abound in organised remains.

In attempting an explanation of these appearances, can any assistance be derived from recourse to the ingenious suggestion of Bakewell, that *the matter of these crystalline beds and strata has been ejected from beneath the crust of the earth in a state of chymical solution.* These sub-marine eruptions may have been numerous, and may have happened at different and remote periods; hence the alternation of rocks, consisting of particles mechanically aggregated together with those of chymical deposition. Hence the existence of metallic ores overlaying recent marine sandstones and compact limestones; for these ores, in a state of solution, may have been the matter thrown out in some of the latest eruptions.

This supposition may derive some confirmation from the well known fact that this region is still in a remarkable degree subject to subterranean concussions and earthquakes. These concussions centring apparently in this range of mountains, and felt at times throughout all the western parts of the United States, are certainly too considerable in force and extent to be attributed to the operation of a cause so limited and superficial as the decomposition of beds of lignite lodged among the alluvion of the Mississippi. We do not insist upon the accounts that have been so often circulated, of the blowing, smoking, and burning mountains, said to exist in the country west of the hot springs of the Washita, because these accounts want confirmation.

Though this range of mountains has probably a nucleus of primitive rocks running through its whole extent: yet these appear but rarely at the surface. We have seen such only in the places already mentioned, and have been informed of others in Washington county, near the sources of the St. Francis, and about Lake Superior.*

From the information we have been able to collect, we are induced to believe that secondary rocks occupy the country on both sides of Red river, from its sources to its confluence with the Mississippi. If this be the case, the primitive of the Ozark mountains must be considered a small and insulated mass.

The inequalities of surface in this great secondary formation are considerable. It has often been called the "basin of the Mississippi," but with little propriety, since it might with equal accuracy be called the basin of the St. Lawrence, the Saskatchawin or Mackenzie's river. The form of that part of it which contains the Mississippi, is however similar to that designated by geologists as *a basin-shaped cavity*. As far as our acquaintance extends, it is bounded on all sides, except a narrow space at the outlet of the Mississippi, by a surface of greater elevation than itself. But whether this surface is not sometimes of second-

* Schoolcraft.

ary formation is doubtful. It is dangerous to infer the existence at a former period of an insulated inland sea from any formation of secondary rocks, without being acquainted with its whole extent, with its elevation at different points, and its connexion with other rocks. On the south-east, secondary sandstones and depositions of coal are met with in some of the most elevated parts of the Alleghany mountains. The positive elevation of the primitive mountains of New England is, except at a few points, scarce equal to that of the secondary in the western parts of the state of New York. From the primitive rocks near Philadelphia, to the secondary of the Alleghanies, is an almost uninterrupted ascent. The clay-slate and granite of the Washita, occupy nearly the lowest part of the surface of the Mississippi valley. We are as yet destitute of barometrical or other observations, by which we might determine the actual height which the secondary rocks reach on the sides of the Rocky Mountains. Pike estimates the elevation of the plain at the foot of the mountains, at 8000 feet above the level of the ocean. This is doubtless overrated. We have already observed, that secondary rocks are found upon the sides of the Rocky Mountains, considerably above the level of the plain. It is probable, that this estimate of Pike's far exceeds the truth, yet any one who considers the great length and rapidity of the rivers which flow from that region, the severity of cold in winter, the rapidity with which evaporation is carried on in summer, the transparency and peculiar aspect of the sky, will be convinced that those tracts are highly elevated; and there is unquestionably good reason to believe, the secondary rocks along the eastern base of the Rocky Mountains have in many points an elevation at least equal to the summits of the Alleghanies.

This vast formation of secondary, extending as it probably does from the Gulf of Mexico to the Northern ocean, and from the Bay of St. Lawrence to the Rocky Mountains, must of necessity occupy in various parts different and sometimes great elevations: like other great fields of the same formation, its borders are marked by high and broken ridges, which become less elevated and less frequent towards the centre. Sandstone appears to be the basis and predominating rock occupying the borders contiguous to the primitive and transition, and passing under the more recent secondary. In this sandstone on the outskirts of the secondary, have been found most of the extensive coal beds hitherto known, also gypsum and brine springs.

Horizontally stratified limestone is met with in many parts of this formation, but is most abundant in the central portions, about the beds of the great rivers, and in those parts which have the least positive elevation. Compact limestone is a name sometimes used to designate all the varieties of that rock occurring in districts of secondary, but is certainly inapplicable to the limestone about Cape Girardeau and in many other places, which is notwithstanding manifestly secondary. Some of the limestone northwest of the primitive on Hudson's river, about the Coatskill and Hellebergh mountains, is of this crystalline variety, but abounds in marine exuviæ. That of Lake Champlain, as well as the greater part of that in the interior and western parts of the state of New York, is of the compact blue variety. From the falls of the Ohio at Louisville to Cincinnati, a mixed kind, partaking of the character of both of the before-mentioned varieties, is found along the river, and for some distance on each side. From Dr. Drake we learn, that this limestone is confined to a small district, and is on all sides bounded by sandstone, which rises from below it, and on which it is supposed invariably to rest. Whether the red sandrock which is found on the south-west branches of the Arkansa, in a horizontal position, and in an highly inclined one skirts the Rocky Mountains, extends to other parts of this formation of secondary, we are unable to say.

Throughout the country adjacent to the Ohio river, the prevailing and basis rock is a gray horizontal sandstone, often approaching in character those varieties which contain coal. It embraces extensive beds of coarse conglomerate, and supports or alternates with compact limestone.

Of the Alleghany Mountains.

By this name we intend to designate the great range of mountains extending parallel to the Atlantic coast, from the sources of the St. John's river in New Brunswick in the north-east, to the confluence of the Alabama and Tombigbee in the south-west. An outline of this great chain has already been traced by Maclure, and particular accounts of portions of it are to be found in the works of Eaton and others; we shall, therefore, confine our attention to those strata, which, forming the north-western side of the range, are most intimately connected with the great secondary formations of the west.

1st. *Granular Limestone*—Appears in every part of the United States, where it has hitherto been observed to be the uppermost in the series of primitive rocks. It is true, it is often found to graduate, by minute and imperceptible shades of difference, into that which is decidedly secondary. Instances of this have been observed so frequently that the fact can be no longer questioned. This fact, and others of the same kind, ought not, perhaps, to be considered as invalidating the received opinions with regard to the classification of rocks according to the doctrines of Werner. If a division is to be made of the rocky strata of the earth into primitive, transition, &c. it is, perhaps, of little importance whether the boundaries thus instituted shall traverse beds of the same substance, or separate contiguous strata composed of different materials.

That series of rocks next in order to the primitive limestone above mentioned, has been very generally denominated the Transition Class. It comprehends the following strata: *Metalliferous limestone, Clay-slate, Graywacke,* and *Graywacke-slate,* and *Old Red sandstone.* If we confine our attention to the consideration of these rocks as they exist in our own country, we shall find them appearing in their different localities under circumstances of considerable uniformity.

2d. *Metalliferous Limestone.*—The prevailing colour of this rock is blue, of various shades and intensities, varying into yellow and gray. It has usually a close texture, an even, large conchoidal, or somewhat splintery fracture. In many varieties the surface, by long exposure, becomes coated with an incrustation of a yellowish white powdery matter, which adheres closely. It is frequently traversed by small reticulating veins of quartz or calcareous spar, which, during the gradual decomposition of detached masses, resist the progress of disintegration, and are left standing out from the surface, giving it a chequered appearance. It is the lowest and is considered as the most ancient of the rocks containing organized remains, which are those of cryptogamous, plants and animals without sight.

Geographical distribution.—This rock occurs extensively along all the north-western side of the primitive of the great chain of the Alleghanies. In lower Canada and Vermont, it is accompanied by granular limestone and granular quartz, which separate it from the mica slate and talcose rocks on the east. [See Eaton's Index to the Geology of the Northern States.] It is there usually inclined towards the west, at an inconsiderable angle. It is separated from the compact fletz limestone of the valley of Lake Champlain by a stratum of old red sandstone, which forms the upper part of a range of hills, called, in Vermont, the Snake mountain. In Berkshire county, in the western part of Massachusetts, and along the eastern side of the Hudson in New York, a stratum of primitive clay-slate intervenes between this rock and the granular limestone. The New Lebanon mountain, which is of slate, and divides the primitive limestone of Pittsfield, Richmond, Stockbridge, &c. from the transition which occurs at New Lebanon springs, and along the western base of this range, is considered primitive. (*Dewey in Silliman's Journal.*) To the north-east of the Hudson river, the transition limestone nowhere occupies any great extent of surface from east to west, but is a narrow strip running along the margin of the primitive, and in a few miles is succeeded either by red sandstone, or clay-slate resting upon it. In Vermont, in the same neighbourhood, it alternates with clay-slate, and supports red sandstone.

Crossing the Hudson above the highlands, and proceeding south-west, little of this stratum is seen in the lower part of New York; but it becomes more abundant in the western parts of New Jersey and Pennsylvania. If we suppose the whole of the Alleghany mountains of Pennsylvania, Maryland, and the western parts of Virginia, removed to a level with the surface at base of their eastern declivities, it is probable their foundation, which would be thus exposed, would be found through their whole extent to be of transition limestone. This rock is almost the only one which occurs between the primitive limestone. About twenty miles west of Philadelphia and Harrisburgh, Cove Hill, the North and South mountains, and the other eastern ranges of the Alleghany, are all based upon metalliferous limestone. It is seen emerging from beneath the sandstone which forms the body of these mountains at O'Connel's town, and in most of the vallies between the Alleghanies. We learn from Maclure, that it extends itself to the south and west, nearly to the termination of this range of mountains at the confluence of the Alabama and Tombigbee rivers in Mississippi.

3d. *Transition Argillite.* — This name is intended to comprehend not only the common varieties of the clay-slate of transition, but also some varieties of graywacke, and the siliceous slate by some considered a distinct stratum. It is believed, that throughout the range of country occupied by the several rocks here mentioned, they will be found too intimately blended, and too closely entangled with each other, to allow of their being considered as separate formations.

Geographical distribution. — The formation including the above mentioned rocks, may with propriety be denominated clay-slate of transition. As far as our acquaintance has extended, it occurs in all its localities associated with metalliferous limestone, or old red sandstone. It is not to be confounded with the primitive argillite which occurs below transition limestone, and is met with in the highly primitive parts of New England, nor with the aluminous schist of the great secondary formation to the west. It is distinct from either; and in most instances its character is marked with sufficient distinctness. It occurs in the central portions of that extensive field of transition which skirts the western margin of the primitive of New York and New England, and forms the great body of the Alleghany and Cattskill mountains. It is wider and more extensive in the north, occupying much of the surface in Vermont, the northern parts of the state of New York and Canada. In the Alleghany mountains of Pennsylvannia, Maryland, and Virginia, its beds are of great thickness, and form, in some instances, the prevailing rocks, being, however almost invariably overlaid by sandstone. It has, in several instances, been observed to contain impressions of organized remains, but these are usually those of zoophytic animals, and are exceedingly unlike those found so abundantly in the schist of coal formations. Its colours are variable, it is, however, most commonly blueish, black, or dark brown. Between Albany and Pittsfield, it is met with of a green colour, and a few miles to the south-east of White-hall, New York, it is bright red.

The *graywacke*, which in this very general and hasty view we have considered as in part belonging to the clay-slate of transition, appears to us to form the connecting link between that clay-slate and the old red sandstone. In attempting to give a more detailed account of these formations, we might perhaps speak of the graywacke as others have done, as a distinct stratum. We have, however, usually found it so intimately blended either with the sandstone or clay-slate, that in this enlarged view we see no necessity for a separation. We cannot agree in opinion with some who have considered the graywacke as the substratum of the great secondary formation of the valley of the Mississippi. We have found it almost invariably overlaid by an inclined sandstone, separating it from the secondary rocks towards the west. This may not be as often the case at the north, as in Pennsylvania, Maryland, and Virginia. Mr. Eaton is of opinion, that "graywacke underlays all that district of country in the interior of the state of New York, which would be bounded on the north by a line drawn from Albany westward to the Onondaga salt springs; on the west, by a line running from the salt springs by Bath to the Pennsylvania line; on the south, by a line running thence to Newbergh on the Hudson, above the highlands; and from thence to Albany, by a line running parallel to the river, at a few miles distance." We are informed by Governor Clinton*, that coal strata exist in the western part of the state of New York, and we are induced from the analogy of the other parts of the same great secondary formation, to believe that the brine springs of Onondaga rise not from graywacke,

* See his speech at the opening of the session of 1822.

but from the sandstone of that coal formation. According to Maclure*, old red sandstone appears from under the limestone and other strata at Lewestown, ten miles below the falls of Niagara, and also near the salines of Onondaga in Genessee county. "This," says he, " would give some probability to the conjecture that the old red sandstone is the foundation of all this horizontal formation, and is perhaps attached to some series of rocks laying on the primitive north of the Great Lakes."

Sandstone of Transition. Old Red Sandstone of Werner? — Throughout the whole extent of the transition formation before mentioned, a sandstone occurs, evidently belonging to the oldest depositions of that rock. It is for the most part distinctly stratified, and in all cases its stratifications are inclined. It consists of grains of quartz, united by a scanty cement, and usually more or less rounded, as if by attrition and the operation of currents of water. Their fragments vary in magnitude from the finest sand to boulders of several pounds weight. Among the Alleghany mountains are many extensive beds of pudding-stone or coarse conglomerate, usually coloured by oxide of iron. It is also to be observed, that this formation of transition sandstone sometimes embraces extensive beds, whose integrant particles have by no means the appearance of having been rounded by attrition. As in the case of almost all the rocks of secondary formation, there appear to have been periods during the time of its deposition when the waters of the superincumbent ocean ceased to throw down the mechanical *débris* of former rocks, and deposited earthy matter from a state of chymical solution. It is perhaps one of the most interesting and most difficult problems which remain unsolved, to account for the alternation through the whole series of lower secondary and fletz rocks, of

---

* Observations on the Geology of the United States, p. 57.

beds of strata of mechanical with those of chymical deposition.

The Alleghany mountains in New York, Pennsylvania, Maryland, and Virginia, are made up principally of rocks belonging to the transition class, and among these sandstone is perhaps of more frequent occurrence than any other aggregate. We are aware that Maclure has not considered the sandstones of the Alleghany mountains generally, as belonging to the old red sandstone formation of Werner; and it must be acknowledged there is some difference, at least in colour, between the ferruginous sand-rock, which commences on the shore of Tappan bay near Nyac, and extends south and west by the way of Newark, Amboy, and Brunswick, in New Jersey, and that which forms the body of the Cove, Sideling and Alleghany ridges farther to the west. But we cannot discover so marked a difference between the sandstone of the localities last mentioned, and that which occurs about the South mountain in Pennsylvania, that at Hagerstown in Maryland, and near Harper's ferry, in Virginia, which Maclure considers as the *old red sandstone*. Indeed, this last appears to us in almost every respect to resemble the inclined sandstone which prevails so generally throughout the middle and eastern ridges of the Alleghany mountains in Pennsylvania and Maryland. We have already stated the opinion, in part sanctioned by the observations of Maclure, that the old red sandstone is the great substratum of the part of the secondary formation south of Lake Ontario. If this be the case, what stratum, if not the old red sandstone, should be seen emerging from beneath that secondary along its south-eastern margin? We will not, however, contend for the name. It is sufficient for our purpose to state, that the sandstone so abundant in all the principal ridges accessary to the Alleghany on the east, has the character of a rock belonging to the transition class of the Wernerians; that is, its strata have a somewhat regular dip and inclination; it contains no beds of bituminous coal, though many of anthracite, and few organised remains. Near the summit of the ridge called particularly the Alleghany, the change to secondary begins to appear. Without the interposition of any other stratum, and without any sudden change of features, the strata of sandstone become nearly horizontal, assuming gradually all the characters of secondary rocks. About one mile west of the summit of the Alleghany, on the road from Philadelphia to Pittsburgh, the first indications of coal are observed. Descending into the vallies, the transition strata again emerge to the light. The same thing happens in the case of Coatskill and other mountains west of the Hudson, their basis being of transition, and their summits crossed with secondary.

The horizontal sandstones connected with the depositions of coal occurring along the Ohio from Pittsburgh to the confluence of Green river, assume various characters, and often support extensive formations of compact limestone. [23]

NOTES.

NOTES.

NOTE [1]. Page 7.

In places where the absence of crocodiles permits people to enter the river, Humboldt and Bonpland observed, that the immoderate use of baths, while it moderated the pain of the old stings of zanceadores, rendered them more sensible to new. By bathing more than twice a day, the skin is brought into a state of nervous irritability, of which no idea can be formed in Europe. It would seem as if all feeling were carried towards the integuments. *Humboldt*'s Personal Narrative, vol. v. p. 105.

NOTE [2]. Page 22.

Maclura Aurantiaca, NUTTALL.—A description of this interesting tree may be seen in Mr. Nuttall's valuable work on the Genera of North American Plants, vol. ii. p. 233. That description was drawn from specimens cultivated in the garden of Mr. Choteau, at St. Louis, where, as might be expected, the tree did not attain its full size and perfect character. In its native wilds, the Maclura is conspicuous by its showy fruit, in size and external appearance resembling the largest oranges. The leaves are of an oval form, with an undivided margin, and the upper surface of a smooth shining green; they are five or six inches long, and from two to three wide. The wood is of a yellowish colour, uncommonly fine and elastic, affording the material most used for bows by all the savages from the Mississippi to the Rocky Mountains. How far towards the north its use extends we have not been informed; but we have often seen it among the lower tribes of the Missouri, who procure it in trade from the Osages and the Pawnees of Red river. The bark, fruit, &c. when cut into, exude a copious, milky sap, which soon dries on exposure, and is insoluble in water;

containing, probably, like the milky pieces of many other of the urticæ, a large intermixture of caotchouc, or gum elastic. Observing this property in the milky juice of the fruit, we were tempted to apply it to our skin, where it formed a thin and flexible varnish, affording us, as we thought, some protection from the ticks.

The fruit consists of radiating, somewhat woody fibres, terminating in a tuberculated and slightly papillose surface. In this fibrous mass the seeds, which are nearly as large as those of a quince, are disseminated. We cannot pretend to say what part of the fruit has been described as the " pulp which is nearly as succulent as that of an orange; sweetish, and perhaps agreeable when fully ripe." In our opinion, the whole of it is as disagreeable to the taste, and as unfit to be eaten as the fruit of the sycamore, to which it has almost as much resemblance as to the orange.

The tree rises to the height of twenty-five or thirty feet, dividing near the ground into a number of long, slender, and flexuous branches. It inhabits deep and fertile soils along the river valley. The Arkansa appears to be the northern limit of the range of the maclura, and neither on that river, nor on the Canadian, does the tree or the fruit attain so considerable a size as in warmer latitudes. Of many specimens of the fruit examined by Major Long, at the time of his visit to Red river, in 1817, several were found measuring five and an half inches in diameter.

Note [3]. Page 27.

This tree, the populus angulata of Pursh, has received its common name from the downy cotton-like appendage to the seed, which being ripened and shed in May, or the beginning of June, is then seen floating in the air in great quantities, and often proves somewhat troublesome to the eyes and noses of persons who are much in the open air. Baron Humboldt in speaking of the unona aromatica of South America, says, " Its branches are straight, and rise in a pyramid nearly like those of the poplar of the Mississippi, falsely called Lombardy poplar." Pers. Nar. vol. v. p. 163. As far as our observation has extended, the poplar most common in the country of the Mississippi, and indeed almost the only one which occurs, is the angulata, very distinct from the populus dilatata, the Lombardy poplar of our streets and yards, which is not a native of this country. The branches of the cotton-wood tree are not very numerous, particularly where it occurs in forests, as is the case on the Mississippi, below the confluence of the Missouri, and in the alluvial lands of most of the rivers in the United States, and show less tendency to arrange themselves in a pyramidal form than those of almost any other tree. In the open country west of the Mississippi, where, in the distance of one hundred miles, some dozens of cotton-wood trees may be found scattered, their tops are peculiarly low and straggling, as is the case with individuals of the same species which have grown in open fields, and by the road sides in various places. This tree is, perhaps, as widely distributed as any indigenous to North America, extending at least from Canada to Louisiana, and from the Atlantic to the lower part of Columbia river. It is, however, so peculiarly frequent in every part of the country watered by the Mississippi and its tributaries, that it may, with as little absurdity as usually attends names referring to locality, be called the Mississippi poplar. It is probable, that nearly one half of the whole number of trees in the recent alluvial grounds or bottom-lands of the Mississippi and its tributaries, are of this species. Whether it was considered by Humboldt as identical with the Lombardy poplar of our streets, we cannot decide.

The cotton-wood varies in magnitude in proportion to the fertility of the soil; and on the Ohio, the Mississippi, and the Arkansa, it attains the size of our largest forest trees. It is sometimes exceeded in girth, and in the number and extent of its branches, by the majestic sycamore; but in forests where the two are intermixed, as is commonly the case, it is seen to overtop all other trees. A cotton-wood tree mentioned in the journal of the exploring party who ascended Red river in 1806, and spoken of as one of many similar trees standing in a corn-field three or four days' journey above Natchitoches, measured one hundred and forty-one feet and six inches in height, and five feet in diameter. [*Freeman's* MS. Journal.] Though we have not actual admeasurements to compare with this, we are of opinion that many trees on the Arkansa would rather exceed than fall short of these dimensions. The cotton-wood affords a light and soft timber, not very durable, except when protected from the weather Before expansion, the buds of this tree are partially covered with a viscid, resinous exudation, resembling that so conspicuous on the buds of the populus balsamifera, and diffusing in the spring and the early part of summer an extremely grateful and balsamic odour.

NOTE [4]. Page 54.

We do not know that any writer has visited these Indians since the expedition of Mr. Bourgmont, Commander of Fort Orleans of the Missouri, which took place in the year 1724. They were then, and have since continued to be, distinguished collectively by the name of Padoucas. Du Pratz informs us, that they were then very numerous, " extending almost two hundred leagues; and they have villages quite close to the Spaniards of New Mexico." And that " from the Padoucas to the Canzes, proceeding always east, we may now safely reckon sixty-five and a half leagues. The river of the Canzes is parallel to this route." From this statement of the course and estimate of the distance to the country of the Padoucas, it is evident, that at this day these Indians do not habitually wander in that direction so near to Missouri as they then did, owing probably to the hostilities of the more martial nations residing on that river.

NOTE [5]. Page 55.

Bufo cognatus. — FUSCOUS, with cinereous lines; *head* canaliculate, groove abbreviated before. *Body* above, dark brownish, papillous, the papillæ and their basal disks black; they are more numerous, prominent, and acute, on the sides and legs; not prominent on the back. A vertebral cinereous vitta, from which an oblique cinereous irregular line is drawn from the vertex to the side behind the anterior feet; another double one from the middle of the back to the posterior thighs. *Sides* and *legs* with irregular cinereous lines. *Head* with a groove, which hardly extends anteriorly to the line of the anterior canthus of the eyes; verrucæ behind the eyes, moderate; *superior maxilla* emarginate; *beneath* granulated.

Length from the nose to the cloaca, $3\frac{3}{4}$ inches. A specimen is placed in the Philadelphia museum.

NOTE [6]. Page 63.

Amongst the herds of these animals, we frequently saw flocks of the cow bunting (*emberiza pecora*). The manners of this bird, in some respects, are very similar to those of the

Tanagra erythroryncha of Lord Stanley, in Salt's travels; flying, and alighting in considerable numbers on the backs of the bisons, which, from their submission to the pressure of numbers of them, seem to appreciate the services they render, by scratching and divesting them of vermin. This bird is here, as well as in the settlements, remarkably fearless. They will suffer us to pass very near to them, and one of them to-day, alighted repeatedly on the ground near our horses' feet: he would fly along our line, and balance himself on his wings, to gratify his curiosity, within striking distance of a whip.

NOTE [7]. Page 72.

We have since learned, from Major O'Fallon, that *Ietan*, the distinguished Oto partizan, had informed him, within a few days of this date, that he had just then returned from a war excursion in company with a small party of Otoes that he led. And the narration of his adventures satisfactorily proved, that it was he and his party that reduced the Ietan war-party to the condition in which they presented themselves to us.

NOTE [8]. Page 117.

Agama collaris. — *Scales* of the back, neck, and head beneath, anterior legs, and superior and posterior portions of the posterior legs, small, slightly convex, mutic, rounded, or a little oblong, obsoletely arranged in transverse lines; those of the abdomen and breast larger, slightly hexagonal or quadrate, and distinctly arranged in transverse lines; those of the tail rather smaller than the abdominal ones, arranged in bands, quadrate, mutic towards the tip of the tail, oblong, carinated, and acute; front, middle of the head, vertex, and anterior portion of the inferior jaw, with scales approaching the size of plates; *colour*, back with five or six dusky, broad bands, alternating with narrow fulvous bands, which have each a series of yellow or cinereous spots; a few spots are also scattered on the dusky bands; *sides* greenish-yellow; *sides of the neck* fulvous, more or less varied with brilliant vermilion red, a deep black band, and another on the shoulder, both obsolete above, and terminating near the anterior legs; *beneath* pale; *posterior thighs* with a series of pores; *eyes* silvery, pupil round, black; tail long, tapering, cylindrical. Length from nose to cloaca 4 inches, tail 5⅔ inches. A specimen is deposited in the Philadelphia museum.

Note [9]. Page 121.

Ixodes molestus. — *Body* reddish brown, punctured, orbicular very slightly approaching ovate; *scutus* rounded or subangular, hardly attaining the middle of the body, and with two distinct, indented, longitudinal lines; *tergum*, with about four dilated, black, distinct radii behind the middle; margin from near the middle of the side, with ten or twelve impressed, acute, equal, equidistant lines, which do not crenate the edge or upper surface. Length rather more than $\frac{1}{20}$ of an inch.

Note [10]. Page 125.

The word Masserne, applied by Darby as a name to the hills of the Arkansa territory, near the boundary of Louisiana, and by Nuttall, to the mountains at the sources of the Kiamesha and the Poteau, is supposed to be a corruption of *Mont Cerne*, the name of a small hill near Belle Point, long used as a look-out post by the French hunters.

Note [11]. Page 133.

Mr. John Rogers, a very respectable and civilized Cherokee, told me that one of the regulators happening to have a relation who had been repeatedly guilty of theft, and finding him incorrigible, he destroyed his eyesight with a penknife; saying, "As long as you can see you will steal; I will, therefore, prevent your thefts by the destruction of your sight." Nuttall's Travels into the Arkansa Territory, p. 135., to which work the reader is referred for an interesting sketch of the history, and of the present condition of the Cherokees. We think it unnecessary to dwell longer upon a subject which has been so frequently discussed.

Note [12]. Page 136.

The confluence of White river with the Mississippi, has been said to be " situated fifty miles above the mouth of the Arkansa." It has also been asserted, that its bifurcation is at " about thirty miles above its junction with the Mississippi." See *Schoolcraft*'s View of the Lead Mines of Missouri, p. 248.

253. There is, however, little reason to fear, that errors of this sort, upon a subject so familiarly known, will obtain general currency. In the same work, the length of White river is said to be thirteen hundred miles.

Note [13]. Page 138.

The mine of Merameg, which is silver, is pretty near the confluence of the river which gives it name, which is a great advantage to those who would work it, because they might easily, by that means, have their goods from Europe. It is situate about 500 leagues from the sea. *Du Pratz'* Louisiana, vol. i. p. 294.

Note [14]. Page 151.

" There are four principal springs rising immediately on the east bank of the creek, one of which may be rather said to spring out of the gravel bed of the river; a fifth, a smaller one than that above mentioned, as rising on the west side of the creek; and a sixth of the same magnitude, the most northerly, and rising near the bank of the creek; these are all the sources that merit the name of springs, near the huts; but there is a considerable one below, and all along at intervals the warm water oozes out, or drops from the bank into the creek, as appears from the condensed vapour floating along the margin of the creek, where the drippings occur." This extract from the " Observations" of Hunter and Dunbar, when compared with our account, will show that some changes have happened in the number and position of the springs, since the time of their visit in 1804.

Note [15]. Page 151.

On the 1st of January, 1818, the thermometer, in the air, at sunrise, stood at 24°, at 2 P. M. 49°, at sunset 41°.

Immersed in the water of the creek, below the springs, at 61°.

In spring No. 1. being the lowermost on the creek, 122°, water discharged, 4 gallons per minute.

No. 2. A feet few from No. 1, 104°, discharges 1 gallon per minute.

No. 3. Twenty-five yards from the last, 106°, discharges two gallons per minute.

No. 4. Six yards above the last, 126°, discharges 2 gallons per minute.

Temperature of a spring issuing from the ground, at a considerable distance up the side of the hill, 64°.

Springs, No. 5, 6, and 7, 126°, 94°, 92°. These rise very near each other, the warmest being more elevated than the rest; the three discharge about 8 gallons per minute.

No. 8. Issuing from the ground, fifty feet above the level of the creek, uniting, as it rises, with another at 54°; temperature of the mixture, 128°, discharge of the two, 10 gallons per minute.

No 9. Rising on the point of a small spur, sixty feet above the level of the creek, 132°, discharges two gallons per minute.

No. 10. Forty feet above the creek, 151°, discharges 10 gallons per minute. Green bushes in the edge of this, which is the hottest spring.

No. 11. Three feet above the creek, 148°, discharges 12 gallons per minute.

No. 12. Twenty yards above the last, 132°, discharges 20 gallons per minute.

No. 13, 14, 15. Near the last, 124°, 119°, 108°, discharges each 4 gallons per minute.

No. 16, 122°, discharges 2 gallons per minute.

No. 17. The uppermost on the creek, 126°.

No. 18, 126°; 19, 128°; 20, 130°; 21, 136°; 22, 140. All these are large springs, and rise at an elevation of at least 100 feet above the creek. In the same area are several others, and what is more remarkable, several cold ones. In any of the hot springs I observed bubbles rising in rapid succession, but could not discover any perceptible smell from them. Not only confervas and other vegetables grow in and about the hottest springs, but great numbers of little insects are seen constantly sporting about the bottom and sides. Temperature of the water of the creek, above the springs, 46°. The entire quantity of water flowing in the creek, after it receives the water of the hot springs, may be estimated at from 900 to 1000 gallons per minute.

Note [16]. Page 152.

The temperature was, however, no more than sufficient to raise the mercury in Fahrenheit's thermometer to 160°. It has been represented by Bringier, in a paper published in Silliman's Journal, that " the heat of the water is 192° Fah." On what observations this assertion rests we know not. See

"The American Journal of Science and Arts." Vol. iii. No. I. p. 29.

Note [17]. Page 164.

" The south side of this river, quite to the rapid part, is entirely different from the opposite side; it is something higher, and rises in proportion as it approaches the height I have mentioned; the quality is also very different. This land is good and light, and is disposed to receive all the culture imaginable, in which we may assuredly hope to succeed. It naturally produces fruit trees and vines in plenty; it was on that side muscadine grapes were found. The back parts have neater woods and meadows, intersected with tall forests. On that side the fruit trees of the country are common, and above all, the hiccory and walnut trees, which are sure indications of good soil." *Du Pratz'* Louisiana, p. 166.

Note [18]. Page 184.

Several persons, passengers on board a steam-boat, ascending the Mississippi, in 1820, went on shore near New Madrid. In one of the houses which they entered they found a small collection of books: as they were amusing themselves with the examination of these, they felt the house so violently shaken, that they were scarce able to stand upon their feet; some consternation was of course felt, and as several of the persons were ladies, much terror was expressed; " Don't be alarmed," said the lady of the house, " it is nothing but an earthquake."

Note [19]. Page 284.

What explanation the advocates for the doctrine of the recent *emersion* of our continent will give of the highly and exclusively primitive character of the Rocky Mountains, we are at a loss to conjecture. The organized remains hitherto observed in the secondary aggregates along the base of those mountains, are mostly of animals supposed to have inhabited the depths of the ocean. But if the granite of the Rocky Mountains has been *forced up* at a recent period, where are the traces of all those older secondary, and fletz rocks, which should have intervened between it and the horizontal sandstones? If these mountains had formed the shores of that ocean, in which the greater part of our continent was so long immersed, after the elevation of the *old world*, we should have expected to find along their base, the remains of littoral animals, and not of those which inhabited the depths of the ocean. It would be proper, however, before we refer to the character of the Rocky Mountains, as invalidating or confirming any system of opinions, to ascertain that their eastern and western sides are in all respects similar.

NOTE [20]. Page 301.

The valley of Red river abounds in limestone, often presenting the shells of oysters and other moluscous animals in a state of petrifaction, scattered in profusion over the surface of the ground, and retaining their original form entire, while on the Arkansa, the rocks are generally sandstone, no limestone being found, except of the Illinois, Grand, and Canadian rivers. *Major Long's* MS. Journal. Several organic relics from the country about the confluence of the Kiamesha, have been obligingly communicated by Mr. Nuttall: among these is a shell which approaches nearest to the variety of the gryphœa dilatata of Sowerby, 149. fig. 2, but the lobe is far less distinct, and the shell is more narrowed towards the hinge, and is somewhat less dilated, and much more like an ostrea. It may be thus described: G. *corrugata*, SAY.—Small valve, flat, and very much wrinkled, and like the other, narrowed near the hinge. The beak is short, and curved upwards, and laterally, and the sulcus is very distinct. Length, and greatest breadth of the small valve nearly equal; from $1\frac{1}{2}$ to 2 inches. It is in a very perfect state of preservation. Mr. Nuttall brought also from Red river, a species of ostrea, which to the eye appears hardly changed. The anterior portion of the specimens are wanting, but the greatest breadth of the remaining portion of the largest one is nearly three inches. The hinge fosse in this species is proportionably much more contracted, and smaller in every respect, than any other species of the genus we have seen; that of the specimen above mentioned is less than one-half of an inch. The specimens were evidently those of old shells, being much thickened. Another species of ostrea, a hinge fragment of an old and thickened individual, which appears to have been long, and narrow; the hinge fosse itself is long and wide. Length of the hinge more than three inches, greatest width more than one inch.

Note [21]. Page 307.

" A very extensive bed of native argil occurs on the right bank of the Mississippi, commencing near the head of Tiawapeti Bottom, at the Little Chain, about forty miles above the junction of the Ohio and Mississippi, and extending with very little interruption near six miles above the Grand Tower, a distance of thirty-four miles. Beyond these limits I have not observed it. Its colour is snow-white; 'structure fine, pulverulent; fracture dull earthy. It is amorphous, and adheres to the tongue. It does not effervesce with acids, even in the slightest degree. The bed of argil reposes on horizontal strata of siliceous sandstone, and is overlaid by shell limestone. In the vein of argil, nodules and veins of flint are arranged so as to make with the horizon an angle of about fifty degrees. The argil has been taken to New Orleans, Pittsburgh, St. Louis, &c. in considerable quantities, supposing it to be chalk, for which substance it has been used." *Mr. Jessup's* MS. Report.

" *Flint.* — This occurs in nodules and veins in a bed of native argil, above Tiawapeti Bottom. Its colours are bluishgray and greenish-black. It gives fire with steel; the fracture is conchoidal, and the edges are translucent. The veins of flint dip to the south-east." *Ibid.*

Imbedded in the chalk of Cape Girardeau, are occasionally found nodules of flint, which are enveloped by a hard crust of calcareous carbonate, arranged in concentric layers. Its colour is grayish-black, breaks with a perfectly conchoidal fracture, is translucent on the edges, and readily gives fire with the steel. *Schoolcraft's* View of the Lead Mines, p. 180.

Note [22]. Page 313.

" *Fluate of Lime.* — This mineral occurs in great abundance seventeen miles south of Shawaneetown, Illinois, on Peter's creek, and proceeding about thirteen miles in a south-west direction, it again appears on and near the surface of the ground; at the three forks of the Grand Pierre creek, maintaining the same course, it breaks out in several places for near twenty miles. This beautiful and useful species of lime occurs at Peter's creek, almost invariably in a crystallized form; the crystals are universally cubes: at the three forks of the Grand Pierre creek, it occurs in masses of several feet in diameter. Both the crystallized and massive varieties, possess almost all the shades of colour that have been observed in the European specimens: viz. green, violet, blue, red, yellow, white, black, and rose-coloured. This mineral varies in transparency, some specimens being perfectly limpid, others opaque. Some of the violet and rose-coloured specimens, when recently fractured or pulverized, yield a strong bituminous odour; this character (which has never been observed heretofore as belonging to this species of lime) is perceptible only in the crystallized specimens.

"The vein of fluate of lime is apparently very extensive; very few minerals have been found associated with it, at the above localities. I saw at Peter's creek a few specimens of laminated calcareous spar, and a few of sulphuret of lead. Excavations have been made by several gentlemen who reside in that vicinity, for lead, but no veins or beds of this ore have been found.

"From examination of the situation of those specimens which I found, and the general appearance of the vein of fluor spar, I do not think that there is a sufficiency of lead ore, to reimburse the expenses that would be necessarily incurred in mining. The accompanying rocks of the vein of spar are compact limestone, sandstone, and oolite." *Jessup's* MS. Report.

"*Concreted Carbonate of Lime, variety Oolite.*—This occurs on Peter's creek, seventeen miles south of Shawaneetown, Illinois, associated with compact limestone, and sandstone, in the gangue of the fluate of lime. It is composed of globular masses, about the size of English mustard-seed, which are united by a calcareous cement; the nucleus of the globules are detached, leaving a small cavity in the centre of each; its colour is yellowish-white; fracture dull." *Ibid.*

"*Sulphuretted Hydrogen Gas.*— This gas is very abundant in the water of many of the springs and wells in Missouri territory. Its origin is probably owing to the decomposition of sulphuret of iron. Six miles west of St. Louis is a large spring of water strongly impregnated with this gas; its odour is perceptible to the distance of four or five hundred yards from the spring. It is reported, that the water has proved beneficial in cases of cutaneous disorders and rheumatic complaints." *Ibid.*

"*Red Oxide of Iron.*—This occurs, though not very abundant, in the hills near Isle a Loutre, on the Missouri river. Its texture is compact, fracture earthy. Its external colour is brownish red; its streak and powder is blood red. This variety of ore produces good iron, and yields from sixty to eighty per cent." *Ibid.*

"*Hematitic Brown Oxide of Iron.* — This variety of iron ore occurs in considerable quantity in the vicinity of the vein of fluate of lime, near Shawaneetown, Illinois. It occurs there under a number of imitative forms, such as tubular, stalactitical, nodular, botryondal, and reniform. Its colour is blackish and yellow brown; it is easily fused, and will produce near sixty per cent. of good malleable iron." *Ibid.*

"*Argillaceous Oxide of Iron.* — This variety of iron ore is abundant in the western parts of Pennsylvania and Virginia, and in Kentucky, where it is almost the only ore of iron that is worked. The principal furnaces in Pennsylvania, are in Cumberland, Northumberland, and Centre counties, and on the Juniata river." *Ibid.*

"*Columnar Argillaceous Oxide of Iron.* — Near the confluence of the Ohio and Tennessee rivers, is a locality of argillaceous oxide of iron, of a columnar structure, and so rising from the surface of the ground as to have some resemblance to cypress trees. This mineral has by many been thought of volcanic origin; at least, that the cause of its peculiar form is, in some measure, connected with the operation of volcanic causes." *Ibid.*

"*Sulphuret of Lead, or Galena.* — This mineral is abundant in Missouri territory, about sixty miles south-west of St. Louis; but as I had not an opportunity of visiting the mines I cannot say any thing respecting its geological situation or quantity. There are two reservations for lead in the vicinity of the United States' Saline, Illinois. From external appearances, I should judge, the ore was abundant; but from the success of former diggings, and the situation of the ore, which has not as yet been found there, either in beds or veins, but sparingly diffused in small masses (attached to the fluate of lime) not exceeding in weight two or three pounds, I think the quantity inconsiderable. Every specimen of sulphuret of lead that I saw there, possessed a crystalline form." *Ibid.*

"*Sulphuret of Zinc, or Blende.* — Fifteen miles south of Shawaneetown, Illinois, uniform masses of argillaceous iron ore enclosed in concentric layers of slate clay, are found in a bed of slate clay. In the argillaceous iron ore small particles of sulphuret of zinc occur. This is the only locality west of the Alleghany mountains that I have seen of this ore." *Ibid.*

NOTE [23]. Page 330.

The following are descriptions of the rocks that alternate with each other as they occur, in connection with the coal-beds at Pittsburgh; commencing with the uppermost and proceeding in a regular gradation to the lowest, that we have had an opportunity of examining.

No. 1. A loose-grained argillaceous sandstone, composed of minute grains of quartz and decomposed felspar, united by an argillaceous cement. Its colour is yellowish gray; fracture uneven; stratifications imperfect. It contains no organic remains; depth of the bed near four feet.

No. 2. Bituminous shale; natural colour brownish black, that of the streak dark gray. Before the blow-pipe it decrepitates, burns with a bright flame, emits a bituminous odour, and soon becomes nearly white. Its structure is slaty; no animal or vegetable is contained in it, small veins of clay are dispersed irregularly between the layers. Depth of the strata ten feet.

No. 3. A bed of bituminous coal; its colour is brownish black, cross fracture uneven, longitudinal slaty; fragments tabular, right angled; lustre resinous; is semihard, sectile and very brittle. Vertical and horizontal beds of indurated clay, containing a small quantity of bitumen, occur in the coal. Depth of the bed from two to eight feet.

No. 4. Bituminous shale possesses the same character as No. 2. Varies in depth.

No. 5. Indurated clay; its colour is lead-gray; fracture, in situations where it has been subjected to the combined actions of moisture and the atmosphere, irregularly slatose; in others uneven. Depth of this bed seven feet.

No. 6. Argillaceous chlorite slate, passing by regular gradations into argillaceous chlorite sandstone. Natural colour, yellowish green, that of the streak light gray; cross fracture uneven. Its powder is soft and slightly greasy to the touch; it contains no organic remains. The depth of this bed varies.

No. 7. Compact limestone, intimately mixed with alumine; it contains small veins of calcareous spar dispersed throughout the mass. Veins of angular fragments of carbonate of lime, united by a calcareous and argillaceous cement, extend irregularly through the rock. The fracture, in some specimens, is compact and earthy, in others uneven.

No. 8. Argillaceous chlorite sandstone, consisting of minute grains of quartz, chlorite slate, and talc, united by an argillaceous cement; its colour is yellowish green; fracture uneven; the powder is soft, and feels greasy to the touch; it is destitute of organic remains.

No. 9. A loose-grained argillaceous sandstone, thickly interspersed with thin laminæ of talc; its colour is light gray; fracture uneven; texture loose; it is liable to disintegration.

No. 10. Argillaceous sandstone, irregularly slatose; its colour is gray, with a tinge of yellow. Nodules of clay iron-stone occur in considerable quantities through the mass of rock.

No. 11. Fine-grained argillaceous sandstone, composed of quartz and magnesia united by an argillaceous cement. Its colour is yellowish gray, which by the action of the blow-pipe passes into reddish brown. This rock contains great numbers of the impressions of the phytolites.

No. 12. Indurated clay; its colour is blueish gray, structure slatose; fracture approaching uneven; hardness inconsiderable. Impressions of small leaves occur in this, but are not numerous; they apparently consist of one species alone.

No. 13. Compact argillaceous sandstone; composed of quartz, felspar, and their laminæ of talc, united by an argillaceous cement; its colour is brownish gray. Nodules of clay iron-stone occur in considerable abundance in this rock; they are formed by concentric layers, around a nucleus, which is the same in composition as the mass of their bed. Their size varies from that of a nut to an apple.

From *Mr. Jessup*'s MS. Report.

END OF THE THIRD VOLUME.

www.ingramcontent.com/pod-product-compliance
Lightning Source LLC
Chambersburg PA
CBHW061931220426
43662CB00012B/1865